D0553994

IN AN UNKNOWN LAND

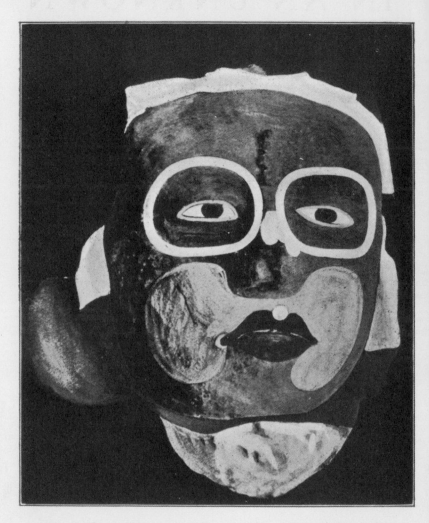

ONE OF THE HEADS FROM THE CASA DEL GOBERNADOR, UXMAL.

[*See p. 246*

IN AN UNKNOWN LAND

By

THOMAS GANN

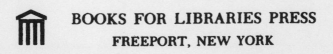

BOOKS FOR LIBRARIES PRESS
FREEPORT, NEW YORK

First Published 1924
Reprinted 1971

INTERNATIONAL STANDARD BOOK NUMBER:
0-8369-5695-8

LIBRARY OF CONGRESS CATALOG CARD NUMBER:
76-150182

PRINTED IN THE UNITED STATES OF AMERICA

CONTENTS

5

CONTENTS

6

PAGE

8 CONTENTS

CONTENTS 9

LIST OF ILLUSTRATIONS

SKETCH MAP OF YUCATAN, SHOWING THE PRINCIPAL
TOWNS AND RUINED SITES VISITED.

1.	BELIZE	15.	ISLA DE LAS MUJERES
2.	COROZAL	16.	BOCA DE IGLESIAS
3.	BACALAR	17.	HOLBOX ISLAND.
4.	PAYO OBISPO	18.	YALAHAU
5.	XCALAC	19.	SILAN
6.	PUNTA HERRERA	20.	PROGRESO
7.	ESPIRITU SANTO BAY	21.	CAMPECHE
8.	CHACMOOL	22.	CHAMPOTON
9.	CAYO CULEBRA	23.	MAYAPAN
10.	ASCENSION BAY	24.	CHICHEN ITZA
11.	CENTRAL	25.	UXMAL
12.	TULUUM	26.	KABAH
13.	SAN MIGUEL COZUMEL	27.	CAVE OF LOLTUN
14.	CANCUEN ISLAND	28.	MERIDA

29. HOLACTUN

IN AN UNKNOWN LAND

CHAPTER I

Arrival in Belize—Population of the Colony—Belize Market—Belize founded by Buccaneers—Efforts made by Spaniards to eject them unavailing—Battle of St. George's Cay—The " Poke and Go Boys " —Celebrations of the Anniversary of the Battle in Belize—Mahogany Cutters—Their hard Lives—Case of Piracy on the High Seas occurring recently in the Caribbean.

FOR several years Dr. Sylvanus G. Morley, of the Carnegie Institution, and myself had contemplated an expedition to the East Coast of Yucatan, one of the least known and most inaccessible parts of Central America, and the last place on the American continent where the poor remnant of the great Maya race, whose civilisation was the most ancient and highly developed in the New World 1,500 years before the coming of Europeans, still holds its own, unconquered and unsubdued, in the dense, impenetrable forests of the interior.

Belize, the capital of British Honduras ever since the early forties, when John L. Stephens set forth from here on his celebrated search for a Central American Government, has been the jumping-off place of nearly all archæological and exploratory expeditions into Central America, being a good place to outfit in, and conveniently situated for all the Central American republics, as filibusters, gun-runners, and refugees, from their interminable revolutions are well aware. Here, then, we found ourselves early in January, with at least four months of assured dry weather in front of us before the rainy season set in which renders travelling through the bush practically impossible.

The population of Belize is an extraordinarily mixed one. English, Spanish, French, German, and representatives of nearly every nation in Europe rub shoulders with Chinese, East Indians, and other Asiatics, while the indigenous

13

population is represented by negroes, Caribs, Maya, and Quichè Indians from the far interior, and the extraordinarily mongrel races which inhabit Southern Mexico and the five republics of Central America. The scene at the market each morning is an extremely lively and animated one. Everyone comes down about six to buy the day's provisions. Burly negresses, in spotless white, their heads wrapped in gay cotton handkerchiefs, their vast feet thrust into still vaster unlaced boots belonging to their husbands, clump happily along, screaming, laughing, and chattering like a flock of parroquets, and chaffering over the price of their fresh fish and plantains. Saturnine Spaniards and Mexicans, thin, yellow, and cigarette-pickled, laying in supplies of frijoles, chili pepper, garlic, and corn cake ; coolies, shining and odoriferous from their morning rub-down with coco-nut oil, purchase rice, oil, and fish ; coal-black Caribs, their faces and hands covered with white, leprous-looking patches, who, notwithstanding constant sea baths, always retain an unpleasant mousey smell, seek their daily rations of fish and cassava bread, and even an occasional pale-faced, starchily-clad English housewife may be encountered, cool, business-like, and unhurried amidst all the excitement. They form a shouting, gesticulating, chaffering, laughing, quarrelling, noisy throng, their skins varying from lightest olive through snuff and butter and *café-au-lait* to coal-black, their bright-coloured clothes making a constantly changing kaleidoscope around the market square.

Belize was founded in the early part of the seventeenth century by English and Scotch Buccaneers, who for many years had driven a thriving trade along the coast in robbing Spanish vessels laden with logwood. Finding at length that the supply of victims was beginning to run short, and that it was really easier to cut logwood for themselves in the neighbourhood of Belize, where it grew in practically inexhaustible quantities along the river banks, they formed a settlement for this purpose, and imported a number of

THE MARKET PLACE, BELIZE.

By H. S. Tuke, R.A

[*p.* 14

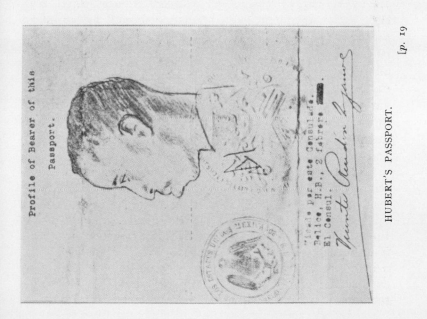

[*p.* 19

HUBERT'S PASSPORT.

African slaves, who worked for them. Repeated efforts were made by the Spaniards to eject these hardy settlers from their territory, but without avail, till early in the last century a large Armada was collected by the Spanish Governor of Yucatan at Bacalar and despatched south to St. George's Cay, a sandy island about nine miles from the mainland, and at that time the capital of the colony. The inhabitants got wind of this invasion, and, collecting their slaves and servants and every crazy old canoe, dug-out, and sailing vessel they could muster, gave battle valiantly to the much superior force of the invaders.

The slaves were armed for the most part only with palm-stick lances hardened in the fire and sharpened, but they rendered such a good account of themselves with their primitive weapons, that after several hours fighting the Spaniards had had enough of it, and, getting on board such vessels as were still left them, turned tail, and retreated north again, never to return. The natives were christened, from their method of fighting at this battle, the " Poke and Go Boys "—a term which has clung to them ever since, though some etymologists have recently promulgated the theory that the name was derived from the rations supplied to the slaves, and should be " Pork and Dough Boys."

Every year, on the anniversary of the battle of St. George's Cay, the event is celebrated with music, dancing, fireworks, and processions of mahogany and logwood cutters through the streets, dressed in their ancient costume of red flannel cap, blue jersey, white trousers, moccasins, and machete, or cutlass, and carrying axe, lance, or paddle, symbols of their occupation, during the procession. An endless ditty, composed by some local poet, of which a single verse is here given, is chanted to the tune of " Villikins and his Dinah."

We jooked them and we poked them and we drove them like fleas,
Right into salt water right up to their knees,
And each greasy Spaniard to the other did say :
O vamonos compadres de St. George's Cay.
(O campadres, let us get out of St. George's Cay.)

The descendants of these same black slaves, who fought side by side with their owners at St. George's Cay, form to-day the backbone of British Honduras, and probably one of the finest coloured citizenry in the world, black and white respecting each other, and working amicably hand in hand for the advancement of their country.

The lot of the negro labourer is not altogether a happy one. In January of each year he sets forth to his mahogany, logwood, or chicle camp at the head waters of one of the numerous rivers, or buried in the recesses of the thick jungle which covers most of the country. Here he constructs little palm-leaf shacks for himself and family, and spends from nine to ten months in strenuous labour with axe and machete, felling mahogany and logwood, or bleeding chicle (chewing-gum, the sap of the sapote tree), living on a diet of straight flour dough and salt pork, supplemented only by such game as his gun can obtain in the neighbouring bush, or coarse fish from the streams. No wonder that during the month or six weeks he spends at Belize at Christmas he endeavours to make up for lost time by a too strenuous devotion to pleasure, chiefly represented by the flowing bowl, and that when the time comes for him to start off into the bush again he is as often as not without sufficient cash from his advance to buy even the cooking-pots and clothes absolutely essential for a nine months' sojourn in the woods, perhaps one hundred miles from civilisation.

The matrimonial bond is worn lightly by the mahogany cutter. Marriage is not infrequent, but perhaps more as an excuse for the spree which the wedding entails than with any idea of forming a permanent bond, and the lady, if she finds her partner unsatisfactory, thinks nothing of accompanying some other man into the bush on the following season, so that it is not infrequent to find women with families each member of which is by a different husband.

The small settler in the colony has an easy time of it ; he is troubled neither by the housing problem nor by the

H.C.L., as he can put up quite a comfortable thatched shack in a couple of days on a five-acre tract purchased from the Government at two dollars per acre. He will find his building materials—palm leaf for roof, pimento for walls, and sapodilla for posts—within a hundred yards of his future front door, and on this fertile soil he will have no difficulty in raising as many plantains, bananas, yams, and as much corn as he wants, while chickens, eggs, and pigs provide means of obtaining what luxuries he may desire in the form of clothes, rum, and tobacco.

That piracy as a profession is not quite dead along the shores of the Caribbean Sea, even in the twentieth century is shown by the following incident. A short time ago a small sailing vessel set out from Belize for La Ceiba, a port in Spanish Honduras, with a coloured captain and crew and several passengers, amongst whom were two Belize negroes. The captain had very imprudently let it be known that he was carrying a considerable sum in silver dollars, of which the two negroes determined to possess themselves. When well out at sea they coolly took possession of the vessel, after shooting the captain and several of the other men and throwing their corpses overboard. Amongst the passengers was a Carib woman, whom they neglected to shoot and threw overboard alive, either because they felt some compunction at shooting a woman, or more probably because, being several miles from land in the midst of shark-infested waters at the time, they felt that such an act would be merely a waste of ammunition. This, however, proved to be a fatal oversight on their part, as the Caribs are wonderful swimmers, and as much at home in the water as on land, and with the aid of a piece of floating wood, which she fortunately encountered, the woman made her way safely ashore, landing on the coast of British Honduras, and, proceeding promptly to Belize, reported the matter to the authorities.

In the meantime the vessel had reached her port in Spanish Honduras safely, and the two negroes not only got

BL

away safely with the silver dollars, but actually succeeded in selling the vessel herself and her cargo. Considering themselves now quite safe, and never dreaming that the Carib woman could have escaped, they coolly made their way back to Belize, where they were greatly surprised at being arrested on a charge of "piracy on the high seas "— probably the first occasion upon which such a charge had been preferred in the colony. The case aroused a great deal of interest amongst all classes, and the police were indefatigable in collecting evidence for the prosecution, with the result that, after a long and careful trial, the two men were found guilty, as charged, by a jury of their country-men, and were sentenced to death, which sentence was promptly carried out in the Belize gaol.

CHAPTER II

WE left Belize on February 2nd in the Government yacht
Patricia, which had been kindly lent us by H. E. the
Governor for our trip to Corozal, where we were to pick up
our own boat, the *Lilian Y*, a 22-ton sloop with 36 h.p.
auxiliary engine, which had been despatched with provisions for our trip, instruments, photographic material,
etc., the previous day, in charge of my factotum, Amado
Esquivel, generally known as "Muddy." At the last moment
on the somwehat negative recommendation of Muddy that
he had "never been in gaol in Belize," we engaged as cook a
youth named Hubert, a procedure which we never ceased to
regret during the whole trip. As no photograph of him
was available, Held sketched him in profile on the blank
space left on the passport for the photograph, which satisfied
everyone but Hubert himself, who said there was "too
much lip about it to please him."

The trip to Corozal was devoid of incident. Morley
endeavoured to improve the occasion—and his Spanish—
by translating English proverbs into his own language for
a Spanish gentleman to whom we had given passage. "*El
gusano tempano coje el pajaro*"—"The early maggot

catches the bird "—one I happened to overhear, seemed a doubtful recommendation for early rising.

We spent the night at Corozal, the northernmost town of British Honduras, and next morning it was "all aboard the *Lilian Y.*" The party consisted of Sylvanus G. Morley, of the Carnegie Institution ; John Held, artist ; myself ; Captain Usher ; " Muddy " ; Hubert ; George—an immense negro from the Bay Islands, always cheerful, grinning, and ready for work ; a colourless old negro supposed to be cook for the crew, but whose only function appeared to be keeping the stove from falling overboard in heavy weather ; Alfredo, our Honduranian engineer ; and " Boy "—a negro youth from Belize, making his first voyage, ostensibly as oiler to Alfredo, though, as far as we could observe, he never did a stroke of work during the entire voyage, but lay about on deck, getting dirtier and dirtier—for we had no rain— and fatter and fatter, till his only pair of pants, splitting from stem to stern under the strain, became so indecent a spectacle that whenever we touched at any port he had to be segregated in the engine-room.

We arrived at Payo Obispo, capital of the Mexican territory of Quintana Roo, next morning, and were very hospitably received by General Octaviano Solis, Governor of the territory, a veteran of thirty-three or thereabouts, who had risen in and through the revolution. Morley and Held were persuaded to stop over a couple of days, giving and receiving dinners, dances, and suppers, punctuated at frequent intervals by liquid refreshments. I, however, having experienced twenty years of the lavish hospitality of Spanish America, fled in the *Lilian Y* the same evening, arranging to join them at Xcalac, which they could reach in a few hours by crossing the peninsula separating Payo Obispo from the east coast of Yucatan.

I spread my mattress on deck that night to get the most of what little air was stirring, as the cabin was hot and stuffy, and, anyway, a 5ft. 10in. bunk offers no real hope of comfort to a 6ft. individual. About midnight I was roused by

VARIOUS AVATERS OF GEORGE.

[p. 21

SANTA CRUZ INDIAN CHIEF WITH GENERAL SOLIS,
GOVERNOR OF QUINTANA ROO, MEX.

[p. 20

George singing. Standing—or rather crouching—on top of the wheel, the spokes of which he grasped with his prehensible toes, and leaning up against the after house, he reminded one of a great black ape. His voice was a squeaky tenor, and sounded curious coming from such a gigantic individual, but every now and then the bottom seemed to drop out of it, and it became a hoarse bass. I listened for nearly an hour to an apparently inexhaustible repertoire, catching such fragments as, " Oh, where shall ah be when de las psalm is sung ? " " Lard, ef yo doan hep me doan hep de grizzlen bar," and " Kiss me, kiss me." Anyone glimpsing George's kissing apparatus will notice that he should be an adept in the art.

I was aroused about 3 a.m. by a grinding shock, and found that we had run aground on the rocks off Blacadores Cay. A stiff breeze was blowing, and the *Lilian Y* was endeavouring to rip her bottom out on the reef. Ridge after ridge the staunch old tub scraped over, till at last we arrived in deep water, and anchored till daylight. The accident had been caused by George's taking us several miles out of our course, and it was unanimously decided that in future steering should be done in the usual manner, and without musical accompaniment.

About 10 a.m. we ran in through the opening in the reef and anchored off San Pedro, the chief settlement of Yucatecans and Indians on Ambergris Cay. The people here are all fishermen, coco-nut growers, and chicle, or chewing gum, bleeders.

We landed for a bath, breakfast, and a run ashore. During the latter, however, a strong north-east wind set in, and we found ourselves in the same position as two small sugar freighters, bound to Progreso with sugar from Guatemala, who had been held up here unable to pass the opening in the reef for four days. The entire east coast of Yucatan is a nightmare to the small sailing craft which trade along it, as in a strong east or north-east wind they have to run behind the reef for safety, where they may be bottled up for a week, or even longer, waiting for the weather to moderate.

Next morning, the wind having died down somewhat, we set sail, and with the assistance of our 36 h.p. engine negotiated the opening in the reef safely, and found ourselves in the open sea again. Holding a course due north along a low, barren, sandy coast, about midday we sighted Xcalac. A brisk north-eastern was blowing, piling up a ribbon of white surf on the reef, which here and along the whole east coast of Yucatan runs parallel with the shore, hugging it closely in some places, in others retiring a mile or more out to sea. We made for a break in the surf line which looked like a passage through the reef, only to discover, just in time to sheer off, that it was one of those deceptive false openings where, the water being a little deeper than on other parts of the reef, the surf does not show up so conspicuously. This nearly proved the end of our trip before it had well begun, as we missed the jaws of the reef by feet, and had the *Lilian Y* grounded she would very soon have had the bottom torn out of her on the sharp coral fangs, with the heavy sea then running.

Morley and Held turned up in Xcalac within an hour of my arrival. They were accompanied by two members of the Governor's staff to speed the parting guests, and showed distinct signs of wear and tear, bringing with them tales of a truly gorgeous time and most flattering letters of recommendation to all officials in the territory, advising them to give the expedition every assistance in their power.

Xcalac is a miserable little isolated place, perched in the centre of an inaccessible stretch of barren sandy shore. Its population consists exclusively of Mexican soldiers, sailors and officials, the dull monotony of whose life is only broken by the arrival of a gunboat from Vera Cruz, bringing fresh troops for the territory. Like all settlements on the east coast, it has never recovered from the hurricane and tidal wave of the previous year, which simply wiped out the houses and shipping, and tore great *barrancas* through the site occupied by the town.

From Xcalac we ran north all night, arriving at five next morning in front of the opening to Espiritu Santo Bay. At Punta Herrera is a small lighthouse, where we put ashore, and secured one of the light keepers as a pilot for the bay. It is a desolate waste of grey water, running some twenty miles inland, whose western limits have never been thoroughly explored. The shores, flat, barren, swampy, are entirely uninhabited, and covered with mangrove, salt water pimento, and low wiry scrub, while the water shoals off to 2ft. or less a mile from the beach. By means of the pram—an invaluable little boat, which without her Evinrude engine did not draw over 6in., and was absolutely impossible to upset in any sea—we reached the eastern shore, where we found ourselves separated from the land by 100 yds. of evil looking grey ooze. Muddy, stripped to his shirt, waded laboriously ashore through this, which reached well above his knees. Morley—always to the fore in adventures, great and small—next essayed the trip. He had forgotten, however that the soles of Muddy's feet were calloused by many years of shoelessness, and on planting his own tender sole full on a sharp point of rock, with which the bottom of the mud was liberally supplied, he endeavoured to shift the weight to the other foot, which, however, encountered an even sharper tooth. It is not an easy matter to change one's footing rapidly when sunk in two feet of mud, and the performance ended in a series of spasmodic jerks, a shower of mud, collapse, and a shirt much in need of washing. Held and I from front seats in the pram enjoyed the show immensely, and, profiting by the experience, waded slowly ashore with the aid of a stick, never lifting one foot till the other had found at least a tolerably smooth resting-place.

We slept that night on the veranda of the lighthouse, and early next morning set out in the pram with the lighthouse keeper to find a ruin, said to exist somewhere on the south coast of the bay. We passed innumerable sandy and swampy islands, on one of which we discovered an old fishermen's camp, consisting of a few primitive palm-leaf huts—or, rather, conical hut roofs, for they were wall-less—a well of brackish water dug in the sand, and a crawl, or small enclosure of sticks, built in the sea a few yards from the shore, in which the turtle captured may be kept alive till enough have accumulated to make it worth while sending them to Belize or the nearest market.

After nearly two hours' passage along tortuous channels separating mangrove-covered mud swamps, disturbing in our course thousands of water fowl of all kinds, including the beautiful white egret—whose time, however, had not yet arrived, for it is only during the breeding season that he is shot for his plumes—we arrived at a small rocky island covered with almost impenetrable low scrub, near the centre of which we came upon our ruin. It was a small sanctuary, or altar, built of stone and tough mortar, 8ft. square and 5ft. high. The roof and upper part had fallen in. In front was a small door, and in the back wall a square window. The building was covered with eight layers of stucco super-imposed one on the other, each of which had been decorated in red, yellow, blue, and black. On the front, to the right of the door, were the imprints of four red hands, so commonly found on all the buildings of this region. They were made by dipping the hands in red paint, and applying them to the surface to be marked, and may have been the builders' sign manual. Indeed, so clear are they on some interior walls that the maker might still be identified, if in the flesh, by his finger-prints.

The ruin is known to the Indians as Canchè Balaam, or Tiger's Seat, which is probably its original name, handed down from the ancient Maya. It is an insignificant little place, but of interest to us as the first building of this kind we had seen on our trip. Later we were to become well acquainted with the type, which we named the Tuluum style, from the remarkable conformity of all the examples with the architecture of Tuluum, presently to be described, which was evidently the capital city of this east coast civilisation. The solitary little shrine is apparently the southern-most outpost of this civilisation, as to the south and west of it quite a different type of ruin is found, representing a much earlier period of the Maya civilization.

These east coast buildings, whether single or in large or small groups, exhibit certain characteristics in common which distinguish them from both earlier and later Maya architecture. The masonry is crude and rough, and covered both internally and externally by layers of smooth, hard stucco, which nearly always show traces of painted designs. The main entrances of temples and palaces are usually supported on one or more circular stone columns, above which are lintels of sapodilla wood, often still *in situ*, hardly altered by their five hundred years of weathering. The façades are frequently decorated by figures of gods and geometrical devices moulded in exceedingly hard stucco. Stone altars, or shrines, such as that just described, are of frequent occurrence all over the area, and at the larger sites ruins are found of extensive flat-roofed, arcade-like buildings, standing on terraced, stone-faced mounds, and supported by rows of great round stone columns, which were probably used as market-places.

The east coast culture was the dying effort of the great Maya civilisation, and was most probably the work of refugees from Northern Yucatan after the conquest of Mayapan about A.D. 1450, which finally destroyed all central authority amongst the Maya. The whole country was divided into a number of small provinces, each under its own cacique, or ruler, all in a constant state of warfare with each other, up to the arrival of the Spaniards a century later, whose conquest of Yucatan, as of Mexico, was greatly facilitated by the internecine strife of the natives. This lonely, deserted-little shrine, looking out over a vast stretch of grey sea and desolate, uninhabited country, last decadent effort of a once great civilisation, appealed somehow more strongly to our imagination than any of the ruined cities which we later discovered.

Leaving Espiritu Santo at 1.30 p.m., we arrived about 5.30 at Culebra Cays, a group of mangrove islands lying right in the mouth of Ascension Bay. We landed at the easternmost island, where, on a small spit of sand, the only solid spot in the mangrove swamp, we found a curious bee-hive-shaped hut built of palm leaves, occupied by five ancient mariners, inhabitants of the island of San Pedro, who came here every year for some months during the turtle and barracouda fishing season. Wooden frameworks covered with drying fish, and a crawl well filled with green or edible turtle a few yards off shore, showed that their efforts had not been unsuccessful. Hundreds of yards of seine net were hung out to dry, while dozens of the little cedar models of turtles, used as net-floats and decoys for the precious " Caray," or tortoiseshell turtle, strewed the beach. These old fellows, friends of many years' standing, were all married, but liked to get away from their families and have a good time together, camping out here on the bay for six months or so every year, fishing and hunting, and all agreed that the procedure greatly enhanced the joys of matrimony. Their life seemed an ideal one. All they brought with them was corn, tobacco, and coffee, the sea and the bush supplying every other need, even to the material for their house, while the constant sea breeze kept off mosquitoes and sand flies, which are at times such a pest on the mainland. We offered them whisky and cigars. The latter each accepted, but refused the former, all being total abstainers, except the youngest of the party, a youth of perhaps sixty, who said it was so long since he had had a drink that it was hardly worth acquiring the taste again as he would have no means of gratifying it after we had gone.

Next morning we bade good-bye with real regret to our venerable hosts, sorry that, driven by the exigencies of a long route and limited time, we could not give their simple life a longer trial.

A few hours later we reached Ascension, a little settlement perched on a sandbank bounding the northern shore of Ascension Bay. A few years ago it was the headquarters of the Mexican troops sent to subdue the Santa Cruz Indians, and a place of considerable importance, with a fine pier and many large buildings. Like all other east coast settlements, however, it was practically wiped out by the cyclone, and all that remains of its former glory is the gaunt skeleton of the pier and a few ruined buildings. A *celador*, or minor Custom's official, resides here, after reporting to whom we set out for Vigia Chica, higher up the bay, our next port of call, passing on the way the rusting wreck of the old Mexican gunboat *Independencia*, once a participator in the Mexican campaign against the Santa Cruz Indians, now— fit symbol of that campaign—ending her days stuck in the mud opposite the scene of her former activities, like the soldiers she carried, slowly becoming an integral part of the soil of the country she was sent to conquer.

Vigia Chica, once the port of the flourishing city of Santa Cruz de Bravo, and terminal of the National Railroad of Quintana Roo, a 55-kilometre line joining the latter with Santa Cruz, is now little more than a depressing dump of ruined houses, wharf, and rolling-stock. Of all places on the coast it suffered most severely from the cyclone, the houses being flattened out, while the surface of the stone wharf, with the iron rails and rolling-stock, was literally skimmed off and dumped in the sea alongside. A Mexican lieutenant and a dozen soldiers are all that remain of the once large garrison, while the civil population is represented by a few depressed chicle bleeders and contractors, whose business it is to get out as much of the precious chewing gum as they can from the *hinterland*, which is in the territory of the Santa Cruz Indians.

Mule-drawn flat cars still run between Vigia Chica and

Santa Cruz, chiefly for the purpose of taking in chicle bleeders and their supplies, and bringing out chewing gum. Two of them, with the necessary mules, were kindly lent us by the lieutenant and Messrs. Martin & Martinez, chicle bleeders operating in the interior, and on these we set out for Santa Cruz about 2 p.m. On reaching Kilomètre 9 from Virgia everyone had to get off, and with the assistance of the mules carry all the luggage over to Kilometre 11, where two fresh cars awaited us, as the rails had been torn up across this interval to prevent the Santa Cruz Indians making sudden incursions upon the town.

At dusk we arrived at Central, thirty-four kilometres from Vigia Chica, formerly a considerable military depôt, the only relic of which is a large tin-roofed house, the former *cuartel*, or barracks, now used by Messrs. Martin & Martinez as quarters for their chicleros. These chicleros, recruited from the scum of the Mexican peonage, are probably the dirtiest people on earth, and as the *cuartel* was crowded with them and a large pack of their mangy dogs, I erected my folding cot and mosquito curtain on one of the flat cars, which I had pushed about half a mile up the line in order to escape what might be termed the odoriferous zone which surrounded the house. Unfortunately, in the early hours of the morning it came on to pour with rain, and I had to make a break for the house in a tangle of mosquito curtains and blankets, arriving wet through. I found Muddy and Held sitting sadly and wakefully in chairs. The former, who had tried to woo sleep on a blanket in the hall, said he had at last got tired of picking dog fleas off himself, while Held every time he dozed off had been awakened by the incursion into his room of some picturesque brigand apparently in the last stages of consumption—a fairly apt description, for chicleros in their immense wide-brimmed conical hats, machetes, revolvers, bandoliers, cotton shirt and trousers, red blankets and sandals, are certainly picturesque, and all keep up a constant staccato coughing and expectoration upon the floor, while wandering about at intervals during the night smoking innumerable cigarettes.

Next morning we found a small party of Santa Cruz Indians had arrived during the night with a letter from their chief, General Mai, for Mr. Martin. They are small brown men, shy, uncommunicative, and rather anxious-looking, dressed in short bell-shaped trousers, shirtlike coats of cotton, palm-leaf hats and sandals, all of native manufacture. We were exceedingly anxious to meet their chief, as we wished to obtain from him guides and an escort to extensive ruins in the interior of his territory, never before visited by Europeans. The Indians, however, refused to carry a letter to the chief. Neither money nor argument—the latter perhaps not very lucid, as they could only understand Maya—moved them, their contention being that the chief had given them a letter to deliver, which they had accomplished, but had said nothing about bringing a letter back, and if they exceeded their instructions by doing this they might on their return be macheted—or chopped to death by a machete—and would undoubtedly be flogged. We pointed out, however, that if they refused our request we should certainly inform the chief of their discourtesy when we met him. This opened up an unpleasant probability of punishment whatever course they took, and proved so disconcerting that while we were at breakfast the whole party decamped incontinently into the bush, and we saw them no more.

The place was full of sullen, swarthy, unclean Mexican chicleros, who, now that the season was over, and chicle would no longer run from incisions in the bark, had several months of enforced leisure to look forward to, though in order to keep his working force together the employer is obliged to feed them, and even advance them money on account of next year's work.

The chicle bleeder's is a hard life, and only the toughest element of a pretty tough population will sign on for it. It necessitates living all through the rainy season in the heart of the virgin bush, soaked by day and crowded into dirty palm-leaf shelters by night, with poor and insufficient food. The work, which consists in climbing the sapodilla trees and cutting spiral grooves in the bark, along which the sap runs out, to be caught in receptacles at the base of the tree, is not devoid of danger, and many accidents from falls, cuts, and snake bites occur where the patients are separated from the nearest doctor by one hundred miles or more of virgin forest.

The easiest part of the work is boiling down the semi-liquid sap in great iron kettles, to drive off the water, till it becomes a tough, plastic solid, which is put up in oblong blocks, which are carried on mule back to the nearest river or port. In purchasing these blocks, " Caveat emptor " is the motto of the employer, for the ingenuous chiclero frequently inserts a core of wood bark, or even dirt, and sometimes the block consists of a mere skin of chicle, enclosing a core of judiciously weighted alien material.

Later in the day we started on a mule-drawn *plataforma*, or flat car, for Santa Cruz de Bravo. On reaching Kilometre 48 we found the line torn up, and walked on to 49, where we expected to find another car ready to take us on to Santa Cruz. This, however, owing to some misunderstanding, had not been provided, and we were obliged to walk the seven kilometres into Santa Cruz over a very bad and muddy path.

The town of Santa Cruz has a curious history. Founded, as indicated by the old church, towards the end of the sixteenth century by the Spanish *conquistadores* of Yucatan, it appears to have led the placid, uneventful life of a Spanish provincial town up to the year 1848, when in the general uprising of the Maya Indians, driven to desperation by the cruelty and oppression of their Spanish masters, the inhabitants were all either massacred or driven out. From 1848 to 1902 the town was occupied by the Maya, but in the latter year was reconquered by General Bravo on behalf of the Mexican Government. General Bravo renamed the

town Santa Cruz de Bravo, built the railroad over which
we had just come to the town from the port of Vigia Chica,
projected railroads to Payo Obispo in the south and Merida
in the north, imported large numbers of convicts for forced
work from Mexico, held out every inducement to merchants
and settlers, and actually succeeded in creating within a
few years a prosperous Mexican town of 4,000 or so
inhabitants in the heart of the mid-Yucatecan wilderness.
The Indians, however, though driven into the fastnesses
of the bush, never ceased a guerilla warfare against the
garrison and inhabitants. Whenever they encountered a
party of soldiers or civilians in the bush, not too formidable
to be dealt with, they promptly chopped them to pieces,
and on one occasion, on securing a corporal and three
soldiers, tied them securely in a little palm-leaf house,
saturated them with kerosene, and set fire to the house.
The Mexicans, on their side, whenever they came across an
Indian settlement in the bush promptly wiped out the
inhabitants and destroyed their corn plantations. Notwithstanding the fact that the bush had been cleared for
two or three hundred metres on either side of the railroad,
the Indians constantly attacked the trains, massacring
soldiers and civilians and looting baggage. Finding at last
that the land in the vicinity was of little agricultural value,
that the town itself was cut off from communication with
other places on all sides by dense bush, and that the Indians
were a constant menace, the Mexicans determined to
abandon the town and hand it over again to the Santa Cruz
Indians, though its acquisition had cost them rivers of
blood and millions of dollars.

The following year this abandonment was effected ;
soldiers, convicts, and civilians were withdrawn, and,
scattering over various parts of the Republic, left the town
without a single inhabitant.

It was in this town, abandoned for over a year, that we now
arrived. The wooden houses, some of them really magnificent structures, were falling into decay, the streets and the

beautiful little plaza (with its stone fountains, promenades, and seats, surrounded by an orange grove) were choked with bush and weeds, the fountains were dry and filled with leaves, and the town was occupied by a single family of Santa Cruz Indians, who had taken up their abode in a two roomed mud-floored shack, though they might have occupied the Governor's palace, and were gradually pulling down the wooden houses to use the lumber as firewood. The fine old sixteenth century Spanish church was the only building which stood forth unaltered among the ruins of the modern gingerbread Mexican city ; it is 105 ft. by 36 ft., and 80 ft. high, with massive walls 8 ft. thick. During the Maya occupation of the city it was the centre of that remarkable religious cult, the worship of the Santa Cruz, or Holy Cross, from which the Santa Cruz Indians derive their name. Between the expulsion of the Spaniards by the Indians and the conquest of the latter by the Mexicans in 1902 no priest of any denomination was permitted to enter the Santa Cruz country. The Indians, however, appointed priests from among their own number, who carried out a sort of travesty of the rites of the Roman Catholic Church, freely interspersed with those of their ancient religion. The headquarters of the cult was at the capital, and centred round what was known as the Santa Cruz, a plain wooden cross some two to three feet high, probably removed from some church after the expulsion of the Spaniards. It was gifted with the power of speech—probably owing to the ventriloquial power of one of the priests—and acted as an oracle, to whom all matters of importance, civil, military, or religious, were referred. It need hardly be said that the cross never failed to return an answer to any of these questions in entire conformity with the wishes of the chief.

In 1859 a mission was despatched by the Superintendent of British Honduras to the chiefs of the Santa Cruz Indians, with the object of endeavouring to rescue some Spanish prisoners held by them. One of the members of the

SANTA CRUZ DE BRAVO: OLD CATHOLIC CHURCH.

[p. 32

BACALAR: RUINS OF THE OLD CHURCH WHERE THE MASSACRES
OF SPANIARDS TOOK PLACE BY THE SANTA CRUZ INDIANS.

[p. 34

expedition, in a manuscript account left of its failure, says :

" That night all the available Indians arrived in front of the house where the Santa Cruz is kept. The boy attendants, or sentries of the idol, called " angels," with the subordinate chiefs and soldiers, knelt outside, and did not rise till the service was over, when they crossed themselves, and rubbed their foreheads in the dust. About 11 o'clock the Indians were heard running backward and forward, and an order was given to bring out the prisoners, who were placed in a line before the Santa Cruz, and a large body of soldiers was placed with them. They all knelt down in the road. There were about forty female prisoners with one arm tied to the side, and twelve or fourteen men pinioned by both arms. All were calm except the children, although it was known that Santa Cruz was pronouncing their doom. A squeaking, whistling noise was heard proceeding from the oracle, and when it ceased it was known that the Santa Cruz wanted a higher ransom for prisoners."

This, apparently, was not forthcoming, for later the chronicler says :

" Some of the women and children were separated from the rest, amongst whom was a young Spanish girl well known in high circles. A procession was then formed, and marched off to the east gate ; first came a strong body of troops, and then alternately, in Indian file, a male prisoner and his executioner, who drove him on with his machete, holding him by a rope. Next came the women, thirty-five in number, driven and held in a similar manner ; then another body of soldiers closed the rear. The Englishmen were not allowed to follow. The procession halted under a clump of trees about 150 yds. off
CL

Soon the butchery commenced and shrieks were heard, but in ten minutes all was over.

" The Santa Cruz was mixed up with some Catholic rites, but retains the leading characteristics of the god, who was best propitiated by placing bleeding human hearts within his lips."

As we contemplated this solid, ugly old church, still standing square and uncompromising amidst the surrounding ruin and desolation, we could not help thinking, if an aura of the human emotions experienced within them clings to buildings, what a black cloud of misery and despair must environ and fill it ; first of victims of the Holy Office under the Spanish occupation ; later of unfortunate wretches brought for the judgment upon them of the Santa Cruz, which almost invariably in its squeaking whisper condemned them to death by *machetazos*, or being chopped in pieces by a machete ; and last, and perhaps worst, of the miserable prisoners under the Mexican occupation, when the church was used as a gaol, and hundreds of prisoners were crowded promiscuously into the nave—men, women, and children— with the offscourings of the criminal population from Mexico City, locked in together at night.   Free fights were common, and often wound-covered corpses were removed in the morning, while filth, vermin, and immorality were rampant always.

With these thoughts running through our minds we entered the lofty nave, silent, gloomy, acrid with the smell of bats, dank and cold by contrast with the warm sun outside. We did not remain long, however, but, chilled and depressed, soon made for the open air again, and hunted up the single Indian family left in charge of the deserted city.   None of them could understand a word of any language but Maya. Our wants, however, were easily indicated—food, plenty of it, and right away.   We were soon provided with a sort of omelette made from eggs and tiny round tomatoes fried together, with plenty of tortillas, or corn cake, and sacha,

INCENSE BURNER.

Found in considerable numbers throughout the Santa Cruz country, the figures are believed by the Maya to come to life by night.

[p. 38

BACALAR CHURCH INTERIOR.

Here took place the massacre by the Indians of the Spaniards in 1848; their bones were till recently piled in a great heap on one side of the nave, and splotches of blood are still visible on the walls.

[p. 34

a very unattractive drink made from ground corn and water. The tomatoes were delicious, and sweet as sugar, though it was not till later that we discovered the plants from which they came climbing luxuriantly over the graves in the churchyard.

CHAPTER III

WE left Santa Cruz without regret, and were agreeably surprised to find a *plataforma* awaiting us at the railhead. Harnessed to it, however, was a gaunt mule ominously named " Floja " (lazy)—a name which her conduct did not belie, for never at any stage of the journey could we get more than three miles an hour out of her, though the driver tried every device known to muleteers, pulling the car up by the traces so that its front edge caught her hind legs, which manœuvre she lazily met by trotting a few paces to escape the car, and when she felt the strain on the traces aiming a murderous flying kick at the driver over the top of the car during the manœuvre. We coaxed her with sticks, stones, and even scraps of burning palm leaf, while the driver, after cursing her by all the saints in the calendar without avail, tried *cariño*, or soft sawder, calling her " *Chula Mula*," " *Dulce corazon* " (sweetheart), " *Mulita bonita* " (pretty little lady mule), till at last, hoarse and tired, even he resigned himself to the inevitable.

While we plodded slowly along, Don Julio Martin told us of a graveyard where were situated some old tombs, a few miles outside Central, and next morning early we set out to visit them.

After retracing our route of the previous day for a few miles up the tram-line, we turned off into a *milpa*, or maize plantation, where we found a number of small tumuli, built of earth and large boulders, probably burial mounds of the ancient Maya. Passing through this, we soon entered the forest, and after a quarter of an hour's walk came upon the first " tomb," which proved to be a little two-storied Maya shrine, standing upon a stone platform 20ft. by 15ft. It was constructed of roughly squared stones held together by very tough mortar. The upper story was 3ft. 4in. high, 4ft. long, and 3ft. 10in. broad, and possessed a single small doorway facing due west ; the lower was 6ft. 9in. long and 6ft. 4in. broad, and had doorways in all four walls, over each of which were oblong recesses 5in. deep.

Small Maya Shrine.

The figure shows the ground plan of the building, with a median core or column of masonry passing up through its centre, and rounded interior angles, leaving a narrow oval passage into which opened a small doorway on each side of the building. The whole structure was covered throughout with hard, smooth stucco, which at the bottom of the recesses above the doorway, where it had been protected from the weather, still showed traces of red, black, and white pigments.

Don Julio informed us that some years ago this little shrine was surmounted by a stone cross about 2ft. 6in. in height, which had been thrown down and smashed in pieces by the Mexican soldiers stationed at Central, to whom the sight of a cross is as a red rag to a bull. His story was probably true, as on the roof of the upper storey we found a depression surrounded by cement, evidently made to support a square column.

This opens up a . very interesting problem : was the building erected by the Maya, after they had become Christianised, as a shrine, such as one sees at the stations of the cross which surround many modern Indian villages, their old style of architecture remaining unaltered, except by the addition of a cross ; was it erected in pre-Columbian days, and later adapted to Christian uses ; or was it (as Don Julio supposed) a tomb built over one of their chiefs who had embraced Christianity ? Interesting but unfortunately futile speculations, which can now probably never be answered.

The Santa Cruz Indians, degenerate, traditionless descendants of the ancient Maya, call these shrines " *Kahtal alux*," " houses of the little people." All through this territory are found in considerable numbers large pottery incense burners, upon the outside of which are sculptured in high relief human figures, two to three feet high, covered by a wealth of ornament and decoration. The Indians firmly believe that at night these figures come to life, leave the vases to which they are attached, and visit these little houses, the scene of their former life, returning by day to lifeless pottery. There were four more of these shrines scattered through the bush within a radius of half a mile, all replicas of the one described, but none in quite such a perfect state of preservation.

Returning to Central, we passed a dance platform built of stone, with flat, cement-covered top, 27½ft. long by 16ft. broad, and 3½ft. high. These platforms are found at even the smallest ancient Maya sites, and were used by the people for ceremonial dances and dramatic entertainments, of which they were inordinately fond, for, according to the ancient chroniclers, the Maya of Yucatan were at the time of the conquest at once the gayest and most pleasure-loving people, and the most fettered by religious observance, possible to conceive

Close to the platform we came across a stone-faced pond, or cistern, 30ft. in diameter, still containing good drinking water, though much silted up with the mud and the vegetal accumulation of several centuries. These sunken stone-lined cisterns are fairly common in this part of Yucatan, and probably form the solution of the problem of how the former inhabitants obtained their water-supply in a country void of rivers and springs, where for four months in the year it hardly rains at all.

Within twenty-four hours we had been brought in contact with relics of the three civilisations which during the last thirteen centuries had dominated Yucatan—the Maya represented, by the shrines, the dance platform, and the cistern, lasting from the sixth to the sixteenth century ; the Spanish represented by the old church at Santa Cruz, from the sixteenth to the early nineteenth ; and the Mexican, represented by the ruined city of Santa Cruz, from the end of the Spanish occupation to the present day. While the works of the Maya and Spanish architects stand to-day almost untouched by the hand of time, practically in the same condition as on the day when they were first completed, the meretricious remains of the modern civilisation, though only deserted for a few years, are rapidly falling into decay, and in but a few more years will have disappeared completely—streets and plazas, private houses and public buildings, stucco and woodwork—before the all-devouring bush, leaving no smallest trace of their existence.

The same afternoon we started back from Central for the coast in a single flat car, seven of us perched insecurely and uncomfortably on top of our mountains of impedimenta. Five kilometres from Central two Indians dodged out of a little bush path on to the track, and on coming up with them we were delighted to find that they were First Captain Desiderio Cochua, Commander-in-Chief of the Army of General Mai, the head chief of all the Santa Cruz Indians, together with the General's nephew, a precocious youth whom I had encountered before, when he formed one of a

deputation sent to interview the Governor of British
Honduras on behalf of the Santa Cruz Indians. Their
clothes gave no indication of their high rank, consisting
merely of sandals, straw hats, loose, shirt-like cotton coats
and bell-shaped trousers rolled up to the knee, while their
modest luggage, consisting of a hammock and roll of *toto-
poste* (large, hard, thin corn cakes, specially made to carry
on a journey) slung in a net over the shoulders by a strap
passing round the forehead, put our own vast carload of
bags, boxes, suit-cases, pots, pans, firearms, canned goods,
wraps, etc., completely to shame. We all got off the car,
and, sitting on the railroad embankment, formed ourselves
into an entertainment committee for the two Indians with
the help of Scotch whisky and cigars for the Captain, and
chocolate creams and cigarettes for the boy, to the accompaniment of American ragtime on the horrible, cheap little
gramophone, the delight of Morley's heart, which accompanied us on all our travels by land or sea.

The Captain spoke only his native language, so our sole
means of communication with him was through Muddy,
my knowledge of Maya being Ollendorfian, and confined to
such useful commercial phrases as : " *Yan tech ha, he, chicken
caax, imixua*"—" Have you any water, eggs, chickens,
corn cake ? " and " *Bahux takin hakatiola ?* "—" How
much do you want for them ? " with " *Tech hach kichpan
Xchupal* "—" You are a very pretty girl "—" *Tzaten,
tzetic, tzutz* "—" Will you give me a kiss ? "—for social
small coin.

The Captain informed us that he was going to Central
to transact some business for the chief, who was laid up
with whooping cough in a village a couple of days' journey
off in the bush. Whooping cough, like measles, mumps, and
scarlatina, is an extremely fatal complaint amongst the
Indians, to whom it is a comparatively new disease, against
which the immunity acquired after centuries by European
has not yet come as a protection. He was very friendly
and cordial, expressing unbounded admiration for the

English—amongst whom Morley, notwithstanding his New England accent, was included—and promised that if he could possibly manage it he would meet us with a guard a week from the following Sunday, and take us to a ruined city behind Tuluum, far larger, finer, and in better preservation than the latter ; in any case, if he could not turn up, he promised that the chief should send messages to the head man at Acumal, the nearest village to Tuluum on the coast, instructing him to have guides ready to take us to the ruins. We were greatly elated at these promises, as no European had ever been permitted by the Indians to approach these ruins, rumours of whose good state of preservation and extent had already reached us. Unfortunately, as it turned out, we were not to visit them on this occasion, as, though we waited three days at Tuluum for Desiderio, he did not turn up, being detained at Central, and on reaching Acumal we were unable to get the *Lilian Y* in through the opening in the reef, which is here very narrow. Our visit, however, is only postponed, not abandoned.

Before leaving them for good some description of the Santa Cruz Indians, with whom we had probably come in closer contact in this and former expeditions than any other Europeans, may prove of interest. They are the last independent tribe of aboriginal Indians in Central America, and are probably the purest representatives of that great Maya race, written records of whose civilisation have been found antedating the Christian era. The territory at present occupied by them reaches from Acumal, in the north of Yucatan, to the head of the Bacalar Lagoon in the south, a distance of approximately 200 kilometres, extending inland for about 70 kilometres. They are the direct descendants of those Maya who, about the middle of the fifteenth century, after the fall of Mayapan, emigrated to the east coast of Yucatan, and founded what may be called the east coast civilisation, whose ruins it was our object on this trip to explore.

Physically these Indians, though short, are robust and

well-proportioned, the men averaging 5ft. 2in. to 5ft. 3in. in height—the women perhaps a couple of inches less. The hair in both sexes is long, coarse, black, and luxuriant on the head, but absent on other parts of the body. The complexion varies from nearly white to chocolate colour, the skull is very broad, the features and extremities small and finely modelled, and the eyes large, dark brown, and (except in the younger girls, where they are sometimes languishing, but more frequently mischievous) sad, or merely bovine in expression. The teeth are beautiful, but in middle life get worn down very much from constantly eating corn cake impregnated with grit from the rubbing-stone—indeed, they say themselves that every old man or woman eats a rubbing-stone and three *brazos* (the stone with which the corn is ground) in the course of their lives. Many of the younger women are extremely handsome, measured even by the most exacting standard, though they reach maturity at a very early age, and when a European woman would hardly have begun to show the ravages of time they are wrinkled hags. Bow-legs (*xkulok*) are usually common amongst them, due probably to the fact that the children from the time they can toddle are taught to carry the *macapal*, a netted bag slung from the forehead, resting on the shoulders, and not (as the early chroniclers supposed) because they were carried as infants riding astride their mother's hip. The constant carrying of a *macapal* has given them a curious and characteristic gait—the upper part of the body bent forwards, eyes on the ground, toes turned in—and so used have they become to it that often on going a journey with no luggage to carry they put a few stones in the *macapal* to act as a counterpoise.

Nearly all the Santa Cruz have a peculiar faint, not unpleasant odour, somewhat suggestive of peat smoke, and not affected by washing. It rather reminds one of the peaty smell of the West of Ireland peasant, and, like this, is no doubt due to frequent exposure to wood smoke in the chimneyless room.

The women are much superior in looks and physique to the men, and when got up in gala costume they present a very attractive appearance, with exquisitely embroidered white cotton *huipil* (a loose, sleeveless garment cut very low at the neck and back, closely resembling the feminine evening dress of modern civilisation, but leaving more to the imagination), gold chains, pendants, and earrings of native workmanship, and often a small coronet of fire beetles, resembling tiny electric lamps, in their magnificent hair.

When quarrelling amongst themselves the women and girls use the most disgusting and obscene language, improvising as they go along with remarkable quick-wittedness, not bound down, like more civilised people, by stereotyped forms in oath and invective, but pouring out a ceaseless stream of vituperation and obscenity to meet each case, which strikes with unerring fidelity the weak points morally, physically, and ancestrally in their opponents' armour. They are very industrious, usually arising between three and four every morning to prepare the day's supply of corn cake for their lord and master's early breakfast. During the day they have few idle moments, as they cure tobacco, make cigarettes, gather cotton, which they spin and weave, make palm-leaf mats and liana baskets, cotton and hempen string, and rope hammocks, nets, and cooking and other utensils of pottery—in fact, every conceivable household article, for which her less adaptable civilised sister would have to send to half a dozen different stores, the Maya woman has to manufacture herself from such materials as the bush provides. Nor is she imbued with any tincture of the modern movement for emancipating women from the care of the household, for, in addition to her other multifarious duties, she does the family cooking and washing, and even helps her husband with the livestock.

Most of these independent Indians are utterly lacking in any ambition to accumulate wealth. It occasionally happens, however, that one of them does acquire it, as in the case of the Head Chief of the Icaiche Indians—neighbours of the Santa Cruz, but much more *pacíficos* than they —who was paid a salary by the Mexican Government to keep his people quiet, in addition to royalties on chicle cut on his tribal lands by various contractors. He accumulated no less than two demijohns full of gold coin, which, having no wants requiring money for their satisfaction, he simply buried in the bush, where presumably they still remain, as before his death, which was sudden, and due to a growing unpopularity amongst his people, he neglected to confide the secret of their location to his family.

The Santa Cruz's real god is his *milpa*, or corn plantation, for he knows that if the corn crop fails from any cause actual starvation menaces him and his family till the next crop comes in. The plantation consists merely of a small clearing in the virgin bush, made about December. The vegetation, which is thoroughly dry about May, the end of the dry season, is then burnt, and the corn planted by making holes with a sharp stick in the soil at fairly regular intervals, dropping in a few grains of corn, covering them over, and leaving the rest to Providence. When the corn begins to ripen, about the end of October, the owner constructs a country residence of a couple of dozen or so large palm leaves in his *milpa*, and practically takes up his abode there till the crop is harvested, as deer and wild hog are extremely fond of corn, while the pigs of neighbouring landed proprietors, and even the proprietors themselves, have to be closely guarded against.

In the Indian menu *ixim*, as he calls maize, is the *pièce de résistance*. Corn cakes are prepared from it in the following manner. The grain is soaked overnight in a lye of wood ashes, which softens the kernel and removes the outer husk. The softened kernel is next ground to a paste on a slightly concave oblong stone by means of a stone rolling-pin. This process takes considerable time and labour, and one is always awakened between 3 and 4 a.m. in an Indian hut by the clank, clank of the rubbing-stone, vigorously wielded by a half-naked woman, who literally waters the bread with the sweat of her brow. The mass of ground corn, when finished, is flattened out by hand into little round, thin cakes, which are baked on a pottery or iron disc, and must be eaten very hot—a fact which precludes the possibility of the whole family ever dining together, as the women have to keep preparing the cakes one at a time and handing them to the men as fast as they can prepare and bake them. They sit, when eating, at little round tables about 2ft. high on small blocks of wood.

In addition to these cakes, they make a great variety of drinks from ground corn and water, flavoured with honey, or cacao ; one of them, known as *pinol*, is made from parched corn, and has almost exactly the colour and flavour of coffee, from which it is practically indistinguishable. This *pinol*, a true " coffee substitute," was probably used by the Maya centuries before the genuine coffee-bean was employed in the East.

They obtain fire by means of a flint and steel, or by swiftly rotating a sharp-pointed shaft of hard wood—generally dogwood—in a hole made in a small dry slab of some very soft wood—usually gumbolimbo.

A great variety of game is found in the Santa Cruz country, including deer, antelope, wild hog, armadillo, gibnut, wild turkey, quam, corrasow, quail, pigeon, and partridge. Besides these, iguana, woula—a large species of constrictor snake—and other snakes are eaten, and turtles are often captured along the coast and adjacent islands, while their eggs in the breeding season form a great delicacy for the Santa Cruz in the neighbourhood of Tuluum. The jaguar, puma, picote, monkey, tapir, and squirrel are also hunted from time to time for their skins or flesh. Traps of two kinds are in common use. One is constructed by digging a deep pit with outward sloping sides, the top of which is covered with branches, into which the animal falls and is unable to get out. Another, also used for catching large game, is constructed in the following way. A path frequented by game in going to and from a watering-place is found. Along this is dug a shallow trench opposite a good, springy young sapling. Two stakes are driven in, one on each side of the trench, the one farthest from the sapling being crooked at the top. A piece of hempen cord provided with a noose at one end, and with a stick long enough to extend from one stake to the other, firmly tied by its middle above the noose, is attached to the top of the sapling by its other end. The sapling is then bent down and held in place by the stick above the noose, which is fixed lightly between the crook in one stake and the stake opposite to it, the loop hanging suspended between the two. Lastly a number of sticks and leaves are scattered lightly over the trench, and beside the stakes and loop. An animal coming along the run is very apt to thrust its neck through the loop, and by pulling on this to release the cross stick, whereupon it is immediately jerked into the air by the recoil of the sapling. Animals of all sizes are caught in traps of this kind, the strength and adaptability of which vary with the size of the bent tree and the adjustment of the noose.

The houses are single-roomed affairs, the wells constructed of *tasistas*, or small palm sticks, the roof of palm-leaf thatch, and the floor of hard earth. They contain no furniture beyond the family hammocks, as eating, cooking, and most of the important business of life is carried on in the kitchen. It is difficult to navigate the room without coming in contact with the hammocks, but these should be touched with great caution, as in many cases countless livestock leave the body of the hammock during the day, and secrete themselves in the knots at the junction of the body and arms, a strategic position for night raids and for a transfer to the garments of the unwary at any time. Privacy under these conditions is naturally impossible, but they never seem to feel the need of it, and in the presence of strangers, equally with their own men, the women and girls are quite natural and unashamed, though by no means shameless.

Indian girls married formerly at about fourteen or fifteen

boys at seventeen or eighteen years. After the conquest of Bacalar and Santa Cruz, however, and the expulsion of the Yucatecans from Indian territory, a law came into force making marriage compulsory for all girls of twelve years of age and upwards. This was probably done with a view to increasing the population, which had been considerably depleted by the long-continued war. One would have imagined that, as it was the fighting male population which had suffered chiefly by the war, polygamy would have been the natural remedy to suggest itself, but, curiously enough, this practice seems always to have been repugnant to the Maya, and at no time during their centuries-long history do we find it prevalent. Even the chiefs, kings, and caciques rarely indulged in more than one wife, official or otherwise, while the priests were not permitted to marry at all.

The Maya are by no means an amorous race, notwithstanding the fact that at the coming of the Spaniards they practised certain dithyrambic dances for which the Spanish priests insisted on substituting the ungraceful shuffle known as the " Mestisada," in which the men and women prance solemnly and stiltedly about like marionettes in front of each other, without even circling or touching. I have frequently watched the course of young love in Maya lovers from genesis to consummation, but never have I been able to detect that longing for physical contact as experienced in kissing, hand holding, and waist clasping, or for psychic contact to the exclusion of the rest of the world, as expressed in glances, smiles, and unintelligible mumbles, so characteristic in more civilised lovers. On the contrary, they seem to take it all as a purely business proposition ; the man wants someone to help him in the house, the woman wants someone to provide food—and that is all there is to it. In one particular only do they conform to the code of Venus ; the mating season is almost invariably in the spring. Formerly amongst the Santa Cruz the first question of a father to his daughter's prospective suitor was, " *Hi tzak a kul, hi tzak Taman ? "*—" How many macates of corn and cotton have you ? " At the present day, however, there are not enough men to go round, and he is glad to see anything in the way of a prospective son-in-law turn up.

The babies and small children are pretty, merry little things, generally seen rolling or toddling about in the sun and dust, unclothed save for a string of beads, dried seeds, shells, and stone, clay or wood figures, worn round their necks. Many of these are worn as charms or amulets to protect the wearer from diseases, accidents, and evil spirits, and to bring good luck. A charm worn by nearly all children consists of a small cross of the bark of the *tancasche*, regarded as a sovereign remedy for flatulence, a complaint from which, owing to the nature of their diet, nearly all suffer. A tiny gold key is worn by unbaptised children, with which, should they die without baptism, they may themselves open the gates of paradise.

The ancient chroniclers frequently mention the fact that, at the time of the Spanish conquest, drunkenness was the curse of the Indians, and the cause of many crimes among them, including murder, rape, and arson. These remarks apply equally well to the present day ; indeed, drunkenness is probably even more prevalent now than then, as the rum made by the Indians of to-day is far more intoxicating than the *balchè*, a drink made from fermented honey, water, and roots, used by their ancestors. Moreover, the people drink rum practically whenever they can get it, whereas both the preparation and consumption of *balchè* were to some extent ceremonial, as was the resulting intoxication. Drunkenness is not regarded as in any sense a disgrace, but rather as a beatific state, for which those who reach it are to be envied rather than criticised. The women, especially the older ones, drink a good deal, but they usually do so in the privacy of their own houses. I have, however, seen a little girl of fourteen or fifteen purchase a pint of rum in a village liquor shop, go out on the plaza, swallow it in a few gulps, and then, lying down deliberately in the hot sun, lapse into a state of alcoholic coma. Alcohol effects an extraordinarily rapid change for the worse in the Indian temperament. From a quiet, polite, rather servile individual, he is metamorphosed almost in an instant into a maudlin idiot, staggering about singing foolish snatches of native songs, howling, shrieking, and endeavouring to embrace everyone he comes in contact with. When thwarted while in this condition his temper is likely to flare up at the slightest provocation, whereupon the thin veneer of civilisation and restraint is sloughed in a moment, and he becomes savage, insolent, overbearing, and contemptuous towards the stranger, and ready to draw his machete and fight to kill, with friend or foe alike.

On the death of a head chief of the Santa Cruz Indians the oldest of the sub-chiefs is supposed to succeed him ; as a matter of fact, there are always rival claimants for the chieftainship, and the sub-chief with the strongest personality or greatest popularity amongst the soldiers usually succeeds in grasping the office. There are nearly always rival factions endeavouring to oust the chief in power, and the latter rarely dies in his bed. The power of the head chief is practically unlimited over the whole tribe. Some time ago, when Roman Pec was head chief, one of the sub-chiefs came to Corozal (the nearest settlement to the Santa Cruz country in British Honduras) for the purpose of purchasing powder, shot, and other supplies. He remained some time, as he had many friends in the place, and purchased, amongst other things, a bottle of laudanum to relieve toothache. On returning to his village he was met by three soldiers, who informed him that he was to go at once with them to the head chief, as the latter was angry with him on account of his long absence from the country. Aware that this was equivalent to a sentence of death, he asked permission to retire to his home for a few minutes to prepare for the journey, and, taking advantage of the opportunity, swallowed the entire contents of the bottle of laudanum. This began to take effect very shortly, and, notwithstanding the best efforts of the soldiers, who dragged

DL

him along, prodding him vigorously with the points of their machetes, long before reaching the capital and the presence of the head chief he was dead.

The method of executing those sentenced to death is curious. The accused does not undergo a formal trial, but the evidence against him is placed before the head chief ; if he is convicted he has an opportunity of defending himself, and of producing witnesses in his behalf. Three or four soldiers are chosen by the chief to carry out the sentence, which they do by chopping the victim to death with their machetes when they catch him asleep or off his guard. Several men always " execute the orders of the court," all chopping the victim at the same time, so that no single individual may be held responsible for his death. Imprisonment as a punishment for crime is unknown, fine, flogging, and death being the only three methods employed in dealing with criminals. The severity of the flogging is regulated by the nature of the offence, and after it is over the recipient is compelled publicly to express sorrow for his offence, and go around humbly kissing the hands of all the spectators, after which, by way of consolation, he is given a large calabash of *anisado* (rum with an anise flavour) to drink. The heaviest punishment is meted out for sorcery or witchcraft, as the *pulya*, or sorceress, is greatly dreaded by the Indians. She is literally chopped limb from limb, but whereas the bodies of other victims executed in this way are always buried, that of the *pulya* is left for the dogs and vultures to dispose of.

Both men and women when attacked by any serious malady, are found to be lacking in stamina and vitality ; they relax their hold on life very easily, seeming to regard it as hardly worth a fight to retain. An elderly man or woman will sometimes take to their hammock without apparent physical symptoms of disease beyond the anæmia from which nearly all suffer, and quietly announce to his or her relatives : " *He in cimli* "—" I am going to die." They refuse to eat, drink, or talk, wrap themselves in a sheet from head to foot, and finally, in a very short time, do succumb, apparently from sheer distaste of life and absence of desire to go on living. This point of view is well recognised by the friends and relatives, and they rarely worry the patient with food, drink, medicine, or cheering or encouraging conversation, holding that when an individual is tired of life, he is, if he feels so inclined, perfectly at liberty to leave it.

Smallpox, known as "*kak*," or fire, invading an Indian village is a terrible scourge, far worse than in a more civilised community of the same size, where partial immunity has been conferred by the presence of the disease for many centuries. Sometimes the whole unaffected population departs from the village *en masse*, leaving the dead unburied, and the stricken lying in their hammocks with a supply of food and water, to perish or recover unaided as best they can. Their treatment for this disease is similar to that employed by them in malaria, namely, the production of profuse sweating, followed by sudden immersion in cold water— the colder the better. It need hardly be said that the patient, who might have overcome the disease unaided, not unfrequently succumbs to the remedy. Bleeding is a very favourite remedy, especially for headache and any febrile disorder. Usually the temporal vein above and in front of the ear is opened, but sometimes one of the veins of the forearm, which has first been distended with blood by tying a ligature round the arm higher up. A chip of obsidian, a sharp splinter of bone, or a snake's tooth serves as a lancet, the last being the favourite, as, though more painful than the other two, it is supposed to possess some esoteric virtue, which helps out the cure of the disease. Decoctions from the carcasses of dried and mummified animals form no inconsiderable part of the Indian pharmacopœia, certain animals being regarded as specifics for certain diseases, During an epidemic of whooping cough which I witnessed a decoction of the charred remains of the cane rat was almost exclusively given to the children to relieve the cough.

In this case it is very hard to trace any connection between the remedy and the disease, but some remedies are undoubtedly used on the assumption that " *Similia similibus curantur*," as in the case of *Xhudub pek*, twin seeds closely resembling enlarged glands, the milky juice from which is regarded as specific for glandular swellings in all parts of the body.

The Maya Indians are extremely superstitious, believing that the air is full of *pishan*, or souls of the dead, who are at liberty at all times to return to their old haunts on earth, and at certain seasons are compelled to do so. The *pishan* are capable of enjoying the spirit, though not the substance of human food, especially for some time just after they have left the body ; hence the provision by friends and relatives of food and drink for the dead, sometimes in their houses, sometimes on their graves. Some *pishan* are believed to be friendly to mortals, others inimical. They believe also in spirits known as Xtabai, who have never undergone incarnation on earth. These are always harmful, or at best mischievous, and often take the form of a beautiful woman, whose chief desire is to lead men astray, often luring the victim on into the bush with enchanting voice and backward glances, half disclosing her supernatural beauty, till he is irretrievably lost, and wanders about half demented to die of hunger and thirst. At other times the victim is allowed to overtake and grasp the beautiful Xtabai, but the first touch is death, consequently the cause usually assigned for the demise of anyone found dead on the trails, or in the bush, without any external marks of violence, is " touched by a Xtabai."

Another belief commonly held by the Indians is that the images of Christian saints, like the clay images of their ancient gods upon the incensarios already mentioned, are at times endowed with life, and the powers of speech and locomotion, and that on these occasions they are capable of actively aiding their faithful devotees. A celebrated wooden image supposed to represent San Bernardo, was credited with considerable powers in this respect, and when an Indian wanted rain for his *milpa*, the return of an errant wife, good hunting, or any similar blessing, he would come and pray to the image to obtain it for him.

On one occasion a devotee arrived from a distant village imploring the saint to aid him in the recovery of his pigs, which had been lost, and on returning to his village found to his joy that the pigs had arrived home before him. Next day he returned, with the intention of making an offering to the saint for his good offices, and incidentally, a present to the owner of the house where the saint dwelt. He found the poor *santo* much dishevelled, with torn clothes, and burrs and thorns sticking all over him. On enquiring how this had come about he was informed that the saint had been out in the bush hunting for pigs, a quest which had given him a great deal of trouble before he could find and drive them home, and that when he got back he was tired out, his face scratched, and his clothes torn by thorns and covered with burrs—an explanation which completely satisfied the Indian, and naturally called for a very handsome present to the saint.

The image of San Isidro now reposing at Bacalar is even more celebrated. Some years ago the Santa Cruz Indians wished to remove the saint from his little shrine in Bacalar to the great church in Santa Cruz, a resting-place more in accord with his dignity. For this purpose he was laid in a hammock, and carried by relays of Indians to a swamp dividing the two places, where a halt was made for the night. Next morning, to the consternation of the bearers, the image of the saint was found to be missing. On returning to Bacalar to report the disappearance, they were overjoyed to find him standing as usual in his lowly shrine, crook in hand, halo on head, looking benevolently down on them. Three times in all they tried to remove him, but on each occasion at the night halt the saint returned to his old quarters at Bacalar, till they realised that he preferred his own shrine to the great church at Santa Cruz, and, with reputation greatly enhanced, he was after that left in peace.

Many curious superstitions are associated with the ruins found throughout this country. I was assured by an Indian that he had gone on one occasion to the ruins situated near the village of Benque Viego, and, seeing a pigeon seated on a tree, raised his gun to shoot it. Before he could do so, however, the pigeon changed into a cock, and then almost instantaneously into an eagle, which flew at him and drove him away.

There is a further superstition connected with these ruins to the effect that when the first settlers came to Benque Viego, they wished to build the village near the ruins, where plenty of cut stone is available, and land is excellent for corn growing. They were, however, repeatedly driven off by a little old man with a long grey beard, who appeared when anyone tried to dig a post hole on the new site, and whose appearance was so threatening and terrible that they finally gave up the idea, and contented themselves with the present site, which, it must be admitted, is in many ways inferior.

Nominally they are Christians, but the more one sees of them, and the better one gets to know them, the more one realises that their Christianity is merely a thin veneer, and that fundamentally their religious conceptions, and even their ritual and ceremonies, are survivals—degenerate, much altered, and with most of their significance lost, but still survivals of those of their ancestors in pre-Columbian days. To Christianity, not as a separate faith, but as a welcome addition to their ancient religion, they took kindly from the first. The innumerable saints of the Roman Catholic Church were grafted on the not very extensive Maya pantheon, and at the present day the Sun God, the Wind God, the Rain God, Our Lady of Guadelupe, Saint Lawrence, and Santa Clara, may all be invoked in the same prayer, while the cross is substituted in most of the ceremonies for the images of the old gods, though many of the

MAYA INDIAN CHILDREN.

p. 48

PRIEST BEFORE ALTAR IN THE CHA CHAC CEREMONY.

[p. 55

latter are called on by name, and offerings are made to them.

The Cha Chac ceremony, which we witnessed from beginning to end, whose object is to procure sufficient rain for the ripening of the corn, will be briefly described, as it embraces most of the offerings and procedure of all the other ceremonies.

The day previous to the ceremony the men of the village dug the *pib*, or oven in which the food offerings were to be baked. This consisted of an oblong hole in the ground some 6ft. by 4ft. and 2ft. deep, filled with dry wood, on which were placed a number of large stones. The women worked hard all night at their rubbing-stones, grinding great quantities of *masa*, a thick paste of ground corn, and *sikil*, a thin paste of roast pumpkin seeds, from which their offerings were to be made. Early in the morning of the day of the ceremony the priest arrived with his assistant. He was a thin, solemn, ascetic individual of pure Maya type and evidently unmixed blood, clad in immaculate white cotton shirt and trousers, with sandals on his feet. A site was chosen in the midst of a grove of large trees, in which a circular space 25ft. in diameter had been completely cleared of trees and undergrowth. In this were erected two rude huts, one 12ft. the other 6ft. square, of freshly-cut sticks, thatched with huano leaf. In the centre of the larger hut was erected an altar of sticks, bound together with liana, and arched over with branches of the sacred shrub known as *jabin*. On the altar were placed a number of small calabashes for drinking from, and a cross. Beneath it in large gourds, were placed the corn and pumpkin seed paste made the night before, with a large jar of *balchè*, the sacred drink of the Maya, made from fermented honey, in which has been steeped the bark of certain trees. The gourds of corn and pumpkin seed paste were next removed to the smaller hut, where they were dumped out on the floor, which had been covered with wild plantain leaves. The priest and his assistant soon converted the paste into cakes,

each of which was wrapped in an outer coat of palm leaf
and an inner jacket of wild plantain leaf, and tied up securely
with liana. The firewood in the *pib*, or oven, had been
meanwhile set light to, and the hole was now half filled
with glowing ashes and red-hot stones, in which the leaf-
wrapped cakes were half buried, the earth taken from the
pib when it was dug out being raked on top of them, while
the priest sprinkled a little *balchè* to the four cardinal points
with a branch of sacred jabin, repeating four times the
prayer: "*In kubic ti at epalob, ti noh yum kab yetel nahmetan*"
—" I offer to the majestic ones, to the great Lord, cakes
of corn."

Meanwhile a turkey and four fowls had been placed in
front of the altar. The priest and his assistant seized the
turkey, placed a wreath of sacred jabin leaves round its
neck, and poured a little *balchè* down its throat, murmuring
meanwhile : " *In kubic ti hahnal kichpan kolel ti San Pedro,
San Pablo, San Francisco.*"—" I offer a repast to the
beautiful Virgin, to San Pedro, San Pablo, San Francisco."

The turkey and fowls then had their necks wrung, and
were sent away to be cooked by the women, after which all
returned to the *pib*, which was opened up, and the red hot,
leaf-wrapped bundles of corn bread removed to the small
shed, where their wrappings were removed, and they were
placed upon the altar. The fowls and turkey, roasted and
dismembered, were also placed on the altar, together with
a large calabash of *balchè*, and some freshly made corn husk
cigarettes. All the offerings to the gods were now in place—
bread, meat, tobacco, and wine.

The priest, standing directly in front of the altar facing
the people sitting round in a semicircle, took some burning
incense in a piece of plantain bark, and, waving it towards
the four cardinal points, placed it upon the altar ; next he
took a little of the *balchè*, and scattered some of it towards
the north, east, and west, repeating at the same time in a
low, solemn, droning undertone this dedicatory prayer to
the gods to whom the offerings were made :

" Now my beautiful lady of the yellow-leafed breadnut, as well as you, my handsome father, San Isidro, tiller of the earth ; as well as you, Lord Sun, who art seated in the middle of the Heavens, in the east ; as well as you, Yumcanchaacoob (Lord of all the Chacs) ; I deliver (these things) to you with the majestic servants in the middle of the Heavens. As well as to you, my handsome father Cakaal Uxmaal ; as well as you, my beautiful Lady Santa Clara, as well as you, my handsome father Xualakinck (a male wind god), as well as you, my beautiful Lady Xhekik (a female wind god), as well as you, my handsome father San Lorenzo ; as well as you, my beautiful lady of Guadelupe, as well as you, Lord Mosonicoob, that blows within the *milpa* when it is burnt, I deliver to you this holy grace that you may taste it, and because you are the greatest *santos* on earth. That is all, my masters. Pardon my sins. You have not to follow the holy souls, because I have made this holy offering."

After this the *balchè* was passed round in calabashes and drunk by the participants, while the corn bread and fowls were divided up amongst them, a very insignificant portion of bread, meat, and *balchè* being reserved for the women who were, of course, not permitted to participate in the ceremony, but on whom by far the most arduous part of the labour of preparing for it had fallen. After this the priest distributed the new-made corn husk cigarettes from the altar, and finally everything used in the ceremony including sheds, altar, and vessels, was burnt, and very carefully reduced to ashes. It is absolutely essential in performing the ceremony that everything employed in it be fresh and unused. The huts and oven are made specially for the occasion ; the gourd cups and bowls have never been used before ; the pottery is new, and even the incense, corn husk cigarettes, and black native wax candles are specially prepared for the ceremony.

After the ceremony it is equally important that everything

employed in it be completely destroyed, generally by fire. The Cha Chac would appear to be primarily an offering of food, drink, incense, and tobacco, made to the Christian, *santos* and to their own ancient gods by the Indians, which after they have been presented to the gods, may be consumed by the participants in the ceremony.

Its chief function, no doubt, was to secure the goodwill of the saints and gods, and so ensure a satisfactory rainfall during the ripening of the maize crop, but this was not its sole function, for by the side of the hut containing the principal altar was placed a small wooden table, or subsidiary altar, with a string of gourds, in which were placed small portions of food, drink, and tobacco, at the same time that these were placed on the large altar. The priest also made offerings from this small altar to the gods, which he explained were on behalf of the *tuyun pishan*—literally " solitary souls," meaning souls of the dead—who had not as yet reached paradise, but were wandering about the earth disconsolate and alone—a state obviously suggested by the Christian idea of purgatory.

CHAPTER IV

ON leaving Desiderio Cochua we made an uneventful passage
as far as the break in the railroad nearest to Vigia, and on
portaging our luggage over this found a flat car and fresh
mule awaiting us, the latter an evil-tempered, irritable
animal, known as "Lunatico." Curiously enough, all
the mules on this line appear to possess names descriptive
of their most prominent characteristics. All, without
exception, are evil, and, so far as our experience went, well
merited. Lunatico did not take kindly to the harness,
emphasising his disapproval directly anyone approached
him to put it on by well-directed kicks. At last, however,
by tying him up short and blindfolding him, we succeeded
in getting it on, only, however, to encounter a fresh obstacle,
as our old muleteer, known to us only as *hombre*—i.e. " man "
—who was obviously suffering from a bad attack of cold
feet, refused point blank to fasten the traces to the flat
car, saying he felt sure the blank, blank son of ten million
blank, blank *diablos* would run away, overturn the car,
and prove his finish. A compromise was reached by his
agreeing to give the traces one turn round a central hook
at the front of the car, holding the end in his hand, so that

any moment he might, so to speak, slip his cable, the reins meanwhile being handed over to a *compadre*.

We galloped along in fine style for a mile or two, for Lunatico, whatever his other faults, had not a lazy hair on his carcass. Suddenly, however, for no apparent reason beyond justifying his name, he took it into his head to bolt, on which poor old *hombre* completely lost his head, loosed the traces, while *compadre* let go the reins, and we were left gazing at the gradually diminishing back view of Lunatico disappearing down the line, a tangle of ropes trailing behind him.

Meanwhile our flat car, its momentum exhausted, soon came to a stop, and we found ourselves marooned in the middle of a swamp, eight kilometres from anywhere, night coming on rapidly, and battalions of mosquitoes concentrating for the assault. Disgustedly we drove *hombre* and his *compadre* off down the line, in the faint hope that the mule might have got hitched up by the traces or reins, failing which they were to make their way to Vigia and bring back first aid in the form of a fresh mule. In half an hour or so we were rejoiced to see them returning, leading Lunatico, and accompanied by a third man, who had encountered the beast pelting down the line, and, guessing what had happened, promptly stopped him.

This time we fastened the traces firmly on each side of the flat car, handing over the reins to the old muleteer with the warning that if anything further happened he and *compadre* should act as mules, and drag the car into Vigia, with a liberal ration of whip. Lunatico set off at a magnificent gallop, the light car swaying, bumping, and lurching over the uneven road bed, and threatening every moment to upset us into the vile smelling swamp on either side. Poor old *hombre's* time was divided about equally between petitioning the saints for a safe deliverance, cursing the *gringos*—Americans—holding the reins, and endeavouring to retain his seat on the car. Indeed, the latter feat gave us all as much to do as we could accomplish, for the great pile of baggage, to the top of which we were clinging, endeavouring to keep its component parts from being jerked off into the swamp, everyone grasping his own most valued possessions, swayed about like a ship in a heavy swell, shedding along our track here a pot, there a calabash, and anon a string of dry corn cake, whose loss the darkness temporarily hid from their owners.

With no worse losses than these we reached Vigia between 8 and 9 p.m., where we were treated by Messrs. Martin & Martinez to a real dinner, no single item of which had ever dwelt in a tin.

Next morning early we boarded the *Lilian Y*, and, passing the wreck of the *Independencia*, and the lighthouse at Ascension, arrived at Boca Paila about 4 p.m. This is a narrow inlet through which runs a five-knot current, against which we had great difficulty in taking the pram in. It opens up into a vast shallow lagoon studded with mangrove cays, connected to the south with the Chetumal Bay, and to the north, it is said, by devious waterways, even with Yalahau Lagoon, in the extreme north of the peninsula. This vast shallow lagoon is a sportsman's paradise, as the water is literally swarming with fish—snapper, stone bass, mullet, and many other varieties, which in turn attract sharks, barracouda, and larger fish, with myriads of aquatic birds. We saw great numbers of cranes, spoonbills, curlew, and plover, flocks of the beautiful scarlet ibis, and even considerable numbers of egrets, now becoming year by year shyer and rarer in most places, by reason of the constant war waged against them for their plumes, but in this remote spot, where the foot—or rather the keel—of man hardly ever passes, still common, and comparatively tame.

Opening into this lagoon is a little creek navigable only for small canoes. It leads to the fresh water lagoon of Chunyancha, by the side of which dwell the last few representatives of the Chunyancha tribe of Indians, a branch of the Maya, their miserable hovels of sticks and palm-leaf thatch being placed within a stone's throw of the stone-walled ruins of their more noble ancestors' dwellings.

We left Boca Paila with regret, and, indeed, one might pass an ideal holiday here, camping out on the fine white sandy beach, under the glorious tropical sun, the heat tempered by the almost constant cool breezes from the Caribbean ; fish and fowl in great variety to be had for the taking, driftwood in abundance for the camp-fire, and no troublesome human to break the peace of nature from year's end to year's end.

About 1 a.m. next morning we made San Migue, the capital of the island of Cozumel. Pandemonium seemed to have broken loose on the island, singing, howling, shouting, drums beating, bands braying, guns exploding, dogs barking, all tortured the quiet night, and proclaimed the strenuous observance of the last day of carnival. The noise was so terrific that we could not go to sleep, and so lay on and off some distance from the shore till about 7 a.m., when we landed for an interview with the Administrador del Aduana, or Chief of Customs, an educated Mexican, dressed in nicely-pressed grey silk suit, tight, highly-polished grey kid boots, with silk stockings to match, a grey figured shirt, and—no collar or tie.

The little plaza, or public square, facing the sea contains a pretentious statue of President Juares, and a fine stone clock tower, but is neglected and overgrown with weeds and rank vegetation. These two—the Administrador and the plaza—epitomise in themselves what may be termed the Neo Mexican culture, the keynote of which is meretricious-ness—a constant striving after the grandiose and impressive in architecture, institutions, and culture, a lamentable falling short, and attainment only of the ridiculous.

The island, which is about 50 kilometres long by 20 broad, when Stephens visited it in 1841 was absolutely uninhabited ; now, however, it supports a population of probably 1,500

souls, mostly Yucatan and Indian fishermen, some of whom
also cultivate patches of henequen and coco-nuts. The life
is an easy one. Dinner can be caught off the end of the
wharf at any time in ten minutes ; corn cake is cheap ; and
the coco-nuts, which require practically no tending on this
wonderful sandy soil, provide the rum, tobacco, and cotton
for a pair of trousers and shirt, which are all most of the
inhabitants demand of existence.

The one fly in the ointment is the swarm of Mexican
federal officials—the Judges, the Captain of the Port, the
Paymaster, the Administrador, with their numerous staffs—
who have to be supported—and handsomely supported at
that. It must, however, be admitted that, except in very
lean times, these prey rather off the stranger within their
gates than off the native—a custom prevalent in most small
Mexican ports, where high titled officials with expensive
tastes but very meagre salaries have to supplement the
latter to the best of their ability in order to gratify the
former. We realised this when we had to pay over 200
dollars in port dues of various sorts in our progress from
Payo Obispo to Progreso, though we had cleared directly
from the former to the latter place, with permission to call
wherever we wished *en route*.

Next day, with true Mexican hospitality, our new friends
refused to let us go till we had attended a dance they were
getting up in our honour that night. We pointed out that
the night of Ash Wednesday was no time for good *Catolicos*
to get up a dance ; they replied that, having had a hot time
during the carnival, they felt like keeping it up a little while
longer, for which our presence offered an excellent excuse.
Messengers were sent round to warn the señoritas of the
pueblo, and about 8 p.m. a considerable crowd had collected
in the dance house on the plaza, open on all sides to the
winds of heaven, and to various *mirones*, or onlookers,
without whom no Yucatecan dance is complete. These
consist of dogs, children, loafers, the aged female relatives
of the performers, and, indeed, of all the inhabitants of the

pueblo with nothing particular to do. Most of the guests, in deference to the day, had a smear of ashes on their heads or foreheads ; later on, however, as in response to the stimulus of the *vino del pais*, things became more lively, Held (whose abilities at quick-fire portraiture and caricature proved of inestimable assistance to us throughout the trip), with the aid of a little charcoal, red ochre, and grease, transformed them into a company of demons.

This *vino del pais*—wine of the country—new native white rum, is an insidious liquor, producing, when taken in moderation, merely a gentle exhilaration and sense of *bien être*, but leaving, even with the strictest moderation, a most evil head and stomach on the " morning after " to those not broken in to it.

Like all Spaniards both men and women were excellent dancers, and performed danza, danzon, and Spanish quadrilles as if their hearts were in the business.

The island ladies are fine, slummocky, upstanding young women, perhaps not so slim, graceful, and alluring as the *mestizas* of the mainland.

The few hours' sleep we had that night were taken on the beach, to avoid the noise of the dogs, which are the curse of all Yucatecan villages, where they take complete charge at night, wandering about in bands, rendering sleep impossible for the stranger and a stroll in the streets after dark not unattended with danger, as, though great cowards, they will, when reinforced by numbers, and under cover of darkness, attack anyone they do not know.

Next morning, after a bathe and tea, we started for the ruins of the ancient church situated about a mile from the village, and now buried in the bush. We were particularly anxious to see this venerable building, which is generally regarded as the first Christian church erected upon the American continent, as it stands upon the traditional site of the chapel erected by Cortez on his way to the conquest of Mexico in 1519. The incident as related by Bernal Diaz, who accompanied the conqueror, and was an eye-witness of the occurrence, is as follows :

" The Island of Cozumel, it seems, was a place to which the Indians made pilgrimages, for the neighbouring tribes of the promontory of Cotoche, and other districts of Yucatan, came hither in great numbers to sacrifice to some abominable idols which stood in a temple there. One morning we perceived that the place where these horrible images stood was crowded with Indians and their wives. They burnt a species of resin, which very much resembled our incense, and as such a sight was so novel to us, we paid particular attention to all that went forward. Upon this an old man, who had on a wide cloak, and was a priest, mounted on the very top of the temple, and began preaching something to the Indians. We were all very curious to know what the purport of this sermon was, and Cortez desired Mechorego to interpret it to him. Finding that all he had been saying tended to ungodliness, Cortez ordered the caziques and the principal men among them, with the priest, into his presence, giving them to understand as well as he could, by means of our interpreter, that if they were desirous of becoming our brethren they must give up sacrificing to these idols, which were no gods, but evil beings by which they were led into error and their souls sent to hell. He then presented them with the image of the Virgin Mary and a cross, which he desired them to put up instead. These would prove a blessing to them at all times, make their seeds grow, and preserve their souls from eternal perdition. This and many other things respecting our holy religion Cortez explained to them in a very excellent manner. The caziques and priests answered that their forefathers had prayed to their idols before them, because they were good gods, and that they were determined to follow their example, adding that we should experience what power they possessed ; as soon as we had left them

El

we should certainly all of us go to the bottom of the sea. Cortez, however, took very little heed of their threats, but commanded the idols to be pulled down and broken to pieces, which was accordingly done without any further ceremony. He then ordered a quantity of lime to be collected, which is here in abundance, and with the assistance of the Indian masons a very pretty altar was constructed, on which we placed the image of the Holy Virgin. At the same time two of the carpenters, Alonzo Yanez and Alvaro Lopez, made a cross of new wood which lay at hand ; this was set up in a kind of chapel, which we built behind the altar. After all this was completed, Father Juan Diaz said Mass in front of the new altar, the caziques and priests looking on with the greatest attention."

The ruins of the church, measuring 98ft. in length and 36ft. 2in. in breadth, face east and west. The roof has

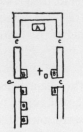

Ground plan of ruins of Ancient Church on the Island of Cozumel.

A. Altar.
B.B.B.Overground Vaults.
C.C.C. windows.

entirely fallen in, while the west wall has completely disappeared. Stucco-covered remains of the other walls still stand, varying in height from two to ten feet. Inside we discovered six large and one small overground vaults, built of stone and mortar, shaped something like an inverted iron bath-tub. These had all been opened, probably by treasure seekers. Inside one we found the complete skeleton of a young Mestisa woman, which had been buried for from sixty to eighty years. This secondary use of the church as a burial-place had taken place since Stephen's visit in 1841, as he makes no mention of these vaults, and states that the island was at that time entirely uninhabited. The altar—probably the identical one which Cortez erected in 1519—is now in ruins; just to the west of it the floor of the Church has been dug up, doubtless by treasure-hunters, exposing a row of seven small, stone-lined chambers, possibly the burial-place of successive heads of the church in the island. Benito Perez, a priest who accompanied the expedition of Grijalva to Cozumel in the year 1518, the first occasion upon which Europeans had ever touched there, applied to the King of Spain for the bishopric of the island, but was put off with the bishopric of Culhua, or Mexico, while the Bishopric of Cozumel was conferred upon a churchman of far greater eminence, whose remains, for all one knows, may have rested peacefully in one of these stone cysts till disturbed by the sacrilegious hands of greedy seekers after buried treasure, who throughout Yucatan have left their mark alike on Christian church and heathen temple.

The island was discovered accidentally by Grijalva while endeavouring to follow the course taken by Cordova in the previous year along the north coast of Yucatan towards Mexico. An itinerary of the voyage was kept by Grijalva's chaplain, who records the landing at Cozumel in the following words :

" On Friday, the sixth of May, the Commandant ordered one hundred men to arm themselves. They embarked in boats and landed. They were accompanied by a priest and expected to be attacked by a great number of Indians. Being prepared for defence, they arranged themselves in good order, and came to a tower where they found no one, and in all the environs did not see a single man. The Commandant mounted upon the tower with the standard bearer, the flag unfurled. He planted the standard upon one of the façades of the tower, took possession in the name of the King in the presence of witnesses, and drew up a declaration of such taking possession. The ascent to this tower was by eighteen steps ; the base was very massive, one hundred and

eighty feet in circumference. At the top rose a small
tower of the height of two men placed one upon the other.
Within were figures, bones, and idols they adored. From
these marks we supposed they were idolaters.

" While the commandant was at the top of the tower
with many of our people, an Indian, followed by three
others who kept the doors, put in the interior a vase with
very odoriferous perfume, which seemed of storax. This
Indian was old ; he burnt many perfumes before the idols
which were in the tower, and sang in a loud voice a song,
which was always in the same tone. We supposed that
he was invoking his idols. . . . These Indians carried
our Commandant with ten or twelve Spaniards, and gave
them to eat in a hall constructed of stones very close
together, and covered with straw. Before the hall was
a large well from which everybody drank. . . . They
then left us alone, and we entered the village, where all
the houses were built of stone. Among others we saw
five very well made, and commanded by small towers.
The base of these edifices is very large and massive ; the
building is very small at the top. They appeared to
have been built a long time, but there are also modern
ones."

This temple, standing on a stone-faced pyramid, from
which Grijalva coolly took possession of the whole country
in the name of the King of Spain by the simple process of
proclamation, and from which the great Cortez himself
threw down the idols of the Indians, and erected close to its
base the first Christian Church in the New World, possesses
associations with the conquest and the *conquistadores*
unequalled possibly by any other spot on the American
continent. When Stephens visited the island in 1841 it was
still standing, and in a fair state of preservation, if one may
judge by Catherwood's drawing. Now, however, the little
temple is a heap of ruins, and nothing remains but the great

mound upon which it stood, the " very massive base " of
Grijalva ; yet one can almost visualise the scene as it occurred
four hundred years ago—the little group of armour-clad
Spaniards, swordsmen, crossbowmen, and arquebusiers,
standing at the base of the pyramid ; farther off great
crowds of half naked Maya, led by their priests, in long,
blood-soaked cotton robes, and their caciques, with immense
feather-decorated headdresses and elaborate ornaments
of gold and jade ; Grijalva, mounting solemnly the stone
steps of the pyramid, and proclaiming through his herald
the sovereignty of the King of Spain over those lands, which
for three centuries were to prove the brightest jewel in the
diadem of Spain, without a thought to the claims of the
unfortunate aborigines, whose native land was being
torn from them, standing round listening to the proclamation, entirely ignorant of what it portended.

On returning to the coast from our visit to the ruins of the
church, hot, tired, and irritated by prickly heat and
encounters with mosquitoes and coloradillos—a micro-
scopic abomination which bores under the skin and causes
intolerable itching, well named *bête rouge* by the French—
we found ourselves on a flat, rock-bound coast, dotted with
deep, clear, sandy-bottomed pools, with edges upholstered
in soft yellow seaweed, suggesting simultaneously to Morley,
Held, and myself the same idea—a bathe.   In two minutes
we were experiencing the delightfully soothing sensation of
cold salt water on our tortured skins.   Before going in the
guide had told us to "*Cuidado jerisos*," or "Beware of *jerisos*,"
but as *jerisos* was a new word to us in Spanish, of whose
meaning we had not the faintest conception, and as there
seemed nothing to be afraid of in a clear, rock-bound,
sandy-bottomed pool, where neither sharks nor barracouda
could enter, we plunged gaily in.

I was the first to discover the meaning of the word *jeriso*,
for on sitting down on the rim of the pool I located one
at once, concealed in the seaweed.   They are small
sea-urchins, or sea-porcupines, hemispherical in shape, and

covered with long, sharp black spines, which when sat upon penetrate for a considerable distance into one's anatomy. Almost every member of the fauna and flora of Yucatan, and the sea surrounding its coast, is armed with some weapon, offensive or defensive—tooth, claw, spine, spike, sting, or poisonous juice. Nearly every bush and tree in the low scrub is provided with its own variety of spine or thorn, one of the worst offenders being the Agave Americana, which is cultivated in vast fields all over the peninsula for the henequen fibre obtained from its leaves, each of these leaves being tipped with a gigantic black thorn, sometimes used as pins by the natives, capable of putting one's eye out with the greatest ease. An even worse offender is a low bush covered with double curved thorns, which not only holds back the traveller through the bush, but vomits over him a stream of vicious stinging ants, who have their homes in the hollow interiors of the thorns, and sally out to the assault on the slightest provocation.

Insect pests include ticks, mosquitoes, sand-flies, wasps— especially in the ruins, where they love to build their nests from the roofs of still intact rooms, and settle in a cloud on the invader—hornets, doctor-flies, various blood-sucking tabanidæ, centipedes, chiggers or sand-fleas, tarantulas, and beef and screw worm flies. Beef worm, so named from its prevalence amongst cattle, is the larva of a fly, which, deposited on the skin, soon burrows its way through, and rapidly develops into a fat, hairy maggot, about one inch in length, which in its uneasy wrigglings and protrusions of its head through the blow-hole it has left in the skin is a constant source of irritation. They seldom attain any size in humans, except on the back, where they are not visible, as the accepted treatment (a plug of wet tobacco over their blow-hole for a few minutes, followed by a vigorous squeeze) usually gets rid of them before they get very large, but to dogs, cattle, and other animals, who may harbour hundreds of them, they occasionally prove fatal. Screw worm is also the larva of a fly resembling a large grey house fly, which crawls up the nose of sleepers and lays its eggs in hundreds over the mucous membrane. The larvæ burrow into this, and grow to about half an inch in length, causing the membrane to slough off in great patches, and usually bringing about the death of the sufferer.

Poisonous snakes are found in considerable numbers. Fortunately, however, they usually get out of one's way. The commonest are the rattlesnake, tomagoff, coral snake, and barber's pole—a beautiful striped red and black snake, whose bite is particularly venomous. Nearly every village has its own snake-doctor, who, as he treats poisonous and non-poisonous snake-bites alike, and the proportion is about one of the former to ten of the latter, naturally soon acquires a considerable reputation, and is able to raise his fees from the eggs, chicken, and corn basis to that of real money.

Nor are the denizens of the sea far behind those of the land in objectionable qualities. Shark and barracouda are found all round the coast, awaiting the bather who ventures into over two feet of water, while in the shallows numerous stinging jelly-fish guard the surface, leaving the patrolling of the bottom to innumerable sea-urchins, sea-scorpions, and sea-centipedes.

If I have perhaps dwelt unduly on these pests by land and sea, my excuse must be that I have suffered deeply, while the experience of the sea-urchin was a particularly harrowing one, treated, moreover, by Morley and Held, not with the sympathy due it, but with gusts of ribald mirth.

Cozumel possesses no medical practitioner, and, whether despite or on account of this fact, is undoubtedly a most remarkably salubrious place. Epidemics of yellow fever and dysentery, such as ravage the mainland, are unknown here, while malaria and hook-worm are rare indeed. To die from any other cause than old age is looked upon by the inhabitants as abnormal, and somehow not quite *comme il faut*.

We encountered a large proportion of ancients, both men and women, in our walks abroad, some of such hoary antiquity as to lead one to believe they must have been contemporaneous with the last of the *conquistadores*.

We obtained in Cozumel a pilot for the north and northeast coasts named Miguel Polanco—a silent, reserved, not undignified individual, with greying hair and face crisscrossed in all directions by a million little wrinkles, and tanned to the colour of saddle-leather by constant exposure to sun and wind. He was reported not only to be an excellent pilot, but to have discovered by accident the ruins of an ancient Maya city not very far inland from the coast. On interviewing him, this rumour was confirmed. Four years previously, when hunting a deer which he had wounded near Punta Santa Rosa, between the Chetumal and Espiritu Santo Bays, he followed it inland for about a mile, and there, buried in the virgin bush, suddenly came upon extensive ruined buildings, which even from his imperfect description we had no difficulty in identifying as Tuluum style Maya ruins. We were greatly elated over this find, and, though all of us had been taken in many a time and oft by natives whose swans had turned out to be geese—and poor geese at that—there was something so circumstantial about Polanco's account, and the details varied so little on repetition, that we were convinced there must be a good backing of truth behind it.

Next morning early we set sail from Cozumel, with nearly 100 miles of our route to retrace in order to reach Punta Santa Rosa. Our pilot, as I have remarked, was reserved and dignified both in manner and appearance. Indeed, clad in steel morion and breastplate, he might well have passed as a reincarnation of one of those intrepid pilots, equally at home with an astrolobe or a sword, who accompanied the *conquistadores* to the New World. No sooner were we under way than I could see Morley's speculative eye upon him, and I knew his hour had come, for Morley has a perfect genius for extracting what he calls " info " from everyone with whom he comes in contact who seems to have any of that valuable commodity to give up. He promptly seated himself beside Migail on the deck-house, and with a bland and ingratiating smile, the New England accent toned down to the gentleness of a sucking dove, commenced the cross-examination.

Miguel stood it pretty well for a time; then, taking advantage of a lull in the barrage of questions, he bolted incontinently forward, though the spindrift, and the smoke from the galley fire combined to render this the least desirable part of the ship. Morley returned to his deck chair and pondered deeply, till in about half an hour I could see he had formulated in his mind a fresh set of questions, when Miguel was again summoned aft to be pumped ; and so it went on all day, till Miguel, with a wild and harassed look, lapsed gloomily into monosyllables.

Both wind and current being against us, we did not make the southern point of Ascension Bay till nearly 7 p.m. Though the night was dark, with a mere nail-paring of moon showing, Morley and I determined at all costs to sleep ashore, and escape for once the horrible rolling of the *Lilian Y.* We bundled our cots, mosquito nets, bedding, and hurricane lamps into the pram, and, taking Alfredo and George, rowed ashore.

A hundred yards from land the water shoaled off so badly that even the pram could not be shoved in any farther, and we had to get out and wade to the low, sandy shore. We soon had our cots and mosquito curtains up, though the latter flapped and bellied so in the brisk breeze that sleep appeared doubtful under them. On returning

Ascension Bay. Tiger tracks following a racoon at our camping place.

to the pram with a lighted lantern, Alfredo discovered tracks on the soft sand, and, of course, had to call our attention immediately to them. They had obviously been made within a very few hours, as they were sharply outlined, and situated well below ordinary high-water mark. The little sketch will give the reader a better idea of their

appearance than a page of description. The front tracks
are those of a gigantic racoon ; the back those of a good-
sized tiger, obviously trailing him. They had both emerged
from the bush, we found, about 100 yds. to the south of our
camp, and as there was a great inlet of the sea a mile or so
to the north of this, it appeared probable that the tiger,
with the racoon stowed inside, would sooner or later pass our
camp to regain the bush. We sent back to the *Lilian Y*
for more hurricane lamps, and with a ring of these around
the cots, and the mosquito curtains flapping and cracking
in the wind, we lay down, I with a shotgun, and Morley
with a revolver handy. We found it difficult to get to sleep,
owing partly to the flapping of the mosquito curtains, but
chiefly, I imagine, to the proximity of the tiger. Nor was
our condition improved by Morley, who kept recalling
instances which he had read, or heard, or imagined, of the
Central American puma, or jaguar, when driven desperate by
hunger, attacking humans. I pointed out, however, that
our tiger was probably peacefully sleeping off the effects
of a large fat coon, and, in any case, an army of tigers would
not dare investigate two flapping mosquito curtains
encircled by a constellation of hurricane lamps.

We struck camp before six next morning, having seen no
signs of the tiger. Miguel thought the best place to land
for the ruins was about ten miles south of our present
location, so we kept on a course nearly due south close in
to the reef. Someone thought of fresh fish for breakfast,
and we remembered we had a couple of spinners on board,
one of which was immediately thrown overboard. In
twenty minutes we had caught two barracoudas, one of
3lbs., one of 10lbs., and two rock fish, one of 12lbs. and one
of 30lbs.

This strip of coast is a sporting paradise, as the neighbourhood of the reef swarms with fish, some of them affording
almost as good sport to the angler as the tarpon, while the
bush is full of deer, peccari, jaguar, puma, gibunt, wild
turkey, and curassow, and the swamps and lagoons abound

in duck, plover, snipe, and innumerable flocks of aquatic birds.

We landed on a beautiful sandy beach, along which we walked in a southerly direction, the pilot carefully scanning the bush to try and locate the spot where he had entered in pursuit of the wounded deer. We passed in the course of a mile eight mahogany logs, worth at least 50 dollars each, two oars, quantities of wreckage, and a lifebuoy with s.s. *Iaqua* upon it, in addition to strange seeds, fruit stones, and beans of all sizes and shapes, corals, sponges, multi-coloured seaweeds, gorgeous shells, and all the wonderful flotsam and jetsam of the Caribbean, laid out before us on a counter of sparkling sand.

It would seem as if this strip of coast has never been visited by a boat of any size, as there must be thousands of dollars' worth of mahogany logs along its whole extent, driven in by the prevailing east winds, from wrecks, and from rafts being towed to the embarking point which, encountering heavy weather, have got broken up and scattered. We seriously contemplated a beachcombing expedition later on to exploit the find.

The pilot at last thought he had located the right spot, and we turned into the bush, which here consisted of low dense scrub, chiefly pimento, buttonwood, and logwood trees, interspersed with the beds of shallow lagoons, now dry, and patches of mangrove swamp. These latter, on account of their arching aerial roots, rendered walking through them a very tedious process. The beds of the dry lagoons were criss-crossed in all directions with the tracks of game, deer, peccari, gibunt, tiger, wild turkey, and many others, some of them quite recent, but we were hunting more important game than these, and had not even brought our guns.

After over an hour's walk in a generally S.S.W. direction we determined to lie down for a rest, and let the pilot continue the search with Muddy, as it was obvious he did not know in the least where he was. In a little more than half an hour we heard shouts to the south of us, and found they had discovered the ruins about a quarter of a mile away. We all set out with great eagerness, and soon stood face to face with the ruined temples, palaces, and public buildings of what had evidently been a good-sized Maya city, now buried in the midst of this dense, impenetrable bush, all tradition of it perished, its very name forgotten, and now being viewed probably for the first time by European eyes.

THE TOWN OF SAN MIGUEL COZUMEL, FROM THE SEA.

[p. 62

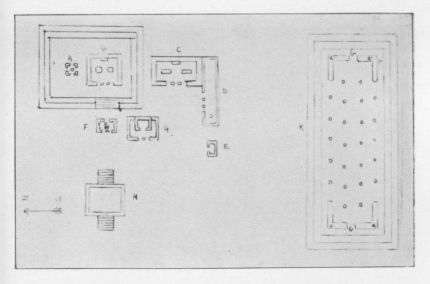

CHACMOOL : PLAN OF THE MAIN GROUP OF RUINS.

[p. 78

CHAPTER V

Soldier Crabs and Bats—Clearing the Bush round the Ruins—Hubert lives
up to his Reputation—Maya never discovered the Principle of the
Arch—Description of the Temples—A Chacmool's Offerings found
buried beside it—Market-place—Curious Stucco Ornaments—Ceremonies Performed at these Temples—The Builders of this and other
East Coast Cities.

WE had noticed an unusual number of soldier crabs crawling
about in the bush as we came along, but at the ruins they
swarmed in countless thousands, from little fellows the
size of a periwinkle to giants nearing four inches in diameter.
They crawled over one if one kept quiet for a few minutes,
dropped on one from the roofs, and crept up the legs of
one's trousers. Why such swarms of them should have
invaded the ruins where there was apparently absolutely
nothing edible is impossible to imagine, unless, as the pilot
suggested, they were the souls of ancient Maya citizens
come back in this incarnation to drive the first white invader
back from their ancient city, reinforced by bats, scores of
which fluttered past us and flew in our faces as we entered
the dark little temple rooms, where for centuries they and
their ancestors had remained undisturbed.

We at once started measuring and planning the ruins,
sending the pilot and Esquivel off to the *Lilian Y* to bring
back all hands with machetes and axes to clean as much of
the bush as possible round the ruined buildings, in order to
let the light in, and admit of their being photographed.
All hands were back in under two hours, having cut a track
from the beach to the ruins about a couple of miles below
our first landing-place, where the distance proved to be
under half a mile. They had improved the time during
our absence by catching a 40lbs. rock fish with the spinner,

and harpooning an immense 8ft. June fish, which, however, got away by breaking the harpoon.

For the first time during the trip we were rejoiced to see Hubert with a kettle in which to boil water, as we were parched with thirst after our morning's work, having had nothing since early tea. Hubert, however, lived nobly up to his reputation as a food spoiler, though it seemed hard to uphold with only tea to prepare, but he accomplished it successfully by smoking the water so badly that, notwithstanding our thirst, we could hardly swallow the tea.

Breakfast over, the men, setting briskly to work with axe and machete, soon had a clearing made round the main group of ruins large enough to admit of our taking photographs of them. A ground plan of this group, which comprises nine buildings, is shown in the figure. Temple A is a little sanctuary almost exactly similar in size and construction to that already described at Central, except that in this case there is no trace of an upper story having existed. The building is 6ft. 9in. in length by 6ft. 10in. in breadth. The roof is supported by a square column in the centre of the building, surrounded by a narrow gallery, into which small doorways, 2ft. 1in. high, open at each of the four sides. Above each doorway is a recessed panel, the bottoms of which still show traces of paint.

The whole structure was originally covered with smooth stucco, and painted. A triangular stone cornice passes all round the building just above the doors. The original height cannot be ascertained, as the upper part of the building has been broken down by the root of a good-sized tree growing from the roof, but it was under 5ft.

Temple B, 23ft. 3in. long, by 17ft. 7in. broad, and 9ft. high, is entered by a broad doorway, on its western side divided into three entrances by two circular stone columns surmounted by square capitals. Above these were originally placed sapodilla lintels, traces of which, much decayed, may still be seen in situ. The roof is flat.

The whole building is covered externally with smooth

stucco, upon which are still to be seen in several places traces of the " red hand," imprinted by the living member dipped in fresh red paint. Round the entire building, 6ft. from the ground, runs an ornamental stone cornice. The interior of the building is supported on two oblong stone columns. The roof, as in all Maya buildings, is supported by a false, or corbal, arch formed by the overlapping of successive courses of masonry till the interval between— usually less than a foot—can be joined by capstones.

The walls are constructed of thick masses of cement, in which stones are firmly embedded, the whole forming practically a monolithic arch.

It would appear that the Maya never discovered the secret of the keystone, which is a remarkable circumstance in people who had made such strides in architecture, who erected such vast stone palaces, temples, and monoliths, and the beauty and finish of whose sculpture is unsurpassed to this day.

Temples A and B stand on a stone-faced platform, or truncated pyramid, 7ft. 4in. high, approached by two terraces, each of which is 3ft. in breadth. On the west side, immediately facing the entrance to Temple B, the summit of the platform is reached by a flight of stone steps.

Temple C very closely resembles Temple B, except that it is somewhat longer and narrower. The entrance, as in B, faces the west, and is divided into three by two circular columns capped by square capitals. The whole structure, inside and out, is covered with hard stucco ; the roof, formed by the usual corbel arch, is supported on two oblong columns. Against the centre of the back wall was a small bench, or altar, of stone, 1ft. 3in. high, 6ft. 3in. long, and 2ft. 3in. deep. One half of this was broken, showing that the interior had been hollow.

We carefully raised the flat flag which covered the top of the other half, and found beneath it a cavity of considerable size, perfectly empty.

Temple D.—This temple was in ruins, the roof having

fallen in, leaving only part of the walls and the columns supporting the entrance standing. The outline could easily be traced, and it was found that the building had originally been 40ft. long by 9ft. broad, approached by two entrances, one on the north supported by two stone columns, and a small narrow one on the west side. The walls were thinner and of more flimsy construction than those of the other temples, while the building itself was evidently of much later date than Temple C, against whose southern wall it had been built, as between the two, where the north wall of D had partly separated from it, the older wall of C, covered with weathered stucco, was plainly in sight. A single circular supporting column was found towards the west end of this temple.

Round the outside wall, 6ft. 3in. from the ground level, were the remains of a plain square stone cornice, upon which were carved circular indentations, the only attempt at this kind of ornament in the whole city.

Temple E was a small, roughly-constructed, one-roomed structure, with a single entrance, 2ft. 8in. wide, on the north side. The room into which this led was 5ft 4in. long, 4ft. 6in. broad, and 4ft. high, from the highest point of the corbel arch to the floor, which was covered with hard cement. In the east and west walls were small oblong slits for windows.

Temple F, though only 10ft. 8in. by 8ft. 9in. in external measurement, was probably the most important sanctuary in the group, as it contained the image of the god to whom apparently the entire group was dedicated. This statue represents a Chacmool, a human figure reclining on its back and elbows, the knees drawn up to the buttocks, the forearms and hands extended along the outer sides of the thighs, the head raised and turned to the left. It is constructed of hard stucco, and represents a man of about 8ft. in height, with chest, arms, and legs of heroic porportions. At the navel is a saucer-shaped depression in which to burn incense. The figure is clothed in a cotton breast-plate, with

CHACMOOL: FAÇADE OF TEMPLE "C"; ON THE RIGHT IS SEEN
PART OF THE RUINED TEMPLE "D."

[*p.* 79

THE CHACMOOL, YUCATAN.

[***p.*** 81

elaborate collar or neck ornament, and a maxtli, or narrow apron, falling between the legs in front. The arms are ornamented with shoulder tabs and gauntlet-like objects above the wrists. Just below the knees are scalloped bands, while on the feet are elaborate sandals. The whole figure was originally painted yellow, decorated in red and black geometrical designs. The head, which was a good deal mutilated, had been broken off at the neck, and was found by the side of the statue. These Chacmool figures are of Nahua, or Mexican origin, and are found at only one other Maya site, namely Chichen Itza, where Mexican artistic and religious influence is found strongly developed, having been introduced about the beginning of the thirteenth century by Aztec mercenaries employed by the King of Mayapan in his wars against the ruler of Chichen Itza.

It was by the merest accident that we discovered this Chacmool statue, as it had been completely buried by the accumulated dirt and rubbish of centuries, leaving only the tops of the knees projecting for a few inches. These were discovered by George, who with racial curiosity commenced excavating with his machete around them, bringing to light the brightly-painted stucco covering the legs. He called our attention to these, and, setting all hands to work, we soon had the whole statue uncovered down to the stucco floor with which it was incorporated. In removing the débris from around the figure we found buried in it at one place a shell gorget, two greenstone beads, an ear-plug, some fragments of the bones of a large animal (probably a tapir) and a small pottery incense burner, with a human head in high relief on its outer surface. Some devotee, faithful even after the fall and destruction of his god and its supersedure by the God of the Christians, must have made this little offering, probably at some period after the mutilation had taken place, but before dirt and débris had begun to accumulate around the statue. The offering itself, consisting of flesh, now represented by dry bones, burning incense, now but a few charred fragments at

FL

the bottom of the incense burner, and personal jewellery, is a typical Maya one of the period, such as are found by the thousand in the great cenote, or sacred well, at Chichen Itza, the Mecca of the Maya religion, to which pilgrimages were made from the remotest parts of Yucatan.

We learn from the early Spanish Fathers that it was no uncommon thing for the Indians baptised into the Catholic Church to apostasize and revert to their ancient gods, making offerings at their shrines, and carrying out the rites and ceremonies of their ancient religion in the depths of the forest, far from prying Christian eyes. Such practices were naturally strongly discouraged by the padres, and the images of the old gods were, where and whenever found, destroyed and mutilated, while the manuscripts of the Maya, handed down in the priesthood for hundreds of years, and containing the history, religious ceremonies, system of medicine, and calendar of the people, painted in their glyphic system on paper made of the fibre of the American aloe, were ruthlessly burnt, so that of the thousands of them existing at the time of the conquest but three remain to-day.

The western opening of Temple F towards which the Chacmool faces is 7ft. 6in. wide, while the eastern opening is only 4ft. wide. The feet of the image occupy nearly the centre of the wider opening, but the head does not come within a couple of feet of the narrower one, so that a procession coming through the temple would naturally divide into two streams at the feet of the image, one passing on either side, meeting again at its head, to emerge from the eastern door.

Temple G, immediately to the south of Temple F, is 15ft. 4in. long by 13ft. wide, and 5ft. high from the top of the roof to the stucco floor. It possesses a single opening on the western side, 5ft. 10in. wide, divided into two by a circular stone column. Like the other buildings, it is faced inside and out with hard stucco.

Temple G has evidently (as shown in the plan) been built

THE CHACMOOL IN SITU WITHIN A LITTLE TEMPLE IN MAIN
LINE OF APPROACH TO CHIEF TEMPLE.

[p. 80

around a much smaller building, which measured but 7ft. 5in. by 7ft. The junction between the walls of the old and the newer structures is very clearly indicated. No attempt had been made to destroy the older building, and it still stands entire, with its narrow doorway, 2ft. wide, within the newer one.

Structure H is a dance platform, measuring 23ft. by 18ft. 9in. It is approached by flights of stone steps, each 8ft. 5in. broad, on the east and west sides. The original platform, the outline of which can still easily be traced, measured 17ft. 6in. by 13ft. 3in. This, however, was enlarged by the construction on all four sides of it of a wall 2ft. 8in. in width.

The great colonnaded structure shown in the plan is much ruined. The whole roof has caved in, and many of the circular columns which supported it have given way. The corner walls, *aa*, at the western extremity have fallen down, while the terraces of the platform upon which it stood are so covered with detritus and vegetal earth, upon which has grown up a thick growth of bush, as to be hardly distinguishable.

The building itself was 102ft. long by 27ft. 10in. broad. It was bounded at each angle by rectangular walls, *aa*, *a' a'*, measuring 12ft. 7in. on the east and west sides and 14ft. on the north and south. The walls were built of squared stones filled in with rubble, and were 3ft. 3in. thick. At the points *bb* on the east and west sides are doorways 2ft. 8in. wide, which leads one to suppose that the north and south sides, now completely open, were at one time either boarded up or walled with adobe, otherwise, two sides of the building being quite open, doors would have been unnecessary.

The roof was apparently flat, probably of thatch, supported on sapodilla beams, which rested on the twenty-four stone columns, many of which are still intact. The building is approached by three broad, stone-faced terraces, and when complete must have been a very imposing structure. It was probably used as a market-place or assembly hall, for either of which purposes it was eminently fitted by its spaciousness, and the coolness which, owing to its high situation, well exposed to the sea breeze, and its palm-leaf roof, it must have possessed.

In the open space between Temples C and D was found the sugarloaf-shaped object shown in the illustration. This was 2ft. 6in. high, made of cement and stone, and covered with a layer of hard stucco. Traces of red paint still remained upon it. It had originally formed the head-dress of a human figure, as the typical Maya ear-plugs can still be plainly seen on either side of the blank space (shaded in the figure) from which the face has been broken away. The upper part of the headdress is ornamented with rows of spines about 1in. in length. A similar object was found to the east of Temple F, but no trace of the figures from which they had been broken.

Chacmool—Stucco incense holder and headdress.

The curious T-shaped object was discovered between Temples C and F. It is 3ft. high, but has been detached below from its base along the line *cc*. The arms have been broken off at the points *aa*, but the two T-shaped prolongations *bb* were discovered close to the figure. These are evidently meant to represent small double incense burners, as the pellets of incense, as used by the Maya, may be seen moulded in the stucco on either side of them at *dd*.

Five yards west of Temple G were found six remarkable objects, all constructed of extremely hard concrete, covered with a layer of smooth stucco, and all firmly rooted in the ground on concrete bases. They consist of :

1. A concrete stool, with supports of the same material at each angle.

2. A cube of concrete resting on a larger concrete base, and supporting a circular column, the top of which has been broken off.

3. A pyramidal column surmounted by a cup-shaped cap, the total height being 1ft. 9in.

4. A square concrete pedestal, 6in. high by 1ft. 9in. in diameter.

5. A square column 8in. high, on two sides of which are still visible traces of human heads moulded in stucco, which had been attached to it.

6. A low square pedestal 16in. in diameter.

These curious objects are unique, as they have been found at no other Maya site either in Yucatan or the south, and they probably belong to the very last phase of the Maya culture before its final extinction by the Spaniards. The actual use to which they were put is doubtful, though they were almost certainly connected with the ritual employed in the worship of the Chacmool, and while two of them were probably used to contain the burning incense, the others may have served as altars, or tables upon which to place the vessels of *balchè* and corn made drinks, the cakes of ground corn, beans, and pumpkin seeds, the roast meats, and other offerings such as we have seen the modern Maya offer to their ancient gods.

The incense burners seen above, containing pellets of artificial incense, have their counterparts in those candelabra which one sometimes sees in churches, in which small electric bulbs at the end of the counterfeit candles supply the illumination.

The group of buildings A, B, C, D, E, F, G, and H was almost certainly religious in character, the earliest of them, with the platform upon which they stand, being A and B ; F containing the Chacmool image, the small simple structure within G, and the original dance platform now forming the core of the enlarged platform H.

In the light of our knowledge of the religious ceremonies of the ancient Maya, derived from their own records and contemporary accounts of the Spanish conquerors, one can easily visualise what took place along this *via sacra* from the dance platform, through the Chacmool temple, up the flight of steps, to the main temple, at some special celebration some five hundred years ago. The procession of wild-looking, half-crazy, unwashed priests, smelling horribly, their gory hair matted, and their white cotton robes smeared with the blood of countless previous sacrifices, marched up the western steps of the dance platform, where certain chants were sung and dithyrambic dances performed, marching down to the eastern steps of the platform. At the conclusion of the dances the procession would come to the Chacmool temple, where at the feet of the god it would split in two as it entered by the broad western gate, to unite again at the head of the god before leaving by the narrow eastern gate. Meanwhile incense was being burnt, food offerings made, and prayers and petitions chanted to the god outside Temple G, and in times of stress—as famine, drought, pestilence, invasions by barbarous Caribs from the south, and later by enemies from the north—the human victim, or victims, the choicest youths of both sexes, were added, bound and partly stupefied by drugs, to the procession of priests. Leaving the eastern gate of the Chacmool temple, the procession, leading the victims, would slowly mount the steps of the great main platform which lay directly in front of it, and then, on the summit of the platform, in front of the main temple, and in full sight of all the people, assembled in their thousands at a respectful distance from the sacred enclosure, and no doubt, after the manner of their kind all the world over, using the great market-place and its terraces as a grand stand from which to view the proceedings, the victim would be sacrificed after the cruel Mexican fashion—stretched on his back on an altar of wood or stone, two priests holding each leg, while two supported each arm high above his head, and a fifth plunged a sharp triangular blade of flint or obsidian deep into his chest well over the region of the heart, and, inserting one hand into the opening, dragged that organ out of the chest cavity and severed it from its attachment of blood vessels, being deluged in the process with a stream of hot arterial blood. The heart was taken, still palpitating, to B, the main temple, where it was offered to the god, and the ceremonies connected with sacrifice were concluded.

Meanwhile, in front of the temple the corpse was decapitated by the priests, the head being their special perquisite, while the body, rolled down the steps of the platform, was eagerly hacked in pieces by the people, who scrambled each for a fragment like starving dogs for a bone, for this quasi-ceremonial religious cannibalism was one of the many evil practices introduced among the Maya by the Mexicans. How many times these ancient buildings have witnessed such cruel and bloody rites it is impossible to tell yet, as we have seen, after the fall of the deity one poor worshipper at least retained faith enough to return and make his offering at the deserted shrine—a faith not always inspired by more beneficent gods.

Structures D and E, with the enclosing walls of G, and the enlargement of the dance platform H, are all of more recent construction than the main group, though what period elapsed between the building of the two it is impossible to say. C is almost certainly a temple, possibly dedicated to one of the two principal gods of the Maya proper, Itzamna, or Cuculcan, while D may well have been the dwelling-place of some of the priests. A was obviously one of those little shrines peculiar to this east coast civilisation, which we have met with before at Espiritu Santo Bay and Central, and will meet with again farther north. We discovered two more of them at Chacmool before we left— one between the ruins and the sea, the other at some distance to the west of the main group.

In order to obtain some clue as to the identity of the builders of these ruins, and of other similar groups along the east coast of Yucatan, all conforming closely to the Tuluum style, it is necessary to give a brief account of the history of the Maya who occupied Yucatan. This we obtain from the early Spanish historians, from their own records— known as the books of Chilam Balaam, which were kept originally by several cities in their own hieroglyphic writings and later transcribed into Maya, written in Latin characters by natives who acquired a knowledge of the Spanish language—and lastly, to a small extent, from their hieroglyphic records on stone still extant at many of the ruins.

CHAPTER VI

Maya History—Its Sources—Methods of Reckoning the Passage of Time—
History of the Old Empire—History of the New Empire—Foundation
of the Various Cities in the Maya Area—Reasons for Maya deserting
their Old Cities for Yucatan—Settlement of New Empire—Founding
of New Cities—Itzamna, the Hero God—Migration from Chichen Itza
to Champoton—Return to Chichen Itza—Entry of the Tutul Xiu to
Yucatan—The Hero God Cuculcan—The Maya Renaissance—The
Breaking-up of the Maya Triple Alliance—Its Cause—Mexican Mercenaries called into Yucatan—The Cocomes Rule in Yucatan for 250
Years—They are overcome by the Tutul Xiu—The Country is divided
up into a Number of Small States constantly at War till the Coming
of the Spaniards—Naming the new City Chacmool—The Period to
which these Ruins belong—Uncomfortable Quarters—We take leave
of Chacmool.

DURING the first fifteen centuries of the Christian era the
Maya developed what was undoubtedly the highest aboriginal civilisation of the New World. Maya history has been
divided by Sylvanus G. Morley, of the Carnegie Institution,
into two main epochs, the Old Empire, or Empire of the
South, and the New Empire, or Empire of Yucatan. Each
of these is again sub-divided into several periods.

PERIODS OF MAYA HISTORY

OLD EMPIRE

i.	Archaic Period	Earliest Times Down	To 9.10.0.0.0.[1] 1 Ahau 8 Kayab. 360 A.D. (circa)
ii.	Middle Period	9.10.0.0.0. 1 Ahau 8 Kayab. 360 A.D.	To 9.15.0.0.0. 4 Ahau 13 Yax. 460 A.D. (circa)
iii.	Great Period	9.15.0.0.0. 1 Ahau 13 Yax. 460 A.D.	To 10.2.0.0.0. 3 Ahau 3 Ceh. 600 A.D. (circa)

NEW EMPIRE

iv.	Colonisation Period	Katun 6 Ahau 420 A.D.	To Katun 1 Ahau 620 A.D. (circa)
v.	Transitional Period	Katun 12 Ahau 620 A.D.	To Katun 4 Ahau 980 A.D. (circa)
vi.	Renaissance Period	Katun 2 Ahau 980 A.D.	To Katun 8 Ahau 1190 A D.. (circa)
vii.	Toltec Period	Katun 8 Ahau 1190 A.D.	To Katun 8 Ahau 1450 A.D. (circa)
viii.	Final Period	Katun 8 Ahau 1450 A.D.	To Katun 13 Ahau 1537 A.D. (circa)

[1] 9 Cycles 10 Katuns o Tuns o Uinals o Kins after the starting-point of Maya
Chronology, which occurred on a certain 4 Ahau the ninth day of the month
Cumhu, approximately in the year 3400 B.C. of our era.

It will be observed that in the Old Empire the passage of time was recorded by the lapse of so many cycles (400-year periods), katuns (20-year periods), tuns (360-day periods), uinals (months ; eighteen of 20 days, one of 5 days), and kins (days), from the starting-point of Maya chronology, while during the New Empire it was reckoned by the passage of so many katuns, or 20-year periods, numbered, in order to distinguish them from each other, from 1 to 13. The Old Empire flourished during the first six centuries of the Christian era in Southern Mexico, Guatemala, and the western part of Honduras ; the New Empire, which was gradually evolved from the old, flourished in the peninsula of Yucatan from the early years of the sixth century to the Spanish conquest.

The history of the Old Empire is derived exclusively from the hieroglyphic inscriptions found chiefly on monoliths still standing among its ruined cities.

The history of the New Empire is derived chiefly from native chronicles, which give brief synopses of the chief events occurring during every katun, or 20-year period.

Of the origin of the Maya civilisation nothing is known. The accurate calendar system, the complicated hieroglyphics, and the wonderful astronomical knowledge, postulating centuries of effort, emerge from the womb of time, and greet us fully developed about the first century before our era. Where and when their civilisation originated, and how developed, are probably among the many mysteries surrounding this remarkable people which will never be solved.

The earliest dated Maya object was found, curiously enough, outside the region where the Maya civilisation as known to us flourished, namely, at San Andres Tuxtla, in the state of Vera Cruz, Mexico. It is a small nephrite statue, and bears a date in the early part of cycle 8 in Maya chronology, or about 100 B.C. If this statuette were made where it was found, it would indicate that we must look for the birthplace of the Maya civilisation in this region rather than 200 miles to the south, where it attained its highest development. We have ample proof, in ruined cities still extant, that during the first century of the Christian era the Maya were firmly established in Northern Guatemala, Southern Mexico, and Western Honduras. The earliest dated object from this region is a small jadeite plate from the department of Yzabal, in Guatemala, close to the Rio Graciosa. It bears a date towards the end of cycle 8 of Maya chronology, or about 50 A.D., while of the larger remains the earliest dated monument, or stele, was discovered by Morley at Uaxactun, and is nearly contemporaneous with the Yzabel plate.

The next earliest is not found till 170 years later. It was erected at the city of Tikal, in Guatemala, in the third katun, or·20-year period, of cycle 9, or about 210 A.D.

After this, in rapid succession, we find at Copan stele, 250 A.D., Piedras Negras, 350 A.D., and finally Naranjo, 360 A.D., the last city erected during the archaic period.

Numbers of cities were founded during the middle period of the First Empire, of which the two most important are Palenque and Yaxchilan. The former, founded at the end of the 11th katun of the 9th cycle (about 370 A.D.), is, owing to the magnificence of its temples and palaces, the beauty of its stucco moulding, and perhaps more than all to the presence of the cross as an emblem of worship on several of the tablets, probably the best known of all the Maya ruins.

Towards the end of this period, in the 15th katun of the 9th cycle (about 450 A.D.), was founded the city of Quirigua, an offshoot or colony from Copan. Here was discovered the largest monument in the Maya area—a gigantic monolith weighing fifty tons, covered with elaborate carving, and projecting above ground to a height of twenty-six feet. This stele, ever since its discovery, has leaned twelve feet from the perpendicular, but a few months before the destruction of the city of Guatemala by the earthquake shocks of

1917, as if to give warning of the impending catastrophe, it fell flat upon its face, though no slightest seismic tremor had as yet been apparent in the vicinity.

During the third or great period of the Old Empire large numbers of cities were founded, including the important centres of Nakum, Seibal, and Ixkun, while all the older cities continued to flourish. This was the golden age of the Maya—the flood-tide of their artistic development and commercial greatness. The country was covered with great cities, and, judging by their architectural output, the population must have been a very large one, to support whom the land (now a sea of virgin forest, buried beneath which from time to time are found the ruined temples and palaces of its former rulers) must have then been intensively cultivated.

Hundreds of great monoliths were erected during this era throughout the country to mark the passage of 5-year periods, or hotuns, and to record the principal events occurring in them—a fortunate thing for posterity, as it is on these tables of stone that our knowledge of this period of Maya history now exclusively rests.

Early in the Great Period an important event occurred— the colonisation by emigrants from the Old Empire of the province of Bakhalal, in Southern Yucatan, which they occupied from about 460 to 580 A.D., when moving farther north. They founded the city of Chichen Itza, later to become the capital city of the New Empire.

From the stele and monuments we are able to form a fairly accurate idea of the customs, religious observances, dress, and appearance of the people of the Old Empire. The cities have been dated with great accuracy, their system of numeration, calendar system, and astronomical knowledge have been worked out, while some idea of the ancient population is to be obtained from the number and extent of the ruined cities scattered throughout the region, and the elaborate sculptural decorations which they contain. Here, however, our knowledge ceases, for the names of their rulers and priests, of the gods they worshipped, of the cities they dwelt in and the events which occurred in them—pestilence, famine, war, dynastic changes—of the origin and growth of their civilisation, in fact, of practically every particular which lends human interest to the history of a people, we are densely ignorant, the reason being that up to the present only about one-third of the hieroglyphic characters inscribed upon the stele and monoliths have been deciphered, and these deal almost exclusively with time counts, and the fixation of the date recorded on the stone in its proper place in the solar and lunar calendar.

The same eager workers, however, who after years of patient research succeeded in elucidating the glyphs already known to us, are patiently at work on the undeciphered glyphs, of which many more have been discovered, and accurately photographed and drawn, in recent years, and it is almost certain that within the next few years we shall be able to obtain from these a pretty accurate idea, not only of the main events which occurred during the 700 to 800 years which the Old Empire, as known to us, existed, but also of the history of the Maya previous to the opening of the Old Empire, when—as previously stated—we find their civilisation already fully developed.

Early in cycle 10 the Maya had entirely deserted their southern cities, and the first katun, or 20-year period, of this cycle is recorded only at three cities—Tikal, Seibal, and Flores—after which complete silence and darkness close down on these once magnificent cities for a period of over a thousand years, and, indeed, in many cases to the present century.

The city of Uaxactum, discovered by Dr. Morley as recently as 1915, contains a stele recording as a contemporaneous date the 14th katun of the 8th cycle, or about 60 A.D., indicating that its ruins have been buried in the virgin forest, unvisited by man, the haunt of the monkey, the jaguar, and the snake, for a period of nearly nineteen centuries.

Why the Maya should suddenly have deserted their cities practically within one katun, or 20-year period, representing, as they must have done, such an immense capital expenditure in labour alone, in the construction of palaces and public buildings, and the erection and sculpture of stele, steeped, as they were, in the history and traditions of their ancestors for nearly a thousand years, hallowed by the temples of their gods and outward symbols of their religion, is one of those inexplicable mysteries which one constantly encounters in the history of this remarkable people. Imagine the inhabitants of England south of Yorkshire migrating *en masse* to the north of Scotland within a period of twenty years or so, leaving their old homes deserted, and settling down permanently in their new environment, and one has a fair picture of what occurred on a smaller scale in Central America in the sixth century of our era.

Various explanations have been put forward to account for this sudden exodus, one being that the primitive agricultural methods of the Maya reduced the land to such a condition that ultimately it became untillable under their system of cultivation, which consisted simply in felling and burning the forest during the dry season, and planting, at the beginning of the rains, a process which in time allows perennial grasses to take the place of the woody growths and renders cultivation impossible.

A second theory is that during the closing years of the Old Empire profound climatic changes took place in this part of Central America, resulting in a great increase in the rainfall, which not only rendered the climate unhealthy, but increased the growth of bush to such an extent as to interfere with agriculture.

The third theory advanced by Spinden is that the decadence in art which became manifest towards the close of the Old Empire was accompanied by moral and physical degenerative changes, which led to its disruption.

My own opinion is that this exodus took place at the command of the gods as voiced by the priests, for we shall see the same mysterious desertion of their cities, and emigration to new localities, without apparent reason, taking place, not once, but many times, amongst the Maya of the New Empire.

Whatever the cause, we find about the year 600 A.D. the southern cities entirely deserted, and the New Empire well under way. The first settlement was made at Bakalal, in Spanish colonial times known as Bacalar, now a deserted city, with the ruins of stately churches, convents, monasteries forts, and palaces, extending on all sides through the all-conquering bush, having been overthrown in the 1848 war of the castes by the descendants of those very Maya whose ancestors the Spaniards had subdued. The blood of the Spaniards who in this rising paid the penalty for their cruelty and oppression of their ancestors, is still to be seen staining the walls of the church, in the nave of which their bones were till recently piled in a gigantic mound.

Bakalal was occupied from about 520 to 580 A.D., and towards the close of its occupancy the city of Chichen Itza was founded by the Chanes, a branch of the Maya, destined later, under the name of Itzas, to become the most prominent nation in the New Empire. In their march northward along the east coast of Yucatan from Bacalar to Chichen Itza, the Itzas no doubt founded the first city of Tuluum, where, nearly a thousand years later, their descendants founded the later city, whose ruins, shrouded in bush, now overlook the Caribbean Sea from this desolate coast.

This migration was led by Lakin Chan, a priest and leader, deified under the name of Itzamna after his death, and later to become perhaps the most widely worshipped hero god throughout Yucatan. It is from him that the Chanes, whom he led in person, derived their later name of Itzas. Meanwhile other tribes of the Chanes related to the Itzas, wandering up from the south, founded the great cities of Motul and Izamal.

Towards the end of the seventh century A.D. the Itzas, for some reason unknown to us, suddenly left their capital city of Chichen Itza, migrated in a south-westerly direction across the peninsula to Champoton, on the west coast, where, having conquered the inhabitants, they settled down in the land, completely abandoning the magnificent palaces and temples, on the erection of which they must have expended a vast amount of time and labour, as their ruined remains prove to-day.

The Itzas remained in Champoton for nearly three hundred years, when, towards the close of the tenth century A.D.—again apparently without rhyme or reason—they returned to their old city of Chichen Itza, which they rebuilt and reoccupied, many of them remaining behind at Mayapan, where they founded a new city of that name, later to become the capital city of the New Empire.

During the passage of the Itzas back to Chichen, a second immigration was taking place into Yucatan from the westward of a tribe called the Tutul Xiu, under the leadership of the chief, Ahmekat Tutul Xiu. They came from Chiapas and Tabasco in Mexico, and spread over the southern and western parts of Yucatan, founding the cities of Xkabukin, Kaba, Labna, Uxmal, and many others, and finally, at Chichen Itza, coming in contact with the Itzas.

Towards the end of the tenth century A.D. the colonisation and transitional periods of the New Empire were over.

For five centuries a stream of Maya immigrants had been pouring into Yucatan from the south and west, till practically the entire peninsula was now occupied. The people had become accustomed to their new environment ; the constant shifting and changing from one locality to another had ceased. They were settling down to build themselves permanent cities, which provided an outlet for the expression of their artistic and architectural ideals so long denied by a nomadic life in a new and sterile environment—in fact the Great, or Renaissance Period, of the New Empire had commenced.

About 1000 A.D. the three great cities of Uxmal, Chichen

Itza, and Mayapan, each ruled by its independent governor, formed a triple alliance, by the terms of which each was to participate equally in the government of the country. This alliance lasted for nearly two hundred years, until the last decade of the twelfth century, A.D. It marks the high tide in the prosperity and artistic development of the Maya of Yucatan, and constitutes their golden age, during which most of the innumerable cities—now mere masses of ruins buried in the bush—were built and flourished ; a period of unparalleled artistic development in both the painters' and the sculptors' art, and under wise, beneficent rulers a period of peace and prosperity, free alike from internecine wars and dissensions, and from invasion from without.

During this period there entered Yucatan from the west a great priest and leader known as Cuculcan (or feathered serpent). He is described as a venerable old man with a long white beard, dressed in a loose robe and sandals. After a residence in Yucatan of some years, preaching peace, concord, and well-doing, he left it by way of Champoton, promising, however, that in after years he and his followers would return.

The coming of the Spaniards (*teules*, or gods, as they were termed by the Mexicans) was—unfortunately for themselves—regarded by the natives as the fulfilment of this prophecy.

Cuculcan soon after his departure underwent an apotheosis, and with the other great priest and leader, Itzamna, already referred to, divided divine honours about equally throughout the land. The disruption of the triple alliance, the plunging of the whole country into war, and the end of the golden age, was brought about by an event which is to a certain extent wrapped in mystery, as no two accounts of it exactly coincide. The quarrel—a matter of *cherchez la femme*—arose between Chac-Xib-Chac, King of Chichen Itza, and Hunnac Ceel, King of Mayapan. It would appear that the latter was deeply enamoured of

GL

the Princess who was betrothed to the former. Notwithstanding this, however, he attended the wedding ceremony
with a number of his followers. At the conclusion of the
feast, while the retainers of the King of Chichen Itza were
lying about on the mat-strewn floor sleeping off the effect
of their potations of *balchè* (the Maya wine, on which it was
considered good form to get intoxicated after a feast),
according to the usual custom, the King of Mayapan,
with a party of armed men, invaded the bridal chamber
and bore off the bride. Chac-Xib-Chac, on recovering
from his debauch, was naturally incensed at such a base
betrayal of hospitality by a friend and ally, and at once
began to collect his people with a view to making war on
the King of Mayapan. He was joined by the rulers of
Izamal and Ulmil, two smaller cities, but the King of Uxmal
wisely kept out of the quarrel between his allies.

The war at first went strongly in favour of Chac-Xib-
Chan, till at length Hunnac Ceel, finding himself on the verge
of defeat, called in to his assistance Toltec mercenaries
from the Mexican provinces of Chiapas and Tabasco,
adjoining Yucatan on the west. With their assistance he
rapidly overcame the King of Chichen Itza, and drove him
from his city, killing and enslaving many of his subjects,
and driving the rest out to the sparsely-populated eastern
coast of the peninsula, where for years they led a miserable
and hunted existence.

On the fall of Chichen Itza and the dissolution of the triple
alliance the supreme command of the country fell into the
hands of the Cocomes, the ruling family of Mayapan. The
city of Chichen Itza was handed over by them to their
Toltec mercenaries, in consequence of which we find here
in the more recent buildings, the strongest Toltec architectural influence of any city in Yucatan. For nearly two
and a half centuries the Cocomes succeeded, chiefly by the
aid of their warlike Toltec allies, in holding the overlordship
of the peninsula. The ruling families and nobility of each
district were compelled to have some of their members in

residence as hostages at Mayapan all the year round, where, within a great walled enclosure, ground was allotted to each for the construction of their temples and palaces, while outside the walls the vast number of their stewards, personal retainers, and attendants, with their families, formed a respectable sized city in itself.

About the year 1450 A.D. the Maya nobles, disgusted with the arrogance of the Cocomes, humiliated at being compelled to reside within the precincts of Mayapan, and oppressed by the heavy taxes, payment of which was enforced by the Toltec invaders, at last entered into an offensive alliance against their enemies, and under the leadership of the reigning Tutul Xiu, King of Uxmal, declared war against the Cocomes. Hostilities were carried on with varying fortunes for a number of years, till in Katun 8 Ahau, or 1468 A.D., the army of the Tutul Xiu besieged and captured the city of Mayapan, completely razing it to the ground, and putting to death every member of the Cocom family, with the exception of one son, who was absent in Honduras, and a distant relative, Cocom Cat.

After the conquest of Mayapan the whole country became divided up into a number of small cacicazgos, or states, each governed by a separate cacique, or ruler, over whom the King of Uxmal exercised a merely nominal suzerainty. Even the last surviving Cocom, returning from Honduras, was permitted to set up a cacicazgo at Sotuta, his principal town being Tbuloon. Ah Moo Chel, a priest of Mayapan, who had married his high priest's daughter, fled to the east after the sacking of the city, with a considerable number of retainers, where round Izamal he founded the cacicazgo of Ah Kinchel. Nine brothers of the Canules, a Toltec tribe, retired to Acanul, where they founded the cacicazgo of that name, though, being regarded as outlanders and barbarians, they were not permitted to intermarry with their Maya neighbours. Noh Capal Peck, a lord of Mayapan, fled to the north, where he founded the cacicazgo of Ceh Peck.

The Cupules, a Maya tribe, returned and ruled in Chichen

Itza, while the Itza themselves retired *en masse* to Peten, in Guatemala, the former home of their ancestors, and there, under the name of Peten Itzas, formed the last important stronghold of the Maya Indians against the Spanish invaders, by whom they were not conquered till the last decade of the seventeenth century.

The Tutul Xiu returned to their strongholds in the Sierra, but for some inexplicable reason deserted their capital of Uxmal, perhaps the largest and most beautiful city, and certainly that containing the most exquisitely sculptured buildings throughout Yucatan, as its wonderful remains still evidence to-day. They retired to the insignificant town of Mani, leaving the vast temples, palaces, and public buildings of their capital completely deserted, as they were found nearly a century later, to be the wonder and admiration of the first *conquistadores*.

Yucatan was now divided into a great number of cacicazgos, all engaged in almost constant strife one with another. The Cocomes of Sotuta, the Tutul Xius of Mani, and the Cheles of Ticoh, were mortal enemies ; the Peches of Motul were at war with the Cheles and Cupules, as were the Cochuas of Tehomeo with the Chanes of Bacalar. These internecine wars continued till the coming of the Spaniards. Nevertheless, so rapidly did the population increase that at the time of the conquest, in the words of one of the *conquistadores*, " the whole country appeared like a single *pueblo*," while " throughout the whole of it there is not a palm of land which has not been cultivated."

It must be remembered that though split up into so many small states at the time of the conquest, the people of Yucatan were in reality all of one race, speaking one language, and descendants of the two tribes who, as we have seen, originally entered the peninsula, the one from the south-east, the other from the south-west. The Chanes (the tribe from the south-west), at the coming of Itzamna, changed their name to Itzas, and ultimately overran the eastern part of Yucatan. The Tutul Xiu from the south-west settled in the Sierra and western part of the peninsula, forming later, with the Itza, the confederation of Mayapan, and it is from this last name that people, country, and language derived their title of Maya.

We claimed by right of discovery the honour of rechristening this ancient Maya city, and opinions were divided between " The City of the Wounded Deer " and " The Stronghold of Soldier Crabs " as suitable names. On discovery, however, that the former, when rendered into Maya, is " *U kahal tsonan ceh,*" while the latter is still more impossible as a place name, we compromised by naming it " Chacmool " in honour of the tutelary deity of the place.

These ruins almost certainly date back to the period between the fall of Mayapan, in the middle of the fifteenth century, and the coming of the Spaniards about a century later. They are of the same type as all the other ruins along the east coast and on the islands, and were evidently the work of Maya, strongly imbued, as the Chacmool indicates, with Toltec culture. The masonry is coarser, and lacks the finish noticeable in the earlier Maya building. Sculpture is absent, and stucco takes the place of cut stone. They are, in fact, evidently the work of a considerable body of people suddenly thrown into a new environment, who endeavoured to construct as quickly as possible temples and other buildings as closely resembling those they had left behind them as might be compassed with the materials at hand. Whether they would ever again have reached the architectural or sculptural perfection of the Great Period is doubtful, as a subtle degenerative change, moral and artistic, seems to have eaten into the life of the Maya, beginning nearly three and a half centuries before the arrival of the Spaniards, manifesting itself in architectural and artistic decadence, in the development of cruelty, treachery, and pugnacity, and the introduction of human sacrifices, amongst this once peaceful, happy, joyous, religious people.

The fall of the Maya civilisation, though possibly hastened by, was not due to, the coming of strangers, but to
something inherent in itself—possibly the fact that for
nearly fifteen centuries it had come in contact with no
outside influence, and of its own initiative had apparently
neither advanced nor retrograded, a stationary condition
in human affairs as repugnant to the high gods as a vacuum
in nature, for no civilisation can mark time for ever.

We spent two strenuous days clearing bush, measuring
and photographing buildings, Morley and I sleeping ashore,
while the others returned at night to the *Lilian Y*. We
were supposed to be at the height of the dry season, yet
on both the nights we slept at the edge of the beach it
rained briskly, saturating our beds, bedding and mosquito
curtains. We both felt, however, that anything was
preferable to the oily roll of the *Lilian Y*, the nearest she
ever attained to stability even anchored inside the reef.

Interesting and exciting as the work had been, we were
not sorry when it was finished, for between sleepless nights,
hard-driven days, and Hubert's unspeakable cookery (his
omelettes were like greasy leather, and his beans things to
dream of—in a nightmare !), we were nearly all in. Moreover, the heat in the low-lying, bush-encircled ruins was
terrific, while the aborigines—mosquitoes, bats, and soldier
crabs—united in their efforts to eject us from the rooms and
temples, till even the *Lilian Y* seemed a haven of rest as,
on the morning of the 16th February, we weighed anchor
and bade a long farewell to the city of Chacmool.

The tops of the ruins could easily be distinguished from
the mast-head as we steamed out, standing sentinel-like
above the bush, and gradually diminishing in size as we
left them further and further behind, and so, after the
first visit from strangers in nearly five centuries, the silence
of the bush closed down once more over this once flourishing
town, to be broken only by the scream of a parrot and the
howl of a monkey.

It seemed incredible that thousands of people had once

lived here, loving and hating, marrying and giving in marriage, fighting their enemies, worshipping their gods, bartering with their neighbours, sowing and reaping their crops, holding their feasts and fasts, rejoicing and mourning, and at last dying, and leaving no trace beyond the ruins of their city, the very name of which is now forgotten. It brought home to us the impermanence of all human institutions and the insignificance and futility of human effort.

From this melancholy reverie of the past Morley and I were aroused by the strains of " Oh, Johnnie ! Oh, Johnnie ! " started by Held in the unspeakable gramophone, and the smell of burning beans resulting from Hubert's efforts to prepare breakfast.

CHAPTER VII

ON resuming our journey north we put in at Point Nohku, the southern lip of Ascension Bay, as we had heard that the ruins of an old Spanish church were to be found there. Disappointment, however, awaited us, as the ruin proved to be that of a small Maya temple, or shrine, such as have already been described. It was in a very bad state of preservation, and in this lonely and desolate situation had probably been used by fishermen, hunters, or travellers as an altar upon which to sacrifice to their tutelary deities.

The name Nohku in Maya means " ancient temple," and might, of course, refer equally well to a heathen temple or a Christian church.

We camped out that night on the sandy beach under the stars, about three miles north of Ascension Bay, and with a tiny breeze gently swaying our mosquito nets, the aromatic smells of the bush coming faintly to our nostrils, and the lapping of the little wavelets on the shore forming a gentle lullaby, we realised what a paradise Yucatan may be under favourable conditions.

Next morning we were under way early, and about 10.30 a.m., passing in through an opening in the reef, we anchored under the ruins of Tuluum.

These ruins are by far the largest and best preserved of all the groups known to us up to the present along the east coast of Yucatan and amongst the adjacent islands. A certain air of mystery—partly, no doubt, due to their inaccessible position—has always clung to them, investing them with a special interest in the eyes of students of Maya archæology. The first European notice we have of Tuluum is found in the itinerary of Juan de Grijalva's voyage along this coast in 1518, kept by Padre Juan Diaz, chaplain to the expedition. He writes :

" After leaving Cozumel we ran along the coast a day and a night, and the next day towards sunset we saw a bourg, or village, so large that Seville would not have seemed larger or better. We saw there a very high tower. There was upon the bank a crowd of Indians, who carried two standards, which they raised and lowered to us as signs to come and join them, but the Commander did not wish it."

The distance from Cozumel, the high tower, and the size, point unmistakably to Tuluum as the " bourg, or village, so large that Seville would not have seemed larger or better " of Grijalva.

For the next 324 years the history of Tuluum is a blank, till in 1841 it was revisited by the American explorer, John L. Stephens, who discovered on the floor of one of the temples the fragments of a stele, or monolith, covered with Maya hieroglyphs. A few years after Stephens' visit commenced the so-called " War of the Castes." The Maya Indians, driven to desperation by three centuries of oppression and slavery, rose against their Spanish masters throughout the whole peninsula, and drove them into Merida, the capital. When, with great cruelty and loss of life, the revolt had been quelled, the Indians still held a large territory along the east coast, where they have retained their independence to this day.

Tuluum is near the centre of this region, and, as the Indians allowed no white persons within their territories, was not visited during the seventy years between 1841 and 1911, which fact has no doubt added greatly to the mystery and romance surrounding the ruins.

The next visitors were Dr. Howe, of the Peabody Museum, and his companion, Mr. Parmalee, who in 1911 reached Tuluum in a small sailing vessel from Cozumel. They spent parts of two days at the ruins, obtaining a few rather inadequate photographs, and then, seeing fire signals at night, and observing Indians creeping about the bush during the day, they became convinced that an Indian attack was imminent, and, having no means of resisting it with their small party, they beat a hasty retreat.

Two years later the ruins were visited by Messrs. Morley and Nusbaum, who made the journey from Cozumel in a sailing dorey, and arrived nearly dead from sea-sickness. Their dorey was swamped in the tremendous surf, which always pounds the shores of Tuluum, and all their equipment, photographic and otherwise, was ruined ; but, worst of all, on visiting the temple where Stephens had found the sculptured stele in 1841, which Howe had seen in 1911, they found it missing, and left the ruins disgusted, after a stay of only five hours.

A short time subsequent to this I met Parmalee in London, and Morley met Howe in Washington, and both learnt almost simultaneously that shortly before leaving the ruins they had conveyed the fragments of the stele from the temple where Stephens found them to the beach, with a view to their transportation to New York, but, being surprised by the Indians before they could get them on board, were compelled to abandon them, first burying them in the sand near high-water mark in a little bay to the north of the Castillo.

Morley and I, each provided with a plan of the location of the fragments, met on a fruit steamer on our way to Belize—the nearest port of embarkation for Tuluum and arranged a joint expedition, which took place in March, 1916, and was so far successful that we discovered and disinterred the fragments, and, placing them in position, got an excellent photograph of the monolith as it now is, which enabled us to make out with reasonable certainty

the Initial Series date recorded upon it—9.6.10.0.0. 8
Ahau 13 Pax, or approximately 304 A.D.

We found five fragments on the beach, where Parmalee
and Howe had buried them, while two smaller fragments
still remained in the temple where Stephens had found them.

On leaving Tuluum in 1916 we buried the fragments in
the sand of the same little bay, near a pyramidal outcrop
of the limestone, easily recognised.

Later in the year I commissioned the captain of a turtle-
fishing schooner to put in at Tuluum on his trip down the
coast and bring out the fragments. As far as we knew
he had done so, but the schooner was unfortunately lost
with all hands somewhere in the neighbourhood of Tuluum
in the great hurricane which swept the coast in 1916, and
sent her, with many another vessel, to the bottom, so our
only hope of seeing the stele again lay in the vessel having
foundered before she had an opportunity of taking it on board.

Tuluum from the sea presents a forbidding and inhospit-
able aspect. Upon the summit of a gaunt, naked, limestone
bluff, honeycombed into all sorts of fantastic designs by
the ceaseless action of the sea, stands the Castillo—a high
rectangular tower, with lower wings on each side, all presenting blank, windowless, doorless, grey limestone walls
to the sea, and buried in a dense growth of the scrubby
bush which covers this part of Yucatan. Landing at the
ruins is always difficult, and in anything like a strong
breeze absolutely impossible, as the opening in the reef is
narrow, and in rough weather impassable, while even on
the calmest day the surf pounds on this ironbound shore
with incredible force, upsetting one's boat into a maelstrom
of swirling, eddying water, with a sandy bottom from which
project sharp fangs of limestone rock at frequent intervals.

Warned by previous experiences, we anchored the pram
about twenty yards from shore, opposite the southern of
the two small sandy bays which indent the high bluff above
and below the Castillo, and, stripping to our drawers and
undershirts, jumped overboard and waded ashore, being

ultimately spewed gently up on all fours by a great breaker on the sandy beach.

The southern bay, though it looks more dangerous, is in reality far safer than the northern, which for fifty yards out is protected by a *chevaux de frise* of jagged rocks. Morley and I at once climbed the tortuous, rocky path to the top of the bluff, made familiar during our former visit, and made a beeline through the ruins at the land side of the Castillo to the small northern bay, where we had hidden the precious fragments of the stele, only to find them gone—evidently removed by the captain of the turtle-schooner, and now presumably lying with him somewhere at the bottom of the Caribbean Sea.

Greatly depressed, we returned to the southern bay to superintend the landing of our camping outfit—a ticklish business, as everything had to be carried ashore on the men's heads from the pram, which was dancing about on the breakers like a cork, while a slip or toe stubbed on a hidden rock by the porter meant a wetting for some part of our precious outfit.

At length everything was safely landed, and the question arose as to whether we should make our camp on the sandy beach or within the Castillo. I was in favour of the former site, as being handy for a sea bath at all times, and saving the back-aching job of transporting our huge impedimenta up the steep bluff, and then up the still steeper steps leading to the Castillo. Morley, however, from the purely senti-mental motive of wishing to camp in the building where the great American explorer Stephens had camped seventy-five years previously (very uncomfortably, it must be admitted, if his account is to be credited), was in favour of the Castillo, as was also Held. Thither, therefore, followed by all hands carrying bedding, food, cooking utensils, photo-graphic outfits, arms, etc., we betook ourselves.

The Castillo was probably the principal temple of the city. It stands upon the crest of the bluff, its back to the sea, its front facing the land and the city. It is an elaborate structure on three different levels, the two-roomed building on top, approached by a broad flight of steep stone steps, probably representing the chief sanctuary of the entire group. The great stairway is thirty feet wide, with twenty-four extremely steep steps, and remains of stone balustrades, now much broken up by the roots of trees, which have grown over the entire stairway. The sanctuary has an entrance divided into three by two stone columns. Above each are square recesses, each of which at one time contained a painted stucco figure in high relief, though only that in the central one now remains. The interior is divided into two rooms, each 26 ft. long, the front one 6ft. 6ins. broad, the back one 9ft. On each side of the doorway leading from one to the other are inset stone rings, probably for the support of the rod for the curtain which screened the entrance to this Holy of Holies. The roofs of both chambers are formed by the same corbel arch already seen at Chacmool.

The columns at the main entrance are specially note-worthy, as they are in the form of serpents, the rattles of the tail held upwards along the side of the building, the heads projecting forward at right angles from the bases of the column, which are formed by the bodies of the snakes. These serpent columns are of great importance in dating the city, as they are purely Toltec, or Mexican, and were not introduced into Yucatan till the thirteenth century, while at Chichen Itza, the Toltec stronghold, they are found in great number and perfection.

The wing ranges are much lower than the central building, from each side of which they project symmetrically. Their upper stories, now much ruined, were, unlike most Maya buildings, flat roofed, the sapodilla wood roof beams being upheld on circular stone columns, which still remain, surrounded by fragments of the fallen-in concrete roof, which, when the sapodilla rotted, soon collapsed, owing to its great weight.

These wings are approached on each side by flights of short stone steps on each side of the main stairway, which lead to the platforms upon which they stand. The platform in front of the temple at the top of the main stairway was covered with a thick growth of small bushes armed with long, sharp thorns, in each of which dwelt a particularly vicious and pugnacious ant, who at the least disturbance sallied forth to attack the invader.

We set George to cut down these bushes, and he remarked of the ants, that " they were putting fire into his meat." The bush cut down and burnt, I erected my cot on the platform, while Morley and Held set theirs up in the front room of the temple.

At our last visit we had thoroughly cleared the great stairway of bush, for photographic purposes, but it was now covered with a vigorous secondary growth of young trees ten to fifteen feet high, in which a small colony of pretty little blue birds had settled, and were fighting furiously over the fruit of a gigantic wild papaw rooted at the base of the stairway, whose top just reached the level of my cot, giving me an excellent view of the proceedings.

Morley and Held were justified in their choice of a sleeping-place, as during the night it came on to pour with rain, and, before I could get them into the temple, blankets, cot, and mosquito curtains were saturated, while a horrible mix-up took place in the dark front chamber between the steel frame of my net and Held's curtains, which blocked the entry, resulting in much torn muslin and mutual recriminations.

Next morning, after tea, Morley set off with the pilot to explore the ruins. I went to renew my acquaintance with the painted stucco, while Held, with youthful optimism, took Muddy and a couple of shovels down to the little sandy bay where we had hidden the fragments of stele, with the belated hope that they might after all be there. On returning to lunch at midday we were greatly rejoiced to hear that Held's " hunch " had been justified, and that he had actually found two fragments buried beneath a mountain of sand well above ordinary high-water mark, as poor Peter Vasquez, the turtle-fisher whom I had

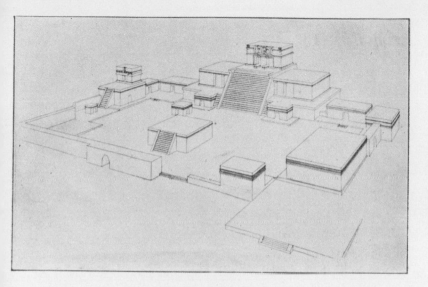

PLAN SHOWING PRINCIPAL TEMPLE GROUP AT TULUUM,
PARTIALLY RESTORED.

[p. 109

TULUUM : TEMPLE WITH ROOF COMB.

[p. 125

commissioned to bring them away, had considered Tuluum too dangerous an anchorage to be visited even for a consideration of 100 dollars ; yet had he only put in for the stone the delay would probably have saved him and the whole ship's company from destruction by the hurricane.

After a frugal lunch on tomato omelette prepared by Muddy—Hubert had been, by general consensus of opinion, disrated as cook, and, being useless as a sailor, had reverted to his normal status as loafer—we all set off to the bay, and before night succeeded in recovering all the lost fragments, with the exception of the smallest, to search for which in that vast accumulation of sand would have been like looking for a needle in a straw stack.

These great masses of stone, some several hundred pounds in weight, had been rooted up from the place where we had buried them, cast like corks well above high-water mark, and then buried beneath a mountain of sand. All this had evidently been accomplished by the hurricane and tidal wave, and it gave us a more realistic idea of their gigantic force than all the wrecked buildings, piers, and ships which we had seen along its course.

We searched very carefully within the temple where Stephens had first found the fragments, but without success. On the platform surrounding it, however, amongst a lot of ordinary stones we found two considerable-sized pieces which had probably been left behind by Parmalee and Howe in 1911, one of which, as will be seen, proved to be possibly the greatest treasure-trove of the entire expedition. The fragments, when assembled, form a monolith 3ft. wide, 8ins. thick, and at present 8ft. long, but as it has been broken off from its base—which is lost—the exact original length is impossible to determine. It was, however, probably in the neighbourhood of 10ft. The stone is cut from the native limestone of the Tuluum cliffs, and piercing it are two large circular natural holes, which had probably originally been filled in with cement, over which the carving was continuous. Upon both faces of the monument are sculptured human figures, slightly larger than life-size, very elaborately dressed. The one on the Initial Series side holds in both hands a two-headed ceremonial bar, or sceptre, the commonest emblem of authority found in Maya sculpture. He wears an enormous and elaborate feather headdress, with highly ornamental breastplate and maxtli, or apron, a network with lozenge-shaped spaces, probably of beads, over the legs, and flame-shaped objects projecting on either side from the waist. Both figure and glyphs on the reverse side are in very low relief—in fact, hardly more than deep scratches on the surface of the stone. On both sides the glyphs are presented in two vertical panels, one on each side of the central figure, connected by a single horizontal panel across the top.

The stone is very much weathered and defaced by its centuries of exposure, but fortunately the Initial Series date inscription—the most important part from our point of view—is perfectly plain and legible.

A short explanation is necessary of the Maya calendar in order to understand this and the other inscriptions which we found later.

The Maya of the Old Empire measured time by the passage of so many cycles, katuns, tuns, uinals, and kins from a certain fixed date. The kin, or lowest unit, was a day, and is represented by the sign ⧈.

This uinal, or month, containing 20 days, by the sign ⧈.

The tun, or year of 360 days or 18 uinals, by the sign ⧈.

The katun, or 20-tun periods, by the sign ⧈ while the cycle, 20 katuns, or 144,000-day period, slightly more than five years under four centuries of our time, is represented by the sign ⧈.

All these signs may be, and frequently are, in the inscriptions replaced by grotesque heads, differing for each period,

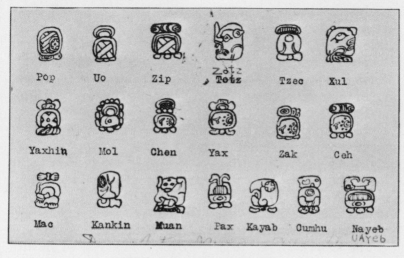

MONTHS OF THE MAYA YEAR.

DAYS OF THE MAYA YEAR.

known as head variants, while the signs themselves are known as the normal forms.

The Maya numerals from 1 to 19 were represented by varying combinations of two elements, the dot . representing 1, and the bar —— representing 5; thus . . . stood for 3; ≝ for 12, and ≣ for 19, while 0 is expressed by the sign 🐚 .

These are known as the normal forms, and may be compared to our Roman numerals. In addition, however, each number from 1 to 19 is frequently represented by a grotesque head, which may be considered as the Maya equivalent of our Arabic notation.

The Maya also divided time into years of 365 days, made up of 18 months of 20 days each and one month of 5 days.

The months were named as follows (Maya symbol) :

Pop	Zac
Uo	Ceh
Zip	Mac
Zotz	Kankin
Tzec	Muan
Xul	Pax
Yaxkin	Kayab
Mol	Cumhu
Chen	Uayeb (5 days)
Yax	

The days were named :

Imix	Chuen
Ik	Eb
Akbal	Ben
Kan	Ix
Chicchan	Men
Cimi	Cib
Manik	Caban
Lamat	Eznab
Muluc	Cauac
Oc	Ahau

HL

To each day sign was prefixed a number from 1 to 13, these numbers following each other in endless succession. The position occupied by the day in the month was also given, and as there were 20 days to each month it is obvious that the day could occupy one of 20 positions. These were not expressed, however, as by us, in terms of current time, for we say first, second, third, etc., January before the first, second, and third days of that month have actually elapsed; the Maya spoke only in terms of time elapsed, as we do in reading the clock, consequently the first day was 0, the twentieth was 19.

The starting-point of the Maya chronology was a certain day 4 Ahau, occupying position 8, in the month Cumhu, written thus : 4 Ahau 8 Cumhu. To illustrate the sequence of the dates let us follow the days for a month from this date :

4 Ahau	8 Cumhu
5 Imix	9 Cumhu
6 Ik	10 Cumhu
7 Akbal	11 Cumhu
8 Kan	12 Cumhu
9 Chicchan	13 Cumhu
10 Cimi	14 Cumhu
11 Manik	15 Cumhu
12 Lamat	16 Cumhu
13 Muluc	17 Cumhu
1 Oc	18 Cumhu
2 Chuen	19 Cumhu
3 Eb	0 Uayeb
4 Ben	1 Uayeb
5 Ix	2 Uayeb
6 Men	3 Uayeb
7 Cib	4 Uayeb
8 Caban	0 Pop
9 Eznab	1 Pop
10 Cauac	2 Pop
11 Ahau	3 Pop
12 Imix	4 Pop
13 Ik	5 Pop

It will be seen that the thirteen numerical coefficients of the days, the days themselves, their positions in the months, and the months, follow an endless succession. Every 18,980 days, or 52 years, the day 4 Ahau 8 Cumhu, or, in fact, any date came round again ; consequently this period was named a " calendar round." It may be likened to a gigantic cogwheel, with 18,980 named cogs revolving throughout all time. The number of cogs between any two given ones is always the same, and at each complete revolution of the wheel, whatever cog one started from must recur again.

The Maya started their chronology from a cog named 4 Ahau 8 Cumhu.

After every Initial Series date the day in the calendar round upon which it fell is almost invariably given as a check on the correctness of the Initial Series ; for example :

The above Initial Series is taken from a stele at the ruins of Quirigua, in Guatemala. It reads : " 9 Cycles, 18 Katuns, 10 Tuns, 0 Uinals, 0 Kins ; 10 Ahau, 8 Zac "— which, being interpreted, means that this stele was set up 9 cycles, 18 Katuns, 10 Tuns, no months, and no days, after the date 4 Ahau 8 Cumhu, and that this date fell upon a certain day 10 Ahau 8 Zac in the calendar round. Now if we reduce 9.18.10.0.0. (generally written thus for brevity) to days we find that it contains 1,429,200, and if we divide this by 18,980—the number of days in a calendar round, we find that it goes 75 times, leaving a remainder of 5,700 ; in other words, 75 calendar rounds and 5,700 days have elapsed from the date 4 Ahau 8 Cumhu to the date recorded by the Initial Series 9.18.10.0.0., and if we count forward 5,700 cogs on the great wheel from the cog 4 Ahau

8 Cumhu we shall find that we come to the cog named
10 Ahau 8 Zac, proving that the entire date is correct.

When several dates were recorded on one monument the
Maya frequently made use of what is termed a Secondary
Series.   Let us suppose that the Initial Series ended on a
day 5 Imix 9 Cumhu, and after this we find recorded

On referring to the glyphs it will be seen that these represent
1 Uinal 1 Kin 13 Ik 5 Pop ; the meaning being that 1 Uinal
and 1 Kin (i.e. 21 days) after 5 Imix 9 Cumhu occurred the
date now recorded—i.e. 13 Ik 5 Pop, and if 21 days be
counted forward from 5 Imix 9 Cumhu, it will be found to
fall on 13 Ik 5 Pop. This saved the repetition of the
Initial Series for each date, and often a number of dates
are recorded on a monument in this way ; they are known as
secondary dates, and the periods which indicate their
distances from the Initial Series date, as 1 uinal 1 kin above,
are known as distance numbers.

The Initial Series and Secondary Series were the only
methods of dating used by the Maya of the Old Empire.
They were perfectly simple and perfectly accurate, but, it
must be admitted, somewhat clumsy and cumbersome.
In the New Empire, throughout Yucatan, they soon fell
into desuetude, and only three Initial Series dates have
been found in the peninsula, as against many hundreds on
monoliths throughout the southern cities. Of these three,
one is at Tuluum, one at Chichen Itza, and one at Xcanchacan.

In the New Empire three distinct methods of recording
time were employed :

1. *The Calendar Round.*—This merely gave the position
of the day in the calendar round, as 4 Ik 10 Pop, which
fixed the date accurately amongst the 18,980 days of the
calendar round, or within a period of 52 years ; but as one

rarely knows to which calendar round it refers, such a form of dating is practically useless to us, unless other dates are found upon the same stele, or in the same temple, which accurately fix the calendar round referred to.

2. *Period Ending Dating.*—This consisted in recording the occurrence of an event as taking place at the end of some particular period in the long count ; that is, in time as measured by the Initial Series. This method involves two, and usually three, factors :

(*a*) The name of the period at whose end the event occurs, i.e. cycle, katun, or tun.

(*b*) The calendar round date on which it fell ; as 6 Ahau 13 Cumhu.

(*c*) A sign or element meaning ending, or it is ended, signifying that the period had come to a close.

Three signs are used in this last connection.

The first and third of these are never used by themselves, but invariably to modify some other sign ; the hand, on the contrary, is rarely used to modify period glyphs, but, connoting ending in general, is used in various connections, one of which is to indicate the completion of a building, when printed in red paint on its walls.

Simple examples of these period ending dates are :

In Inscription 1, glyph (*a*) shows first the ending sign, and following this the cycle sign with the coefficient 9, the whole indicating the end of Cycle 9, (*b*) is the day Ahau, with the coefficient 8, and (*c*) the month Ceh, with the coefficient 13 ; the whole inscription reading 8 Ahau 13 Ceh, the end of the Cycle 9, and as this date can occur practically but once in all time, it is fixed with absolute accuracy.

Inscription 2 reads (a) the end of Katun 14 (note the small ending sign above the numerical coefficient) falling on (b) 6 Ahau (c) 13 Muan, and as this date can occur but once in Maya historic times, there can be no ambiguity about it.

But this period ending system was variously employed, and the accuracy of the dates depends largely on the number and nature of the factors present. Sometimes a day is given as falling within a certain tun, as 3 Chicchan in Tun 7. Now every Tun 7 contained a day 3 Chicchan, and every Tun 7 recurred every 19.71 years, consequently such a date was useful only in indicating a certain day within a period of 19.71 years. The most usual method, as we found in Yucatan, was the recording of a certain tun with the day upon which it ended ; as, for example, Tun 13 ending in the day 2 Ahau. Such a date occurred only once in 256.26 years, and as most of the New Empire sites were occupied for less than 500 years from their foundation to their destruction, it is never necessary to distinguish between more than two possible readings, while almost invariably only one is historically probable.

By adding the day of the month in the above method, as, for example, Tun 11 ending on the day 2 Ahau 18 Xul (a date found by us at Chichen Itza), accuracy within a period of no less than 1,870 years was secured.

Another method even more accurate than the preceding is practised on the rings of the ball court at Uxmal, where the calendar round date is given as 10 Ix 17 Pop, falling within a Tun 17 which ended in the day 12 Ahau, a date which could only recur once in 243,193 years.

The U Kalay Katunob, or procession of the katuns, was much less accurate than any of the preceding. It is the method employed in the books of Chilam Balam, or Maya historical records handed down after the Conquest, and consists merely in numbering the katuns, or 20-years periods, from 1 to 13 in the following sequence : 12, 10,

8, 4, 2, 13, 11, 9, 7, 5, 3, 1. It is obvious that an event so recorded, unless the tun, or year, be given also, may occur anywhere within a period of one katun, or approximately 20 years, and further that, as 30 x 20 = 260, every 260 years each katun will recur. As a matter of fact, however, the tun or year of the katun on which the event occurred is often given, an event being described as occurring on the second tun of Katun 13, just as we might describe the commencement of the Great War as taking place in the fourth year of the second decade of the nineteenth century, and on historical grounds it is usually easy to select the particular round of 13 katuns, or 260 years, on which any recorded event occurred.

It may be accepted that the year 1537 A.D. corresponded to the end of Katun 13 in the procession of the katuns, for it is recorded in the book of Chilam Balam that the death of a certain chief, Napot Xiu, occurred in a Katun 13 Ahau, while yet 6 tuns were lacking before the end of the katun, on the day 9 Imix, and the chronicler further states that the event took place in the year of our Lord 1537.

Now the date 13 Ahau of the new notation corresponded to the Initial Series date 12.9.0.0.0., i.e. 12 cycles, 9 katuns, 0 tuns, 0 uinals, and 0 kuns after 4 Ahau 8 Cumhu, the starting-point of Maya chronology. Therefore 12.9.0.0.0. of the Old Empire = Katun 13 Ahau of the New Empire = 1537 A.D. of the Christian era.

CHAPTER VIII

THE photograph shows all the pieces of the stele found by us, placed together, and upon it the Initial Series is clearly recognisable, though somewhat defaced by time and weather. In glyph 1 is seen the coefficient ⑨ or nine in front of the grotesque head variant for the cycle ; in glyph 2 the coefficient ⑥ in front of the grotesque head variant for the katun ; in glyph 3 the coefficient ⑩ in front of the head variant for the tun ; in glyph 4 the coefficient ⓪ or 0, in front of the head variant for the uinal; and in glyph 6 the upper part of the same zero coefficient in front of the day sign, which has been broken away. The whole inscription then reads 9.6.10.0.0.0. or 9 cycles, 6 katuns, 10 tuns, 0 uinals, 0 kins, after 4 Ahau 8 Cumhu, and if this be worked out it will be found to coincide with a date 8 Ahau 13 Pax of the calendar round. Now the calendar round day always follows immediately at the end of the Initial Series, and should occupy the vacant position shown for glyph 6, which has been broken away, but in glyph 11 we recognise very clearly the month Pax, with the coefficient 13, the whòle date then reaching 9.6.10.0.0.0., 8 Ahau 13 Pax. Nothing could be clearer than this date, which corresponds

I
2
3
4
5
6
7
8
9
10
11
12
13
14

TULUUM.

Front of Stele, showing in glyph 1 the coefficient 9 (one bar and four dots which are partially obliterated), with the head variant of the cycle sign (immediately above glyph 1 is the Initial Series introducing glyph, very much weathered), glyph 2 the coefficient 6 with the katun head variant, glyph 3 the coefficient 10 with the tun head variant, glyph 4 the zero coefficient with the uinal head variant, glyph 5 the upper part of the same zero coefficient, the lower being broken away. Glyph 6, which should be the day sign, is gone, but in glyph 10 the month sign, 13 Pax, is very plain. The whole reads: 9.6.10.0.0 (8 Ahau) 13 Pax. The last two glyphs, 13 and 14, were, as may be seen, found and joined on later. 13 is the sign for the Lahuntun or 10 Tun period, 14 is the day Ahau preceded by the coefficient 7, i.e., 7 Ahau the end of a Lahuntun, which carries the contemporary date of the Stele from 9.6.10.0.0. exactly one cycle forward to 10.6.10.0.0., or in Christian chronology from 305 A.D. to 699 A.D.

approximately to 305 A.D. of our era. But we know from a number of historical sources that Tuluum and Chichen Itza were not founded till towards the end of the sixth century of our era by Maya from Bakalal, led by their Priest-Chief Itzamna. How, then, reconcile the discrepancies in these dates? Three explanations were possible, all equally unsatisfactory :

(1) The stone might have been carried by the Maya from one of their older cities, but as the limestone was obviously exactly similar to that of the Tuluum cliffs, and the stone weighed many hundreds of pounds, this did not sound convincing.

(2) The date of the Initial Series may have referred to some former event in the history of the Maya, and so not have been contemporaneous, but in that case, judging from the analogy of all other Initial Series dates, a Secondary Series contemporary date would have been given.

(3) The whole explanation of the Initial Series system of dating is wrong ; but this is untenable, as all the dozens of inscriptions which have been deciphered by means of it work out to a day with absolute precision.

This problem had occupied Morley's and my own mind ever since our first visit to Tuluum. We had talked it over, and evolved endless hypotheses, each more unsatisfactory then the last, in explanation of it, yet in five minutes after the discovery of the extra fragments of the stele outside the temple where it had rested the whole thing was made perfectly clear to us. This fragment, it will be seen, fits on immediately below the Initial Series inscription, and on it are sculptured the two glyphs shown below.

The upper one is the glyph for the lahuntun, or period of 10 tuns, the lower the coefficient ⅋ or 7, prefixed to a not uncommon face-variant for the day Ahau, the whole reading 7 Ahau, the end of a lahuntun. Now this date occurs exactly one cycle or 20 katuns after 9.6.10.0.0., the date recorded by the Initial Series, so that the contemporaneous date of the stone is 10.6.10.0.0., or 699 A.D., which fits in perfectly with the record of the books of Chilam Balam. The question next arises, 699 A.D. being the contemporaneous date of the stele, what does the date 305 A.D. so carefully recorded by the Initial Series refer to ? And to this I think there can be but one answer. It records some important event in the previous history of the Maya, possibly some great victory or battle, or possibly the date of their setting out on their wanderings north from the southern city of their origin. The stele, in fact, corresponds very closely in idea to a statue of Columbus erected to commemorate the fourth centenary (or cycle, as in Tuluum) of the discovery of America, upon which are inscribed the date of the event commemorated, 1492, and the current date, 1892.

This stone has a curious history. Erected in 699 A.D., it represents with one exception so far as is known the very last Initial Series date throughout the whole Maya area. When exactly the city of old Tuluum was deserted by its inhabitants we have no means of knowing, but the next we hear of the stone is its discovery in fragments by John L. Stephens in 1841, on the floor of one of the temples of the new city, which with other east coast towns was probably founded about the middle of the fifteenth century. Whether the later Maya retained any tradition or written record of the city founded by their ancestors 800 years previously, which influenced them in returning there ; whether they knew of the existence of the stele, or came upon it by accident ; how it got broken ; where the missing fragments have disappeared to ; why it was placed in a temple of its own, are points which will probably never be cleared up.

The principal buildings at Tuluum are surrounded by a

wall on the north, south, and west sides, the east side being guarded by the precipitous cliff overlooking the sea. The wall encloses a space 1,500ft. long north and south, and 600ft. east and west. The area included, measuring about 22 acres, is now covered with dense tropical bush, which renders one building invisible from the next. It is built of rough blocks of stone, the height varying, owing to the rolling contour of the ground, from 10ft. to 15ft. The top is level, and sufficiently wide to admit of four men walking abreast upon it. The sides are pierced by five narrow passages to admit of exit and entry. At the north-western and south-western corners are watch-towers built upon the summit of the wall, 12ft. square, each containing a small altar. When the country was clear of forest they must have commanded a magnificent view for many miles over its flat expanse, but now they look out to the west, far as the eye can reach, over an unbroken sea of almost impenetrable virgin bush, and to the east over the deserted city, shrouded in a veil of bush almost as dense. No more will the guard be changed in these watch-towers, no more the password be given to enter the city by the passages, no more will the alarm be sounded of an enemy in sight, and the women and children collected from the surrounding villages within the fort, while the men arm themselves for the fray, and prepare to repulse the invader from the north, or the cannibal black Carib from the sea. Citizen and enemy alike lie silently side by side without the deserted city walls, awaiting their last summons, unless, indeed, their spirits may return to re-enact the episodes of their former life on its now desolate stage ; to live and strive, to love and hate, and perhaps with ghostly hosts to refight in bloodless battles the sanguinary conflicts of their earthly life.

Mayapan is the only other city in the Maya area, so far as is known, surrounded by a wall, but the Tuluum wall, though shorter, is more carefully constructed, and higher than that of Mayapan. The object of these walls was prob-ably twofold—to surround and isolate from the common people sacred buildings, temples, pyramids, dance platforms, and priests' dwellings, and in time of war to act as a fort, in which the inhabitants from the surrounding districts could take refuge. At Mayapan the first was probably the predominating reason, as we read in contemporary accounts that the vassal nobles to the rulers of Mayapan, with their families, lived within the walls with the higher priests, while their retainers formed a city of their own without.

At Tuluum the wall was mainly defensive, as is shown by the watch-towers standing upon it, and by the presence of narrow passages, with off-sets, passing through it, for in the unsettled state of the country immediately following the fall of Mayapan every man's hand was against his neighbour, and the city was subject to attack on the landward side from neighbouring petty states, and from the sea by Carib pirates. It would probably have been easy of defence against enemies armed only with bows, arrows, and javelins, while starving the garrison out would have been practically impossible, for the only food the fighting man of that day required was a small ration of maize to make into corn cakes, vast stores of which were no doubt always kept in the fort, while unlimited water, somewhat bitter in taste, but quite fresh and drinkable, was to be obtained from a *cenote*, or natural well, close to the north wall.

During our first expedition to Tuluum we located eighteen buildings within the enclosure, to which on this occasion we added two good-sized temples to the north of the Castillo. It is quite possible, however, that a complete clearing of the bush from the space within the walls would disclose further edifices, as it is at present so dense in places that one may stand within a few yards of a building without perceiving it.

Outside the walls we came across ten buildings, chiefly small temples, distributed irregularly round the walls, and for all one can tell there may be many more, as the bush is even heavier and more impenetrable outside than inside the walls. The buildings fall naturally into three groups :

(1) The single story structure with a flat roof, corbel vaulted ceiling, one or more cornices ornamenting the outside, covered internally and externally with hard stucco, similar to those we have already seen at Chacmool and Espiritu Santo, but in Tuluum very much larger and more carefully constructed. The photograph shows one of these structures from which the outside coat of stucco has all been peeled off, as it stands unprotected on the very edge of the cliff, where for five centuries it has encountered the full force and violence of the prevailing easterly wind hurtling in from the Caribbean Sea. This building is the only one at Tuluum, or, indeed, amongst the whole of the east coast ruins, which possesses a roof comb, or ornamental projection from the flat roof—a feature extremely common, and some-times, in the form of a flying façade, greatly elaborated amongst the older ruins in the north of the peninsula.

(2) The second class of building consisted of flat-roofed, concrete-ceiled chambers, such as are seen in the buildings forming the wings of the Castillo. These were roofed in with beams of sapodilla wood resting on circular stone pillars, and covered with a layer of hard concrete. All of these have collapsed owing to the decay of the wooden beams, and consequent falling in of the concrete roofs, all that now remains being masses of great flat pieces of concrete, showing casts of the beams which upheld them scattered about between rows of pillars. This type of roof is very uncommon in the Maya area, the most usual form for stone houses being the corbel vault already described, and in structures too large to admit of this beams covered with palm-leaf thatch, supported on rows of stone columns.

(3) An example of the third type of building found in Tuluum is shown in the photograph. It consisted merely of a low, rectangular structure, with columned entrance, supporting on its roof a similar but smaller building, with a single door in front. Both buildings are ornamented with a double cornice, and both are covered inside and out with extremely hard resistant stucco. Over the entrance

of the lower story are two niches which held stucco figures of warriors. These had been very carefully executed, the limbs and bust being first roughly modelled in pottery, over which the stucco was applied, and afterwards painted in red, black, blue, and green. Over the entrance to the upper story is a panel containing a similar figure ; all are, however, unfortunately greatly mutilated. These figures, remains of which are found in niches above the entrances of several other buildings at Tuluum, are probably intended as representations of the gods to whom the temples were dedicated. Whether they were destroyed by the Maya to prevent their desecration by the Spaniards when they saw that their conquest by the latter was inevitable, or by zealous but bigoted priests, who saw in every endeavour of the Maya to return to their ancient arts of painting, sculpture, and hieroglyphic writing evidence of the handiwork of *el diabolo*, to be sternly and incontinently repressed, it is now impossible to tell.

Into the bright and joyous religion of the early Maya, whose beneficent gods asked only offerings of fruit, flowers, prayers, and incense in return for those gifts which all mortals seek of their gods, was infused the black, cruel, gloomy religion of Mexico, with its bloodthirsty priests and its savage, obscene deities demanding hecatombs of human sacrifices. On this was grafted, three centuries later, the brand of Christianity introduced by the Spanish monks— hard, fierce, zealous men, most of them without real sympathy or kindliness, always at handgrips with the devil for the souls of their unfortunate converts, whose bodies they were ready to sacrifice, and often did sacrifice, with torture, flogging, and fire, to ensure the eternal salvation of their souls. Unhappy Maya ! Joyous, peaceful, care-free, art-loving children of nature, fate indeed dealt hardly with them. Nor is it to be wondered at that the poor remnant left to-day, gloomy, taciturn, secretive, with a religion combining the worst superstitions of three irreconcilable

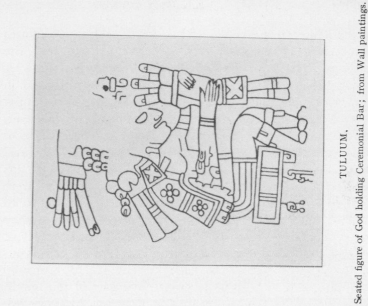

TULUM.

Two-storied building, interior decorated with painted stucco.

[p. 126]

TULUUM.

Seated figure of God holding Ceremonial Bar; from Wall paintings.

[p. 127]

faiths, should hide themselves from their conquerors in the fastnesses of the virgin bush of Yucatan—last stronghold left them in the land which once was theirs.

At Tuluum are found perhaps the finest, and certainly the most extensive, mural paintings now in existence throughout the Maya area. They are executed in red, black, blue, violet, green, and claret colour on the rock-like stucco which covers both the interior and exterior of the buildings. This stucco, though thin, is extraordinarily hard and smooth ; in fact, it was as much as we could do to chip it with a pickaxe. In several places, notably throughout a narrow passage which runs beneath the great stairway which leads to the Castillo, two, and in some places three, layers of stucco have been applied, one over the other, each showing traces of the paintings which originally covered it. On the outer wall of a building just north of the Castillo, facing towards the sea, is depicted a human figure, nearly life-size, outlined in black on the white stucco, with elaborate feather-decorated headdress, maxtli, or apron, plaited cotton breast-plate, and sandals ornamented with bows and tags. This figure, notwithstanding the fact that it has weathered the storms of over four hundred years, is almost as clear in detail as upon the day when it was first painted. In another temple within the sacred enclosure are depicted the gods Itzamna and Cuculcan. Itzamna, as we have seen, was the priest and leader who conducted the Chanes in their migration northward from Bakalal, and soon after his death underwent apotheosis, and became one of the most universally worshipped gods throughout Yucatan. He is known as the "Roman-nosed god" from the fact that he is usually represented with a prominent Roman nose, and is very frequently associated with the symbol of the serpent.

Cuculcan, sometimes known as the "Long-nosed god," was the hero chieftain who led the Tutul Xiu into Yucatan from the west, and who, after his death, was also deified. His name signifies "feathered serpent," and he is also frequently associated with the symbol of a plumed or a feather-covered crotalus.

The whole interior surface of the walls of the chambers within the lower story of the two-storied temple is covered with paintings of gods, and offerings being made to them, with conventional representations of fruit, flowers, jars, vases, bows, knots, and geometrical devices. These are outlined in blue on a claret-coloured background, and are all, unfortunately, in an exceedingly bad state of preservation, owing to the damp and mildew which between them have effected what the sea storms were unable to do, and partly destroyed the iron stucco which covers the walls. From the lower story of this temple are shown two panels of a frieze, probably the best preserved portion of the whole mural decoration.

The first exhibits the Roman-nosed god, whose head-dress is seen to be decorated by two highly conventionalised serpents' heads, while in front of his face is a vase from which projects another similar head. He holds in his left hand a rope-like object, and is apparently receiving an offering of a " ceremonial bar " decorated with flowers from a worshipper who faces him.

The second shows Ah Puch, the god of death, holding in his right hand a " ceremonial bar," the upper part of which consists of a plumed serpent's head. Above this is the symbol ⊙ which, as we have seen, stands for Imix, the first day of the Maya month, but it is also used to denote maize, the Maya word for which is Ixim. This is the only calendar hieroglyph which we were able to discover on the mural paintings at Tuluum, and here it is used probably, not in its calendaric significance, but merely to represent an offering of maize to the deity.

These " ceremonial bars," or batons, are held in the hands of nearly all the figures of gods at Tuluum as symbols of their divinity.

The head of the god of death is, as will be observed, double, and was originally covered by an elaborately

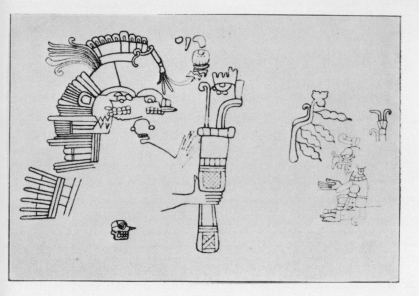

AH PUCH, OR THE GOD OF DEATH, FROM TULUUM ;
BELOW : THE SAME GOD, FROM THE DRESDEN CODEX.

THE GOD CUCULCAN, FROM TULUUM.

[*p.* 128

I AND 2. THE GODS, CUCULCAN AND ITZAMNA, FROM THE WALL
PAINTING AT TULUUM ; BELOW : 3 AND 4. THE SAME GODS
FROM THE DRESDEN CODEX.

[*p.* 130

decorated feather headdress, the greater part of which has now become obliterated, while all down his back plumes of conventionalised feathers are seen projecting. Beneath the figures of Itzamna, Cuculcan, and Ah Puch are shown the heads of the same gods, as depicted in the Dresden Codex, and it will be observed that not only are the representations of the gods alike in each case, but that they are practically identical ; so much so, indeed, that the conviction is forced on one that if not actually the work of the same artist, they were at least executed at about the same period, in the same locality, and possibly from a common model.

Now the Dresden Codex (so called because it at present reposes in the Landes Bibliothek, formerly known as the Royal Library at Dresden) is one of the three priceless aboriginal Maya paintings of hieroglyphs which have been preserved to us. It is painted in red and black on paper made by the natives from the fibre of the Agave Americana, or America aloe, and is folded like a map. Its hieroglyphic inscriptions and pictures deal with the gods, the tonalamtl, or sacred year of 260 days, which of the divisions of these are dedicated to the service of each god, and the ceremonies appropriate to each of them, together with certain obscure astronomical calculations. How or when it was originally brought to Europe from the New World is not known, but it must have come at a very early date, for we know that very shortly after the conquest all the books of the Maya were destroyed by the Spanish priests as works of *el diablo*, irrespective of their subject-matter, so that at the present day only three examples are left to us of the many thousands which originally existed amongst the priests, dealing with medicine, the art of prophecy or divination, the calendar system, the worship of the gods, and the history of the Maya from the earliest times.

The exact date and place of origin of the Dresden Codex are unknown, and have always given rise to a considerable amount of controversy amongst students of Central American archæology. That it comes from Yucatan and belongs to

IL

the New Empire are the only two facts which all admit, but in the extraordinary resemblance, indeed the almost exact identity between the heads of the gods as shown in the Codex and in the mural paintings of Tuluum, I think we have a very useful pointer as to both the time when, and place where, the Codex was painted. It seems, indeed, fairly certain that it was a product of the east coast civilisation, and so belongs to the closing years of the Second Empire, probably within half a century of the arrival of the Spaniards in Yucatan, and, Tuluum being the chief city of this civilisation, it is quite likely that the Dresden Codex originated here, and may even have been the work of the same artist who produced the mural decorations now before us.

The discovery of the city of Chacmool, and the exact dating of the Tuluum stele, would well have repaid us for our entire expedition, but when to them was added the light thrown on that obscure manuscript, the Dresden Codex, we felt that if fortune favoured us with no further discoveries, we could not in justice complain.

The principal gods worshipped at Tuluum were, in order of their most frequent appearance on the mural paintings, and probably of their popularity amongst the people, Itzamna, Cuculcan, Ah Puch (the so-called diving god), a curious figure modelled in stucco over several of the temples of a god with legs in the air and palms together, pointed downwards in a diving position ; Ek Ahau, the black captain, a war deity ; and the maize god, or god of fertility.

The two first of these were by far the most popular, and their common symbol, the serpent, in the form of serpent columns on the main temple, and ceremonial bars, head-dresses, and ornaments on the walls, is to be encountered everywhere.

Curiously enough, the first thing I came across on entering the back room of the main temple was a good-sized rattler's discarded skin lying on top of the small altar, which projected from the back wall—possibly an offering left by the former wearer to his name god.

Alfredo, our engineer, however, in endeavouring to climb to the flat roof of the same temple, had a much more unpleasant experience, for in the act of grasping the edge of the roof to pull himself up he actually touched a snake, which must have been enjoying a sun-bath in this elevated situation. The reptile disappeared amongst the weeds and low bush covering the flat roof, and, search as we might, we were unable to find him, which was rather remarkable, as unless he committed suicide on the rocks beneath it is difficult to see how he managed to elude us. This inexplicable disappearance of a large snake on the open roof of a temple obviously dedicated to a serpent god of course set the men's tongues wagging, for, though a polyglot crew, they were all intensely superstitious, and to the believer—and even half-believer—in the mystic rights of Obeah, practised more or less *sub rosa* by the negro population of all over Central America, the serpent has a peculiar and sinister significance. I noticed, moreover, that they gave the temple a wide berth after this.

On comparing the main temple group of buildings at Tuluum with that at Chacmool, it will be seen that the general arrangement is very similar in each.

Temple B at Chacmool corresponds to the Castillo at Tuluum. Both are divided into a front and back compartment, on the latter of which a low stone altar is placed against the back wall. Both stand on platforms, and are approached by flights of stone steps, those of Tuluum being far higher and more elaborate, as the platform itself contains two ranges of minor temples, or priests' houses. In front of this staircase at Chacmool is the image of the god to whom the whole group is evidently dedicated—the Chacmool, reclining in his own little temple.

At Tuluum, however, the temple was dedicated either to Itzamna, Cuculcan, or possibly both these deities, and the serpent columns of the temple take the place of the image of the god. Farther on, and still immediately facing the stairway, both at Tuluum and Chacmool, is a dance platform

approached by a flight of steps on two sides, where the
procession of priests halted to perform their religious dances
on the way to sacrifice in the main temple. Beyond this
dance platform at Tuluum is an arched opening in the wall
which surrounds the main temple group, through which
the procession of priests no doubt filed on its way to the
sacrifice, just as they filed through the arched doorways of
the idol's little temple of Chacmool.

The sacrifice to the serpent god at Tuluum, carried out
on the platform in front of the temple, at the top of the
high, steep flight of stairs, in front of the twin serpent
images, and in full view of the whole city, right back to the
walls, must have been a far more imposing ceremony than
at Chacmool; indeed, the setting would bear comparison
with those great holocausts which the Spaniards not infrequently witnessed when fighting hand to hand with the
soldiers of Montezuma for the possession of the city of
Mexico, where on the summits of great stone-faced pyramids,
or teocalli, victims were sacrificed by the hundred to secure
the favour of the god of war, the hearts torn out of the living
victims, and the corpses rolled down the steep incline, where
at the base the onlookers were waiting to tear them in
pieces, and perform the act of ceremonial cannibalism which
would endow them with courage from the god to fight the
hated invader, the whole accompanied by the ceaseless
booming on the great snakeskin drum sacred to the god,
which was audible for miles.

Many a time the *conquistadores* of Cortez witnessed such
a scene, and not infrequently saw some of their own companions, who had been captured by the Mexicans, sacrificed
to the god, while looking on powerless to assist them. The
same scenes were enacted at Tuluum, but on a smaller
scale, though probably long after the Spaniards had become
firmly established in Mexico human sacrifice was carried on
in Yucatan, and in this remote region of the east coast,
which was not at any time very securely under the
Spanish dominion, it is possible that the ancient rites may

have been celebrated up to the middle of the sixteenth century.

At our former visit to Tuluum we rather dreaded a visit from the Santa Cruz Indians, whose nearest town is believed to be about nine miles back in the bush, though no white man has ever been there to tell, but though we found evidence that they were watching us, in the form of discarded palm-leaf slings, such as they use to carry small game, upon the floor of a building which we had carefully swept clean the previous day for the purpose of copying some of the mural paintings, we never actually set eyes on a living Indian. Now, however, we looked out eagerly for signs of Indians every day, as our friend Desiderio Cochua, had promised to meet us at Tuluum with carriers for the packs, and to guide us back into the bush to a ruined city which he assured us was far finer and larger, and with more perfect wall paintings than Tuluum. We waited three days for him, but, greatly to our disappointment, he did not turn up, being, as we afterwards heard, unavoidably detained at Central.

As the time at our disposal was limited, we reluctantly made up our minds to move on from Tuluum. We were sorry to leave, for the place fascinated while it repelled us— the absolute silence which pervaded the ruins, broken only by the beat of the surf on the rocky shore, was remarkable, as, with the exception of the little blue birds, attracted by a wild papaw, a few snakes, and an occasional screaming hawk planing overhead, quartering the bush for game, we saw no trace of animal life throughout our stay in the ruins.

The mystery which enveloped these grotesque buildings, with their bizarre paintings, the close airlessness of the bush and its denseness, which made every step an adventure, when one might encounter they knew not what—a few of the descendants of the ancient inhabitants, still surviving in this unexplored region, their ancient religion and customs unaltered, or a band of modern Maya, machete armed, dodging silently from tree to tree, to close in gradually on their victim, and with sharp cutlasses administer the *coup de grâce*—— Then thoughts filled our minds of the terrible things which had been done here in ancient days, till the human sacrifices, the obscene rights, the torturing of captives rose before us as we trod the very spots upon which they had been enacted.

The buildings at Tuluum are, with one or two exceptions, connected with the religion of the inhabitants—temples, shrines, altars, and dance platforms—though a few of the large, flat-ceilinged structures may have served as palaces of the kings, or dwellings for the chief priests. Such an aggregation of sacred buildings must connote a very considerable population, and the question at once arises, where did they live? The answer is, I think, that, like the retainers of the nobles of Mayapan, they lived without the walls, in houses of pimento daubed with mud and thatched with palm, such as are built by the Maya of to-day, and such as leave no trace of their existence after a dozen years. A bird's-eye view of the city must have been a wonderful sight at the time of the first coming of the Spaniards—the buildings covered with gorgeously painted and polished stucco, standing out on the dazzling white background of the limestone pavement, and surrounded by the great white wall, around which clustered thousands upon thousands of the brown bush hovels of the workers, while beyond these, far as the eye could reach, spread the fields of tall green maize waving in the sea breeze. No wonder Grijalva's chaplain—the first European to see it—describes the city as " a bourg so large that Seville would not have seemed larger or better."

CHAPTER IX

WE left Tuluum at 10.30 a.m. on the 19th, and, after a
smooth passage through the reef, sailed due north at the
Lilian Y's usual rate of about six knots. At noon we passed
a narrow, tortuous opening in the reef which leads to the
only landing for Acumal, the village of the northern Santa
Cruz Indians, and the last settlement to the north of the
Indios Sublevados, or revolted Indians, as the Mexicans
call them. We had intended to put in here, weather per-
mitting, but a strong easterly breeze was blowing, the passage
looked very narrow and crooked, and the reef on each side,
with huge waves breaking over it, and churning into a
maelstrom of foam, very formidable, so reluctantly we
passed it by for future reference.

Ten miles north of Acumal we arrived at Playa Carmen,
a small Maya village said to have been settled by Indians
from Cozumel. We anchored about a quarter of a mile out,

while Morley, Held, Muddy, and myself went ashore in the pram in the hope of purchasing fresh provisions, as the unvarying menu of canned goods and biscuits was beginning to pall upon all of us.

The whole settlement, consisting of about fifty Indians, came down to the beach to meet us, and was rewarded by the spectacle of the pram being twisted round and dashed broadside on upon the sandy beach, while her passengers emerged like drowned rats from their immersion under the wave which carried her in. This little contretemps procured us quite a cordial reception, somewhat similar to that accorded the *payazo*, or itinerant clown, so dear to the heart of all Yucatecans, Morley, with his small person, blue eyes, long yellow hair, enormous round tortoiseshell-rimmed glasses, expansive smile, and glibly inaccurate Spanish—a type so totally different from anything they had ever seen before—being regarded as a particularly amusing specimen.

The houses, a dozen or so in number, stood in groups of two and three on a slight ridge a few hundred yards back from the sea. They were of the usual Maya type—walls of pimento sticks and roof of palm leaves, with a hard-beaten earthen floor on which children, pigs, dogs, and fowls mixed indiscriminately. At sight of these last our mouths watered, but, though we offered gold, silver, and notes, we could not purchase a single fowl or egg, nor, though they were obviously well stocked, would the owners sell beans, tomatoes, or corn cake. As a matter of fact, money is of very little use to these villagers, as they have practically no opportunity of spending it, being cut off on the landward side by a dense belt of impenetrable bush from the nearest settlements, while by sea their only communication with the outside world is by means of a dorey which sails across from the island of Cozumel at very long intervals. Fortunately for us this dorey had not turned up for several months and the people had been for a long time without sugar, which they prize highly, as the coffee made of ground parched corn which they drink is a particularly noxious compound when unsweetened. This fact inspired Muddy with the heaven-sent idea of bartering some of our sugar (of which we had a large supply on board intended as a present for the Santa Cruz Indians) with them for the fowls, eggs, and vegetables we so badly needed. The pram was promptly despatched to the ship, and returned with 100 lbs. of sugar and a box of soap, her beaching being very carefully guarded on this occasion. Soon a brisk business was being carried on between Muddy and the Indians, as he was the only one of the party who could speak Maya at all fluently, and they, of course, had no other language. A small calabash of sugar and an inch from a bar of soap were accepted in exchange for one good chicken or eighteen fresh eggs, and on this basis we soon had all the poultry in sight corralled, with the exception of one old rooster, who was rejected by reason of his obvious age and infirmities.

We also secured a good supply of tomatoes, beans, and tortillas on the same exchange basis, and found that if we had only brought a demijohn of rum we might have acquired the village, lock, stock, and barrel.

At each end of this village are small groups of ancient temples, a few of which are still in a fairly good state of preservation, two of them being used by the Indians as drying houses for their tobacco, the leaves of which are hung out on liana cords stretched across the stone walls and left there to dry in the cool, well-ventilated chamber, which the Indians have found by experience to be an ideal curing-house for the weed. All the small temples are typically " Tuluum period " in style, and practically identical with the temples found at Chacmool. The best preserved is 9ft. high and 24ft. long, covered both inside and out with smooth, hard stucco, ornamented by two projecting cornices, and approached by a single entrance, divided into three by two circular stone columns. The roof is flat, and the ceiling formed by the usual Maya corbel vault. This must have been a considerable settlement at one time, as we found remains of at least seven temples in the cleared space occupied by the village, and the Indians told us that about a day's march inland there were the ruins of a large town, which from their description of the buildings was of Maya, not Spanish, origin.

Much as we should have liked to visit these ruins, we decided to leave them till a later visit, as our time was limited, the greater part of our work of exploration still to do, and, no animals being available, we should have had to make use of shanks his mare to reach them. Before leaving I was asked to see two sick people, Muddy having informed the Indians that I was a *doctorah*, as the Maya call a medico. This " ah " was used by the ancient Maya as a masculine prefix to signify lord, or ruler, as " Ah Kin," " Lord Sun," " Ah Puch," " Lord of Death, " Ahau," " Lord or Chief." It is now, however, almost obsolete, and the only name with which I have ever heard it used is as a postfix with the Spanish " doctor," which the Maya have adopted into their language, *doctorah*, signifying " Lord Medicine Man "— remarkable perspicacity on the part of a decadent people, who concede a peerage alone to that profession from which in England it is alone withheld. The X, pronounced Sh, which is the feminine Maya prefix, is still frequently used as a diminutive or endearment prefix to proper names, " Petrona," for instance, being altered to " Xpet," " Lauriana " to " Xlau," and " Maximiliana " to " Xmash."

I found the sick people were two youths in the last stage of chronic malaria—poor skeletons with a covering of yellow, shiny skin tightly stretched over their bones, and immense wood-hard spleens filling their whole abdomen. Each was stretched in a small string hammock, from which he had become too weak ever to arise, and both were sadly neglected, for, as they had been sick for many weeks, their welcome was wearing thin in a community where it is a case of " Root, hog, or die." I gave each a good supply of quinine capsules, and instructions as to diet and cleanliness, which was all I could do, but I left them with no very strong hope of their ultimate recovery.

With calabashes of tomatoes, beans, and eggs, strings of tota poste, hard, dry, crisp corn cakes, which will keep indefinitely, and bunches of fowls, we made a triumphal procession to the shore, again escorted by the entire population, and with expressions of goodwill on both sides pulled off to the *Lilian Y.*

The Playa Carmen ruins, though comparatively insignificant in themselves, possess a decided historical interest as they almost certainly represent all that remains of the Indian town from which Geromino de Aguilar set out to join Cortez, the conqueror of Mexico, at the island of Cozumel in March, 1519. One of Cortez' main objects in landing at the island was to obtain tidings of the Spanish crew and passengers of a caraval which eight years previously had been wrecked off this part of the coast, and who were reported to be still held in captivity by the natives somewhere in the interior. For this purpose he despatched two brigantines to the mainland carrying Cozumel Indians, who agreed to act as intermediaries between the Spaniards and the cacique, who was reported to hold the Christians captive, together with a great treasure in glass beads, copper hawk bells, and similar jewels valued by the Indians. One of the Indians also carried a letter from Cortez to Aguilar hidden in his long hair, as all were naked. The brigantine waited eight days, and then, seeing nothing of either Indians or Christian captives, returned to Cozumel and reported their failure to Cortez, who, though much chagrined, determined to set out without taking any further steps towards their rescue. The squadron, however, had not got very far from Cozumel when one of the ships sprung a leak, and they were compelled to return. Shortly after landing they observed a large canoe, paddled by Indians approaching from the mainland, one of whom, on landing, asked in broken Spanish if he were amongst Christians, and, on being answered in the affirmative, promptly fell on his knees and, weeping, thanked God for his deliverance. This was Geronimo de Aguilar, a Spanish ecclesiastic, who, while on a voyage from Darien eight years previously, had been wrecked on this part of the coast of Yucatan with twenty other passengers, and, escaping from the wreck, had succeeded in landing on the mainland in the ship's boat. Of the eight, five were at once sacrificed by the cacique of the country to his gods—very possibly in the Tuluum temple—and eaten, while the rest, being in poor condition, were penned up in cages to fatten for a similar fate. They succeeded, however, in escaping, and fell into the hands of a cacique who was more kindly disposed, in that he only enslaved them. At the time of Cortez' arrival only two of these unfortunates survived—Aguilar and a sailor named Gonzalo Guerrero, who, having apostatised, took to himself Indian wives, wore nose-and ear-rings, had his body tattooed all over according to the Indian custom, and became a man of some importance in the province of Chetumal. He had heard of the arrival of the Spaniards, but, being ashamed of his apostasy, his harem, and his tattooed face, had declined to make any effort to join them. Aguilar, on the contrary, had refused to worship the gods of his captors, and had kept his vow of continency as an ecclesiastic, though put to tests, according to his own account, which might well have tried the fortitude of St. Anthony. This trait at length won the grudging admiration of the Indians, and Aguilar was placed in charge of the household of the cacique to whom he belonged—a position of some trust and authority.

When the Indian messengers arrived from Cortez at the court of the cacique he was very loth to part with Aguilar, and it was only the sight of the rich treasure of glass beads and copper ornaments offered as ransom which at length induced him to give the latter his liberty. Aguilar at once departed with the messengers to the nearest town to Cozumel, on the mainland (which can only have been the one now known as Playa Carmen), but on arriving there found to his great grief and disappointment that the Spanish flotilla had sailed the previous day. He determined to wait a little while on the coast in case one of the ships put back for him, and next day was rejoiced to see the whole fleet returning, as related, to Cozumel, owing to one of the caravals, which was loaded with cassava bread, having sprung a leak. He set out with the Indians at once in a canoe for Cozumel, where he found Cortez, to whom in his after career he proved of invaluable service as an interpreter between the Spaniards and the Maya.

Aguilar was a man of some education, and, had he wished, could have given us an accurate account of the social life and religious customs of the Maya, together with a key to their hieroglyphic writing, which would have been of inestimable value to antiquarians. The two contemporary accounts handed down to us, written by Bishop Landa and the Abbé Cogolludo, were compiled some time after the conquest, and are records, not of personal experiences, but of second-hand information obtained from priests and leading men among the natives. Aguilar after eight continuous years of life amongst them, must have obtained a first-hand knowledge of their habits and customs such as no other European ever had an opportunity of acquiring, for their whole social and religious system was overthrown on the coming of the Spaniards, yet all he cared to record was a meticulous account of the numerous and ingenious assaults upon his chastity, and the ease with which he overcame them all, till one is inclined to think either that he is not adhering strictly to the truth, or that he was physically incapacitated in some way from indulging in those sins which he takes to himself such credit for resisting.

We arrived about dusk at Punta Maroma, twelve miles north of Playa Carmen, and found good anchorage in three fathoms, close to the shore, well sheltered by a dry reef. Morley and I landed on the sandy beach, where we found the ruins of a fisherman's hut built of palm leaf, which we thought of occupying for the night, but on examining the interior found it looked so " snaky " that we put up our cots on the beach as usual.

Next morning, after a somewhat nervous dip in the shallowest water we could find (for sharks abound along this part of the coast), we rowed on board and set sail for Puerto Morelos, where we arrived in a little over an hour, having caught 60 lbs. of rock fish on the spinner *en route*. We might as easily have caught 600 lbs., but it was useless to go on destroying fish after we had got as many as we required, and the amount of sport in catching rock fish on a spinner is practically negligible, for they allow themselves to be landed with no more fight than a piece of dead meat.

Puerto Morelos some years ago was a thriving settlement, as the remains of a fine wooden wharf, 300 ft. long, attest. The Banco de Londres y Mexico employed 600 chicleros here in bleeding chicle, or chewing gum, from the sapodilla trees in the *hinterland*, which was tapped by a light railroad running back for over 20 kilometres. They were, however, ousted by the Mexican Government, and now the population would probably not reach 50 souls in the surrounding 500 square miles. The rails are slowly rusting away, while the pier, which had a great breach made in its centre by the hurricane, is slowly falling to pieces.

On leaving Puerto Morelos we sailed almost due north past the island of Cancuen, a long, flat bank of sand covered with stunted bush. The mainland to the north of Puerto Morelos is even more desolate than that to the south, as the scrub which covers the *hinterland* behind the sandy zone gives place to sour grass and swamp. This part of the peninsula is entirely uninhabited, and probably forms one of the most desolate wastes on the American continent.

About an hour after passing Cancuen we arrived off " Isla de las Mujeres," or the " Isle of Women," a long, narrow island six to seven kilometres in length by less than half a kilometre across at its narrowest. It is rocky and precipitous at the southern end, low and sandy at the northern. The origin of the name " Isle of Women " seems somewhat uncertain, and many explanations are given of it. On my first outward passage from New Orleans to Belize the captain of the fruit steamer, in pointing out the ruins as we steamed close in to the island, informed me confidentially that it derived its name from the fact that Cortez gathered here a number of native Maya ladies with a view to the formation of a harem ; he even supplied harrowing details. Later the mate (also a storehouse of inaccurate information) explained that Alvorado held on the island an *auto da fé*, at which he burnt a number of heretical women for the good of their souls. He also was primed with information even more harrowing, while an intelligent passenger vouchsafed the information that Grijalva, who passed the island in 1517, found there a colony of Amazons who had so little use for men that they never permitted them to land.

In the account given by Bernal Diaz of the expedition of Cortez, which he accompanied, he relates that, after leaving Cozumel, the fleet was scattered by a storm, but next day all reunited, with the exception of one caraval, which was discovered windbound in a bay on the coast. Several of the soldiers had gone ashore here, and found four temples with large idols resembling women in them, which they had cast into the sea, " for which reason," says Diaz, " we named the place Punta de las Mujeres." No mention is made by any of the contemporary writers of an " Isla de Mujeres," but, considering the ignorance of geography then prevalent amongst the conquerors, there can be little doubt but that the point on which these temples stand is the one alluded to.

The principal village is situated near the north end of the west side of the island, and formerly possessed a population of over 400, now reduced to under 250, owing to the frequent migration of the younger people to the mainland settlements in search of a more exciting existence. They are—like all the islanders and coast people with whom we came in contact—a simple, kindly, hospitable, unambitious folk, " the world forgetting, by the world forgot," interested solely in their own affairs, vaguely aware that a great war had taken place somewhere in the outside world, but concerned about it solely in that it had depressed the price of turtle-shell, their principal export. Theirs is the simple ife reduced to the *n*th power, and we often envied them their care and work-free existence, though, infected by the *wanderlust* microbe, we should probably have been bored to tears with the life in a month.

Fish is extraordinarily plentiful. A net off the wharf will take enough for all the family in ten minutes, and we actually saw one man shoot a cast net into the sea, standing in the back door of his cottage, and haul in a fine catch of mullet.

The streets are covered with fine, loose, white sand, which, till one gets accustomed to it, is very tiring to walk in. It drifts like snow, and, though the side-walks are built of stone, and are very high, it frequently covers them, and blocks up the doors, nor would there be any use in clearing it away, for millions of tons more remain outside to take its place.

A stranger in " Mujeres," as the natives call it, is a rare bird, and we were met on landing by the *Corregidor*, or Mayor, with the whole Municipal Council dragging behind him, who took us on a personally conducted tour of the village.

The plaza is a concreted square, with an ornate stucco basin and fountain in its centre, elaborate enough for a place ten times the size. A very well-preserved Spanish ship's cannon of the sixteenth century is exhibited here, said to have been left behind by Grijalva in 1517, though why he should have abandoned such an essential part of his equipment is difficult to imagine.

Having finished the grand round, we were taken to the house of a Spanish lady who made a speciality of catering to the few belated strangers who arrived on the island— and right nobly she did it, for we looked back with longing to this dinner when partaking of the food at many a more pretentious hostelry on our trip. It started with luscious

PLAYA CARMEN : MUDDY BARTERING WITH THE INHABITANTS.

[*p.* 136

ISLA DE MUJERES : ALL THAT REMAINS OF THE TEMPLE ON THE
EDGE OF THE CLIFF.

[*p.* 146

thick soup made of conchs and ochras, after which came
eggs and tomatoes, fried Spanish fashion, with a liberal
allowance of garlic and chili habanero, and eaten uncon-
taminated by metal by being scooped up with a dog's-
eared tortilla, or corn cake—thin, hot, and just off the fire.
This was followed by an escabeche of fish freshly pickled
with sliced onions and chili perpers. Next the *pièce de
résistance*, a roast fowl, *pollo relleno* or " fowl refilled,"
as the Spanish call it. This was in more senses than one
the *pièce de résistance*, for the coast seems to produce a
breed of reinforced rubber fowls which are at no period
of their career tender. Lastly came pumpkin stewed in
sugar and cinnamon, topped by a cup of excellent coffee.
We were not allowed, however, to devote our undivided
attention to this noble repast, for while we ate the Mayor
and all the Municipal Council sat round the room gravely
watching us, discussing ourselves, our appearance, and
probable business in audible undertones, and asking innumerable questions, a sport in which even our hostess
joined at her periodical entries with fresh courses.

After dinner we discovered the reason of our remarkable
popularity. Though it was well on in Lent, the village
badly wanted to give a *fiesta* and dance. Now, without a
decent pretext of some sort this was practically impossible
to good Catholics. We, however, three distinguished
strangers, with letters from the Governor requesting that
we be well entertained, furnished quite an unimpeachable
excuse. I am sorry to say we refused to fall in with their
hospitable plans, as bed appealed to us far more strongly
than any dance.

On first arriving at the island we had visited the south
end, going half the way in the pram and walking the other
half along a rocky road to the extreme southern point,
where a precipitous limestone bluff on which the waves
of the Caribbean dash endlessly, to be hurled back as great
masses of seething foam and spindrift, forms one of the
wildest and most picturesque spots along the whole coast.

KL

On this point we found two Maya ruins, both distinctively of Tuluum style architecture. One, now almost gone, as many of the square stones have been removed to construct a small lighthouse near by, was a little square sanctuary, or *adoratorio*, of the type already made familiar to us at Espiritu Santo Bay and Chacmool. It had a door at each side, was supported by a circular column in the centre, and differed only from others of the same type in that it stood upon a circular, stone-faced, truncated base, with short flights of stone steps leading from the ground level to each door.

The second building, also of typical Tuluum style, is built of squared blocks of stone, and covered internally and externally with hard stucco. It is decorated by two cornices, the upper single, the lower double. The roof is flat, and the interior supported by the Maya corbel arch roof. The interior is approached by a flight of steps leading to a pillared doorway, and is divided into an outer room and a smaller inner sanctuary. It stands upon the extreme edge of the high limestone bluff, down which half of it has already fallen, for the sea is constantly encroaching, and in another century or so the building will have been completely swallowed up. This is probably the best known Maya temple in Yucatan, or at any rate has been seen by the greatest number of persons, for the Central and South American fruit boats from New Orleans and Mobile pass within a few miles, and, perched upon the summit of this high cliff, it forms one of the most conspicuous landmarks along the whole coast, and it may have been from this very temple that the soldiers of Cortez, 400 years ago, threw down the stone female idols over the precipice into the sea. Indeed, were one to go to the expense and trouble, they could no doubt find these same idols buried in the débris of centuries at the foot of the cliff, when a norther is blowing and the tide is low.

On returning to the little village along the shore we came upon a gigantic kitchen midden composed almost entirely of conchs and other shells, amongst which were quantities

of potsherd of all shapes and sizes, some belonging to
artistically painted vessels of fine thin ware, others to rough
clay cooking-vessels. Amongst them I picked up a clay
bead and a small net-sinker. It would almost seem as if
this had been a communal rubbish-heap for the whole
settlement in ancient days, as we found no other in our
wanderings, and on its east side stood a tiny stone sanctuary
similar to, but even smaller than, the one at Espiritu Santo,
which led us to suppose that even such a prosaic operation
as the disposal of rubbish was not carried out by the Maya
without some sort of religious ceremonial.

On returning to the village I went my usual round of
the houses, hunting for *cosas de los antiguos*—relics of the
ancient inhabitants, such as I make at every newly-visited
remote place in the Maya area. The people said that they
came across great numbers of these on the mainland—idols,
pots, flint and obsidian weapons and implements, etc.,
when making their corn plantations, but never brought them
home, as it was extremely unlucky to meddle with the
belongings of the old gods, who always revenged themselves
on those who did.

I was shown an empty house outside the village, which
had belonged to a man who had brought home several
" idols," or large incense burners, with the figure of the god
to whom they were dedicated sculptured on them. This
man and his whole family had died of some unknown disease
within a few weeks of each other, and their deaths were, of
course, attributed to the idols. The latter were thrown out
into the yard, where Muddy and I, after diligent search
amongst the sour grass and rank vegetation which had grown
up since the owners' death, succeeded in finding them, but,
alas ! so broken up and scattered that it was impossible to
piece them together again.

In one of the houses belonging to an old lady I espied
upon the domestic altar a plain unadorned cross, which,
amongst the other objects—gaily decorated with coloured
ribbons, artificial flowers, religious medallions, and pictures

—seemed somewhat incongruous. It was about 16in. high, and rather crudely cut from light porous volcanic rock. The explanation of its presence which the owner gave was that some fifty years previously, when she was a young girl, she dreamt for three nights in succession that a star of dazzling light hovered over a certain part of her parents' yard, remained undimmed for a few moments, and then faded gradually away. After the third recurrence of this dream she told her parents of the matter, and they, greatly excited at the prospect of discovering treasure of some sort, at once started digging in the place indicated, where, at a depth of a couple of feet, they came upon this stone cross, which had been retained in the family ever since as a much venerated heirloom, though the treasure-hunters must have been considerably disappointed at finding neither gold nor silver.

These islands from the early sixteenth to the early nine-teenth century were the haunt, first of buccaneers, and later of pirates, who made use of their shallow, dangerous, in-tricate waters, full of reefs and shoals, as a sure place of refuge from their enemies and pursuers. Untold treasure must have been hidden on their cays and reefs in the old days, which the owners, slain in a fight with some prospective prize, wrecked at sea, or reaping the just reward of their industry on the yardarm of a British frigate, never returned to collect. Hardly an islet but is pointed out as the deposi-tory of some pirate's hoard, and not infrequently bullion, in the form of doubloons and guineas, and even pieces of plate and jewels, have been washed out by the encroaching sea, or accidentally unearthed in the course of excavations. Such treasure-trove, however, is, for obvious reasons, not widely advertised by the lucky finders at the time.

We left Mujeres at 9.30 a.m., and, sailing south-west, arrived at the Boca de Nisucte, the opening of the shallow lagoon which separates the island of Cancuen from the mainland. Cancuen is long, narrow, and flat, nearly ten kilometres in length by less than one kilometre broad in

places. Its eastern part is merely a sandbank, while the
western and central portions are covered with scrub and
high forest growth interspersed with patches of swamp.
Till quite recently it had been entirely uninhabited, with
the exception of a few temporary fishermen's huts along the
eastern shore, but a few years ago an enterprising Meridano
started cutting the bush and planting coco-nuts, and,
finding that they did well on the island soil, he has now
felled nearly the whole of the bush, leaving exposed a great
number of ruins, all belonging to the east coast or Tuluum
type, none of which were previously known to archæologists.

Anchoring the *Lilian Y* at the mouth of the narrow strait
which separates Cancuen from the mainland, we got out
the pram, and, after an hour of hard cranking, which
exhausted everyone before the day's work began, we started
up the strait against a current so swift that the pram could
only just stem it. The strait was fortunately short, however, and soon debouched into a long, shallow lagoon.
Sailing along this for about five miles, keeping close to the
west coast of the island, we passed a number of Indian
mounds (probably temple and burial mounds) and a few
buildings completely in ruins. Near the south end of the
island we arrived at a rustic landing-stage, where amongst
the coco-nut trees we found the bush house of the manager
of the plantation, who kindly consented to accompany us
to the southern point of the island, where the most perfect
ruins were to be found. The walk was a very pleasant one
at first, leading through the shady coco-nut grove, passing
picturesque little groups of labourers' huts built of sticks
and thatched with palm leaf, from whose doors wild-looking
half-clad Indians, with their still wilder-looking women-
kind, stared at probably the first really white people they
had ever seen. This rapidly gave place to a part of the
plantation where the trees were young and the grass and
bush high, and where we soon began to feel the intolerable
itching of red bug attacking our legs, and gradually advanc-
ing upwards. Finally we arrived at a section where clearing

was still going on, and where progress of any kind over the fallen bush and great tree-trunks became difficult. It was here, however, that we came across the best preserved building on the island, known grandiloquently to the labourers—the only people who had seen it—as " El Palacio del Rey." It is an oblong structure, built of squared stones, 26ft. 5in. long by 7ft. 6in. high, covered inside and out with hard cement, and entered by two doors, each 2ft. 4in. broad. The interior is divided into two long, narrow rooms, or corridors, one in front, one behind, by a partition wall having three doorways in it. The exterior is surrounded above the doors by an ornamental cornice, and in a recess in this cornice, just between the doors, stood—or rather squatted—the stucco figure of the King of Cancuen, " El Rey de Cancuen," which gave the building its name. Till quite recently this figure, the head and bust of which were life-sized, the arms and legs comparatively dwarfed, had sat enthroned over the doorway of his palace, undisturbed for four centuries. Unfortunately a mischievous Mexican peon had, with labour incomprehensible in one of his class —except when engaged in some work of iconoclasm—pried the " King " loose and tumbled him down on the ground, smashing the limbs and lower part of the body beyond hope of repair, but fortunately leaving the head and head-dress very little injured. The face, which is very well (though roughly) modelled, is cruel and malignant in expression ; the nose is large and broad, the mouth wide, and the forehead high—by no means typically Mayan in cast. The headdress consists of broad flaps falling on each side of the large circular ear-plugs, attached above to two projecting bands which come down to the centre of the forehead. Above these is seen the head and upper jaw, with projecting teeth, and the large eyes of some mythological animal, attached to the forehead of which by a tenon is an ornament now so weathered as to be unrecognisable. The whole figure had been painted in various colours, but these are now almost entirely obliterated by time and exposure.

The Mexican, we were informed, had died very painfully
within two weeks of his act of vandalism, his death being
looked upon by the other labourers as a direct visitation
of the wrath of the ancient god for desecration of his sanctuary ; and who shall say that his death, however brought
about, was undeserved ?

Undeterred by the fate of the Mexican, I arranged with
the manager to have the head brought over to the landing-
place by some of the labourers, from whence, on my return,
I could carry it away on the *Lilian Y*, as I greatly feared
that it might be smashed by some of the Indians, or carried
off by a curio hunter.   To this he was quite agreeable, and,
in fact, rather pleased at getting rid of a relic with such a
sinister reputation, not without some slight pecuniary
profit to himself.   Unfortunately, I was unable to call at
the island on the return journey owing to contrary winds
and tides, so presumably *El Rey* still rules over his ancient
kingdom of Cancuen.

Just south of El Palacio were the ruins of two good-sized
buildings ; one of these 37ft. 2in. by 23ft., was entered by
a broad doorway divided into two by a square stone column.
The interior contained but a single room, and the roof,
formed of the usual Maya arch, was supported by three
circular stone pillars.   The second building was very
similar to the first, except that its broad entrance was
divided into four by three square columns.

The largest building we discovered at Cancuen was
situated about half-way between El Palacio and the landing-
place.   It was 77ft. 5in. in length by 25ft. broad, the surrounding wall, decorated all round by a narrow stone
cornice, being 11ft. 2in. high.   This structure stood on a
low stone mound, or pyramid, now a mere mass of ruins.
It was probably the market-place or assembly hall of the
town, corresponding very closely to the market-place
already described at Chacmool.   Nearly the whole front
of the building is open, and was divided into nine entrances
by eight circular stone columns.   Running down the centre

of the interior, midway between the back wall and the
entrance, is a second row of ten stone columns, which, with
those in front, evidently served to support the roof, probably made of palm thatch laid over wooden beams. It
will be seen that the chief difference between this structure
and the corresponding one at Chacmool is that the latter
stands on a well-defined terraced stone platform, and is
open both front and back, while the former stands on an
insignificant low mound, and is completely closed in by a
wall behind.

We passed great numbers of ruined temples and buildings all along the coast of Cancuen, together with
innumerable mounds, probably the burial-places of caciques
and chief priests of the ancient inhabitants. There was,
however, no attempt at centralising the main buildings and
raising them on platforms for defensive purposes, as at
Chacmool, or of surrounding them by a wall, as at Tuluum.
On the contrary, they seem to have been dumped down
anyhow, and strung out over probably a couple of miles of
coast, which rather leads one to suppose that the inhabitants
depended rather on the isolated situation of their island
home than on any special fortification, for defence against
their enemies. Surrounded moreover by the sea, from
which a very large proportion of their food supply must
have been drawn, they were probably first-rate sailors,
and in a war with their quarrelsome neighbours of the mainland would elect to fight by sea rather than by land.

Contemporary history is silent as to the dwellers in this
city of Cancuen. It was probably founded, however, by
the same Maya who were driven out of their own country
after the conquest of Mayapan, and settled along the east
coast of the peninsula, as the architectural style is without
doubt that of Tuluum. Both Cortez and Grijalva must
have sailed close to this island on their first voyages to
Mexico, and, if they passed by day, the white stucco-covered
buildings and temples must have been clearly visible to
them, and would undoubtedly, one would imagine, have

provoked a visit to the natives, whom they had found so friendly at other points along this coast, if only for the sake of proselytising, which, after treasure (though a long way after, it must be admitted), was ever the chief aim of the *conquistadores*. None of them, however, mentions Cancuen, nor is any allusion made to it or its ruins by any later historian, and it is possible that even at that early date the city may have been deserted and the people scattered.

We should have liked very much to remain on the island for a week or two, and by excavation in some of the burial mounds obtained further information as to the cultural status of the inhabitants, and the date at which the island was occupied. This, however, was impossible, as time was limited, and we were already considerably behindhand in our schedule.

Next day we weighed anchor, and, sailing due north from the Boca de Nisucte, arrived opposite the ruins of El Meco in less than an hour. The coastline here is formed of the same monotonous, low sandy beach, over grown with sour grass, the *hinterland* covered with scrubby bush, interspersed with stretches of swamp. Just before landing we observed a small tiger-cat tracking along the sandy beach at a great rate, and hurried up our disembarkation in the hope of getting a shot at him. By the time we got ashore, however, he was out of sight, though we traced his tracks for a long distance up the coast very clearly defined on the hard sand, and evidently following a small deer, or antelope, which had passed that way earlier in the day.

The ruined temple of El Meco is a really imposing structure, and standing back, as it does, only a few hundred yards from the shore, forms a landmark visible for many miles at sea, as well known as their own faces (better, indeed, for not many of them use a looking-glass) to all the fishermen along the coast. It is built on a great stone terraced mound 40ft. high, from the top of which a magnificent view is obtained of the island-dotted Caribbean to the east, and the flat, swampy *hinterland* to the west. It stands alone, a solitary sentinel upon the barren coast, with no subsidiary temples, palaces, or market-places near it betokening a former town site, yet it is certainly the largest of all the east coast temples which we saw throughout our trip, and, though small isolated shrines to fishermen's, hunters', and travellers' gods are not uncommon, this appears to be the only instance of a large Maya temple built away from the habitations of men. It was approached by a steep flight of stone steps leading up the east side of the terraced mound, in front of the base of which was a great pillared colonnade and surrounding the whole structure a stone-paved, walled courtyard. Now, however, the temple is in ruins, its débris covering a great part of the stairway. The pillars of the colonnade have fallen, and the courtyard is overgrown with dense low bush, not pleasant to traverse, as it is simply swarming with snakes, who always seem to prefer the neighbourhood of ruins, possibly because the irregular surfaces of the large stone heaps facilitate the removal of their old skins. One point of considerable interest we noticed about this temple, namely, that the original building had been comparatively small, consisting of a single long chamber, round which at a later date a thick wall had been erected on all four sides, in contact—except at the back, where a considerable space existed between the two— with the outer walls of the older structure. A wide entrance was left in front facing the sea, divided into three doorways by two large circular stone columns. Thus the original temple was made to appear far larger and more imposing without in any way adding to its spaciousness or convenience. Such a sacrifice of convenience to appearance is, however, by no means unknown in architecture outside the Maya area. On examining the structure closely, it becomes obvious that the stone terraces themselves have had wings and extensions added to them from time to time, and the probabilities are that the original temple was a structure of quite modest proportions, standing possibly on a single stone terrace, and that later, as it became for some unknown reason more and more popular, and resorted to as a place of pilgrimage from the surrounding towns, it was added to till it reached its present imposing size.

Morley and I slept ashore on the beach in our cots, as usual, lulled to sleep by the lapping of the little waves on the sand, and the gentle slatting of our mosquito curtains in the light sea breeze. We had had an excellent supper, washed down with the last of the whisky, and followed by an interesting chat on the luck we had had in our trip up to the present, with anticipations of even more important finds to come. In fact, at peace with all the world, we lay smoking cigarettes, and watching the stars through our mosquito curtains, commiserating with Held in the stuffy, uneasy cabin of the *Lilian Y*, and looking forward to a peaceful sleep. It was not to be, however, as about 11 p.m. a perfect deluge of rain awoke us, and, though we jumped out at once and spread the great tarpaulin over nets and cots, it was too late, as everything was already saturated, and when we got back under the nets we found them so weighted down by the heavy tarp. that we were enveloped in wet, clammy folds of gauze, with hardly room to breathe. Each in turn, and at last both together, driven to desperation by the discomfort, jumped out and tried to remedy matters, though leaving the warm rugs to face the cold, driving rain in wet pyjamas required a considerable amount of resolution. Nothing, however, could be done without stout stakes to support the tarp., and these we had not got, so, after a half-hearted effort to hail the *Lilian Y*, which we were sure would prove unavailing, even if anyone on board heard it, we returned to bed, and made up our minds to a night of discomfort and semi-suffocation, in which we were not disappointed.

CHAPTER X

WE made an early start next morning, and, passing Cape
Catoche—" *Cabo Catoche Historico*," as the Spaniards call
it (to distinguish it from the present cape of that name,
which is situated on an island a few miles north, and was
the first point of land ever seen by Europeans on the North
American Continent)—arrived about 2 p.m. at Boca Iglesias.
Here a square church tower stands out prominently from
the surrounding bush, some miles inland, and it was this
church which we were anxious to visit by way of a shallow
arm of the sea, which ran almost directly up to it. The
pilot evidently did not want to set out on the trip that day,
and began to make excuses—first that we could not cross
the bar into the lagoon, next that we should not arrive
before dark, and lastly that the bush we had to traverse
was alive with ticks and snakes. Finally, after we had
embarked in the pram, determined to start in spite of all
opposition, the Evinrude settled the matter by refusing

to work, so a postponement till next day became necessary. Hardly, however, had we re-embarked on the *Lilian Y* than the engine started off gaily to take the men ashore to gather green coco-nuts, of which they drink the milk by the gallon, apparently with perfect impunity, though on us it had most disastrous effects, comparable only to a stiff dose of Epsom salts.

Next morning we made an early start in the pram, and, passing up the narrow Boca (or mouth) against a pretty stiff current, found ourselves in a large, shallow, muddy-bottomed lagoon, studded with mangrove-covered islands, and literally swarming with duck, teal, plover, spur wing, spoonbill, and innumerable waders, while the warm, shallow waters were full of small sharks or cazones, all attracted by the countless myriads of small fry for which the tepid, tranquil waters evidently acted as a sort of incubator. We had hardly got half a mile along the lagoon when the pram stuck firmly in the mud, and could not be moved. Morley, Held, and myself, accompanied by George, promptly took to a small dorey which we were towing, and left the pram to Muddy and Alfredo to get off. George proved a noble poler, and for perhaps a quarter of an hour we made fine progress, then we also stuck fast on a weed-covered mudbank.

For two weary hours in the broiling sun we kept trying passage after passage through the cays and mudbanks, but, though we could see the church hardly a mile away, there seemed to be no channel leading to it, for every passage ended in a *cul de sac*. Just as we were contemplating a return to the *Lilian Y* we were hailed from the pram with the joyful news that they had found the passage, but we were separated by over a quarter of a mile of soft, weed-grown mud, covered by only a few inches of water, and the problem of how to cross this at once presented itself. The mud gave no hold for the pole, and it was obvious that only by main force (and a good deal of it at that) could the gulf be crossed. The crew, resolving itself into a committee of the whole crew, elected George (with one dissentient) for the job, partly on account of his giant physique, partly because even small sharks are reputed to entertain a distaste to the Ethiop as an article of diet. George answered heroically to the call, and went overboard like a shot, to disappear at once nearly up to his armpits in the soft mud, into which he sank deeper every moment. Fortunately he had a hold on the stern of the dorey, and, while we steadied her, he was able, by kicking and floundering, to bring himself into a more or less horizontal position on the mud, where, lying mostly on his tummy, and using his gigantic feet, driven by piston-like legs, as a propelling force, he managed to shove us over all obstructions alongside the pram. It was a great performance, and George's thunderous laugh every time he got a mouthful of mud and salt water, and blew it out through that vast ivory-lined chasm with a loud " Hi-yah ! " was well worth the trip in itself.

Having once struck the channel, we soon arrived at the shore of the lagoon nearest the church, where we found a stone-paved causeway leading up through the swamp to the higher ground upon which it stood. The structure itself, built on a slight rising ground, was, like all the old Spanish churches in this part of Yucatan, architecturally very plain, and singularly lacking in adornment. It was shaped like a tau, the head formed by the chancel, the stem by the nave. The chancel is 25ft. high, 58ft. long, and 24ft. 6in. broad. The central part, which contains the altar, opens into the nave by a great round arch. On either side are square doors opening into rooms now occupied by hundreds of bats, which give to the whole place a sour, unpleasant odour. The roof is flat and machicolated, leading us to suppose that the building served the double purpose of church and fort. The nave, 72ft. 8in. long, is approached by three entrances, one on the north, one on the south, and one on the west side. The walls are 9ft. high, and either the building was never roofed in, or—what is more probable—was roofed with wooden rafters and thatch, which have completely disappeared, as no trace of a roof is now visible. Immediately behind the altar a large hole has been torn in the wall, apparently with the object of removing the image of a saint which had been fixed there.

The altar itself, a solid block of masonry, approached by two low steps, had upon it a curious collection of objects, some of which appeared to have been there for years, while others had evidently been placed there quite recently. These consisted of several lumps of native incense made of the gum of the white acacia, and used by the Maya in their religious ceremonies for the last 2,000 years ; a number of loose " lucky beans " ; a few conch shells ; some flowers made from coloured shells ; a glass full of lucky beans ; a roughly made wooden cross, 2ft. high, draped in ribbons ; three crosses—the central one large, the side ones small— on a wooden stand ; and lastly a tablet, upon which was painted a crude picture of the Virgin, pinned to which were several gorgeously coloured butterflies. The pilot told us that the scattered Indians come for miles round to make these offerings, and to perform their *novenas* at this old deserted church.

It is nearly a hundred years since priests of the Roman Catholic Church have gone amongst these Indians, yet the faith dies hard, and devotees still exist who endeavour to carry out something at least of the outward observances of the ritual. We could not help thinking of the few poor offerings which some faithful worshipper had left beside the mutilated Chacmool statue, and which we had found in excavating it. Here was the altar of the god who supplanted the Chacmool, now itself deserted, and honoured only by a few tawdry offerings from the descendants of those same Indians, whose religion is now a barbarous combination of the various creeds held by their ancestors, modified by their own ignorance, superstition, and hatred of the dominant race.

The church is known to the Indians as Xon Hom (pronounced Shon Hom), but when and by whom it was erected, and when and wherefore deserted, no man knows. The probabilities were, however, that it was built some time in the seventeenth century for the use of a poor Indian congregation who lived exclusively in thatched huts, which would account for the absence of any trace of ruined stone houses in the vicinity. Why the whole of the inhabitants should have cleared out incontinently, however, is one of those insoluble mysteries which confronts one on every hand in Yucatan. The isolated situation of the settlement, inaccessible by land, and only to be arrived at from the sea by the passage of a narrow and tortuous passage through the lagoon, was obviously deliberately chosen, probably with a view to defence against the English and French buccaneers and pirates, who harried this coast in the seventeenth and eighteenth centuries. The long passage of the lagoon, which would have to be made slowly and in boats of light draft, would give the inhabitants ample time to make up their minds either to flee with their possessions into the impenetrable bush of the *hinterland*, or to put up a good fight from the fortified roof of their church, whence, without artillery, it would have been practically impossible to dislodge them.

We left Boca Iglesia the next day, and, sailing north, passed the headland now known as Cape Catoche about 2 p.m. The cape forms part of a long, narrow, sickle-shaped island named Holbox, really a vast sandbank capping the north-eastern extremity of the peninsula. From here our course, which had hitherto been almost due north, changed to west, and about 4.30 we put in at Holbox, the principal village of the island—a picturesque little settlement of about 150 people, all engaged in fishing and turtling, who live in bush huts thatched with palm leaf. Even here we found a *Celador*, or Customs official, and a *Juez*, or judge, sent by the Federal Mexican Government, and, of course, a *Municipalidad*, or Town Council, and an elaborately laid-out plaza, without both of which the smallest village in Yucatan seems unable to exist.

The people appeared uncommonly happy and contented, as they did at all these coast settlements, and they were certainly well supplied with corn, vegetables, fowls, eggs, and fish, of which we laid in a supply. As at Mujeres, so at Holbox, we were told that people rarely died of anything but old age, and to pass out under ninety was rather a reflection upon the salubrity of the island.

We anchored that night off Yalahau, on the mainland, and all slept on board, as even Morley and I, much as we loathed the *Lilian Y* at anchor as a bedchamber, were loth to tackle the mist-enshrouded, swampy shore, with mangrove growing to the water's edge, the rotten piles of an ancient wharf sticking up like broken fangs, and the song of the mosquito and the bull-frog, with the melancholy hooting of an owl, the only sounds to break the silence of the fast-falling night.

Next morning early we boarded the pram to go ashore, but could not get within ten yards of the beach owing to a bank of sticky mud, over which it required the united efforts of George, Muddy, and Hubert finally to shove us.

Yalahau is one of the most melancholy and forsaken-looking places it is possible to imagine, as if an aura of the crimes which had been committed there formerly hung like a pall over the place. It is a waste of mangrove swamp and scrubby bush—the home of land crabs and snakes, and the haunt of myriads of mosquitoes. A hundred years ago it was the last stronghold of the pirates who infested this part of the Spanish Main, being excellently well fitted for this purpose, for it commanded a clear view of all shipping passing between the island of Cuba and the mainland, and, being surrounded by many leagues of swampy flats, traversed by narrow, tortuous channels through which only boats of light draft could pass, permitted the pirates, on the approach

Ll

of an enemy vessel too powerful for them to tackle, to retire to their stronghold, and from thence, if pursued by boats, to scatter through the bush, where it would be impossible to hunt them out. These pirates, bloodthirsty and inhuman scoundrels as their acts proclaim them to have been, were popular enough amongst their neighbours along the coast, who enjoyed no inconsiderable share in the flood of gold and prosperity following in the wake of their robberies, without any of the risk—indeed, at Stephens' visit to the place, seventy-six years ago, several of the old pirates were still alive, and regarded by their neighbours as unfortunates whose legitimate means of livelihood had been taken from them by an over-scrupulous Government.

We saw the stone fort, with twelve embrasures, which was originally built with a view to subduing the pirates, but the officers and garrison of which, joining with them, rendered them a worse pest than ever. It was constructed of square stones taken from an ancient Indian ruin a couple of leagues distant. Part of it had been pulled down to erect a private residence, but even this latter is now in ruins.

We left Yalahau at 7.40, arriving a couple of hours later at Cerro Cuyo, a small town of 250 inhabitants, so called because of a large ancient mound or " cue " standing close to the waterside, the top of which has now been truncated to accommodate a small lighthouse. The town is situated on the narrow sandbank which runs parallel with the whole north coast of Yucatan, from which it is separated by a long, narrow, shallow lagoon, known as the " Rio Lagarto," or " Alligator River," though it does not appear to harbour many alligators, and is certainly not a river, being in the dry season a swamp which may be crossed in many places on foot, and, in the wet season a shallow lagoon closely packed with mangrove cays.

We noticed a great difference between Cerro Cuyo and the settlements which we had hitherto visited. In the former every man was his own master, doing a little fishing, turtling, hunting, or agriculture, as the spirit moved him, but for the most part taking things easy with a cigarette, a hammock, and—when times were good—a pint of rum.

In Cerro Cuyo, however, small though it is, a new air of briskness and movement was noticeable; bales of henequen fibre and cedar logs were being taken out from the *hinterland* on light railroads, which ran for many miles back to the south and west, and nearly all the inhabitants were employees of the " Compania Commercial de Fincas Rusticas," or Commercial Company of Rural Estates, which had large sugar, rum, and henequen estates in the interior, took out woods and gums, and manufactured salt on a large scale along the Rio Lagarto. It was, in fact, the first town of the " New Yucatan," the busy, stirring, get-rich-quick, northern part of the peninsula, as different from the mediæval east, which has changed little since the conquest, as the city of New York from a New England village.

At midnight we arrived at the port of Silan, anchoring till the *Celandor* boarded us at six next morning. This is a clean little town of 350 inhabitants, with the usual vast plaza, one side of which is occupied by a church, now—like nearly all churches throughout Yucatan—either closed or employed for secular purposes. It is the port of the town of Silan, three leagues in the interior, with which it is connected by a Decauville light railroad, having covered-in passenger coaches and a small gasolene engine.

The principal export of the place is henequen, or sisal fibre, used by the International Harvester Company for binding sheaves of corn, and without which it would be impossible to harvest the vast American corn crop. Trainloads of great shining oblong yellow bales of this kept coming out on the little flat cars, while we looked on, for shipment to Progreso in shallow draft bungays, from whence they would be transhipped to the waiting steamers. Early as we were, the only passenger train of the day had already gone, drawn by the only available engine; we were therefore compelled to hire a " special," consisting of a mule-drawn flat car, which could only take us about two-thirds of our journey, to a farm where we were told we would have to hire another mule special, as our own animal was urgently needed at the terminus for shunting purposes.

We arrived safely at the farm—a huge adobe structure, thatched with palm leaf, and surrounded by an immense corral, in the centre of which stood the usual windmill and water trough, ubiquitous throughout Yucatan, where practically all the water is pumped up from deep wells and cenotes. The place was really more a cattle ranch than a farm, and in the corral were a few depressed-looking bony steers and horses, while through the great plain outside, covered with short grass burnt to the colour of hay, and plentifully interspersed with patches of wiry bush, many more half-starved animals wandered disconsolately about in search of something to eat.

The farmer's wife would at first on no account hire a tramvia and mule to four suspicious-looking strangers, and it required fully half an hour of Morley's persuasive eloquence, with a deposit in gold, to persuade her that we were not such desperadoes as we looked, and might safely be entrusted with a mule and tramvia, difficult objects in any case to make away with.

We arrived about mid-day at a level crossing, which we found was the junction for Silan, and, tying the mule up, and leaving the car on a siding, had to trudge over nearly two miles of shadeless limestone road, under the scorching midday sun, before reaching the suburbs of the town. These were for all the world like the suburbs of a large village in the west of Ireland—mud-built, small-windowed, earth-floored, thatched cottages, whitewashed outside, with yards surrounded by crazy low walls, built of stones placed on top of each other anyhow, and ready to fall if a cat jumped over them, ducks, pigs, and goats wandering in and out of the living-rooms at will, while the sole sanitary arrangement consisted of a kitchen midden within convenient distance of the window, from which most of the refuse was thrown out.

From the suburbs we suddenly debouched into an immense plaza, with the *cabildo*, or municipal buildings, on one side, and opposite this the fine old church, now closed. Just beyond the churchyard wall is one of the most gigantic mounds in all Yucatan ; it is 50ft. high by 400ft. long, and is closely connected with another of almost equal size. All the stone to build the church, the municipal buildings, and most of the stone houses and walls in the town has been taken out of this vast mound without apparently reducing its size very materially. Stephens, who visited the place in 1841, was told by the then curé that he could remember the time when there stood on one side of the mounds great terraced buildings and pillared porticos, which had since fallen down, and we know that Silan was at the time of the conquest an important city of the Maya, for it was here in 1531 A.D. that Montejo's Spaniards retired after they had been driven out of Chichen Itza, and, disgusted with the hard life, the lack of gold, and the incessant fighting, determined to leave Yucatan for good. They were well received by the young cacique, Anamix Chel, Lord of the Cheles, and entertained by him very hospitably for several months, during which their wounds healed, and they completely recovered from the effects of their terrible experiences at Chichen Itza.

After this, accounts of the further progress of the Spaniards differ somewhat. Herrera says that, accompanied by some of the Silan nobles, they marched across to Campeche by land, whereas Cogolludo, following other contemporary writers, thinks they marched over the route by which we had just arrived to the port of Silan, and from there took ship for Campeche. This latter is far the more probable, as a march through a long stretch of country densely populated by hostile Indians, all of them hating the Spaniards, and many of them at war with the Cheles themselves, seems practically impossible.

Both mounds had evidently formed gigantic substructures for the support of great ranges of stone buildings, as is indicated by the presence of stone-faced subterranean chambers and arches, which are brought to light even now when excavations are being made for fresh stone, and into one of which (a good-sized arched room, recently discovered) we descended.

The fact that these great palaces and temples, actually in use about the middle of the sixteenth century, had practically disappeared, leaving only mounds of ruins, a century and a half later, a most unusual occurrence with Maya buildings, many of which are but little altered after 1,000 years, can only be explained on the hypothesis that they had been removed piecemeal, the fine squared stones of the temples and palaces themselves first, for the construction of the church, public buildings, houses, and walls of the modern town. We were shown a large flat slab of stone, which some years previously had been removed from the mound. It was now plastered into the back wall of the *cabildo*, and exhibited in fairly high relief the legs, with anklets and sandals, of a human figure somewhat larger than life, standing upon a row of five glyphs, which rested in turn upon the heads and shoulders of two smaller figures of slaves, bent nearly double under the burden, and wearing over their foreheads long, dependent feather ornaments.

Of the glyphs, reading from left to right, the first is 7 Muluc (the bar for 5 is very plain, but the two ovals separated by a longer oval, standing for 2, have not come out well in the photograph). The one next this is clearly 2 Kayab, the date recorded being 7 Muluc, the third day of the month Kayab, but this is a calendar round date only, and recurs every 18,980 days, or approximately 52 years, and, as no period ending is given which would fix the date more accurately, it is practically useless to us, and is, in fact, equivalent to fixing a date in the Christian era as occurring on a certain 9th July in the 18th year of an unknown century; thus, 9.7.18. To contemporaneous

SILAN, BROKEN STELE FROM MOUND NOW IN CASA DE LA MUNICIPALADAD.

[p. 166

MESTIZA GIRL OF MERIDA, YUCATAN.

[p. 175

people the century was easily supplied, just as to the Maya who wrote this 2 Muluc 7 Kayab the cycle did not need to be expressed, but to archæologists finding it a few centuries later it is the most essential part of the whole inscription.

The individual who fixed this stone in the wall of the *cabildo* must have been something of a humorist in his way, as he has executed in plaster, standing on the legs of the ancient Maya chief or king, the very crude figure of a Spanish soldier, with musket, fixed bayonet, belt, and shoulder strap.

On visiting the church we were greatly excited at finding, built into the wall which surrounds it, a small stele, having sculptured upon its exposed side the figure of a warrior in low relief, surrounded by rows of glyphs. The top glyph in the left-hand corner was obviously the introducing glyph to an Initial Series, and the other glyphs in the column had evidently had numerical coefficients in front of them, which left no doubt in our minds that this had originally contained an Initial Series date, from which we could have worked out the exact date of the inscription in Christian chronology. Unfortunately the stone, which was a not very tough limestone, was so worn that it was not possible to decipher either numbers or glyphs. We all tried it in every light and from every position. We wet it, and then we scrubbed it, we sat round it for hours like vultures round a dying mule, and at length even photographed it, but all to no purpose ; it completely eluded us.

The pirate Laffite, probably one of the most famous (or rather infamous) buccaneers of the latter part of the eighteenth century, had at one time pursued his calling along this part of the coast of Yucatan, and been buried in the church at Silan, and we were anxious to see his grave, but not only was this not known, but his very name had been forgotten. Such is fame !

The church had apparently been built upon the foundation of a much more ancient structure, part of which, in the form of arches and low walls, was still standing.

Built into the wall of the present church we found a

tablet which had evidently been removed from the older building, and of which we could make nothing. On taking a photograph we found that it had been plastered in upside down, but even right side up it is nearly as incomprehensible. The only easily distinguishable part of the inscription is the date, 1739, with which the second line commences. It is probably the gravestone of a Maya Indian who died and was buried in the church in the year 1739, the curious lettering consisting partly of those weird symbols used by the Spaniards to express Maya letters and syllables not capable of being written in Castillian, and partly of abbreviations. Like the calendar round date in the *cabildo*, the inscription, though no doubt perfectly plain to a contemporary padre with a knowledge of Maya, is a sealed book to the modern.

It was curious that of the three date inscriptions which we found at Silan, the Initial Series probably going back to about the seventh century of our era, the calendar round date to the fifteenth or sixteenth, and the Christian to the early eighteenth, only the last, which from an archæological point of view is by far the least important, should be decipherable.

After our labours in the church were finished we found ourselves exceedingly hungry and thirsty, and promptly went forth in search of something to eat. At the *cabildo* we were given plenty of beautifully cool, clear, well water, but discovered that, this being a purely Indian village, nothing in the way of a restaurant existed, the only articles of food obtainable being fowls, pork, tortillas, and beans, and as everyone produced their own supply of these, it would have been superfluous to offer them for sale cooked. We sent Muddy out to forage, and he returned in about half an hour with an ancient and very small Indian, who had recently lost his wife, and, actuated presumably by the same beneficent instinct which moves a dog to adopt a family of orphan puppies, agreed to supply us—for a consideration—with lunch, which would be ready in about an hour. We passed the time sitting in the cool of the *cabildo* veranda chatting to the Mayor and serveral members of the Municipal Council, who strolled up one by one, hearing that strangers had visited the town. These men were undoubtedly descendants of those Indians who had erected the mounds, sculptured the inscriptions, and later assisted the Spaniards of Montejo in their dire necessity, yet they took not the slightest interest in the history or traditions of their great ancestors, who enjoyed a high degree of civilisation at a period when our own forebears were scratching impressionist sketches on a soup bone chastely clad in a coat of blue paint. Their chief plaint was against the Federal Government, and, indeed, Yucatan is in this, as in many other ways, extremely like the Emerald Isle, in that everyone is " agin the Government." It was useless to point out to them that the peons had recently been liberated from what was practically a state of slavery by the Carranza Government, that wages were never so high, and prosperity never so universal throughout Yucatan, as at present ; they contended that though the poor peon might, and in fact did, now get up to five dollars gold per day as a free labourer, yet was this more than counterbalanced by the increase in price of necessities, forgetting that where in former years the Indian was satisfied with enough tortillas, frijoles, and chili for himself and family, with an occasional egg or a piece of meat as a treat, and sufficient brown cotton to make clothes, for himself, wife, and children, he now wanted European clothes, canned goods, and condensed milk—and, what is more, he gets them, yet is apparently far less contented with his lot than in the old days of peonage.

The discussion was hardly begun when Muddy announced the joyful news that lunch was ready, and we retired to our host's little round hut, away off in the suburbs, to partake of it. An ancient rooster, sacrificed for the occasion, formed the *pièce de résistance*, helped out by corn cakes, beans, and sauce of chili pepper and raw onions chopped together, the whole washed down by coffee made of ground parched maize. We were too hungry to be critical, and were really thankful to our host, who was apparently the only person in the town willing to feed us at any price, though his charge of ten silver dollars (just over five dollars gold) seemed rather steep. We admired our table-cloth and serviettes immensely. Though made of coarse cotton, they were beautifully worked with figures of quaint mythological monsters and cubist figures of birds and animals done in bright-coloured thread, evidently relics of the old gentleman's deceased wife.

Immediately after lunch we set out on the return journey, and when just at the confines of the town heard singing in a house, where we were told that a *santo*, who had been discovered a short time ago in the bush, was receiving a *novena*. Thinking that this *santo* might be one of the large stucco temple figures of the Ancients, we quietly entered the house, where we found a few of the devout seated on forms in front of a very ordinary wooden figure of a Christian saint, evidently taken from an old Spanish church, which, like so many similar buildings put up after the conquest, when labour was cheap and the population large, was soon deserted and buried in the all-embracing bush, as the Indian population became rapidly exterminated under the exactions of their Spanish masters.

We found our mule and tramvia undisturbed, and arrived without incident in the port at nightfall, boarded the *Lilian Y*, weighed anchor, and, after a successful night's run, arrived soon after midnight in the port of Progreso on the 6th February.

CHAPTER XI

Arrival at Progreso—English and Americans popular in Yucatan—We
are Relieved of our Arms—High Cost of Living and Service—Inflated
Wages—Resemblance of Merida to Monte Carlo—Mass no Longer
Celebrated in the Churches—Palace of Francisco Montejo—Sculptured
Façade all the Work of Native Artists—Damage Done in Cathedral
by Mexican Federal Troops—Flower Decorated Plaza Chief
Rendezvous—Boot Cleaning—Reason for Few Entertainments being
Given by Meridanos to Foreigners—Caste Barriers being Broken
Down—Mestizas Formerly Compelled to Wear Special Dress—Native
Dress of Men and Women—High Prices—No Alcohol on Sale—An
Unfortunate Incident—Meridanos All Speak Maya, and many English
—The Governor of Yucatan—A Successful Administration—Señor
Don Juan Martinez, an Accomplished Maya Scholar—Guardians of
the Ruins—Land Barons of Yucatan, their Recent Rapid Enrichment
—Molina Solis, the Historian—Early Start of Trains from Merida—
Arrival in Dzibalché—Hiring a Fotingo—Ranch of San Luis—Decline
of Cattle Ranches in Yucatan—A Bad Road for Motoring—Arrival
at the Ruins of Dzibalché—Descriptions of the Temples—Unde-
cipherable Inscriptions—The Initial Series Inscription—The Date
Recorded by it is the Latest of all Long Count Inscriptions—
Historically not Improbable.

WE were boarded by the Customs and Health Authorities
at 8.30 next morning, and on learning that the party consisted of two American citizens and a British subject the
progress of our baggage through the usual Customs for-
malities was greatly expedited, for the Yucatecans, unlike
most Mexicans, are extremely friendly both to Great
Britain and the U.S.A., one reason being that most of their
imports are derived from the latter country, while henequen
—practically their only export—finds a ready market
there. There is no harbour at Progreso, consequently
ships are compelled to anchor out in the open roadstead to
gigantic sunken chains provided by the Government for
that purpose, for which privilege they pay five dollars
gold daily.

At the Custom House we were relieved of the arsenal

of automatics, revolvers, and belts and bandoliers of cartridges carried by Morley and Held, as no one is permitted to carry firearms in the State of Yucatan—a most excellent and thoroughly sensible regulation, showing a comprehensive knowledge on the part of the authorities of the psychology of their countrymen. If such a law were only enforced throughout Latin America it would do more to civilise the country and abolish the perennial revolutions than all the talk of all the " patriots."

We had heard a good deal about the high wages and high cost of living in Yucatan, but our first personal experience of it consisted in having to pay ten dollars gold for a cart to transfer our baggage from the Custom House to the railway-station, a distance of about a quarter of a mile. We simply reviled the cartman at first when he made this apparently extortionate demand, but soon discovered to our sorrow that the transfer of baggage is a sort of monopoly, for which the fortunate monopolists charge practically " all the traffic will bear "—in other words as much as they think the victim's pocket will stand. Fortunately for us, our own appearance and that of our baggage, after a month of the *Lilian Y*, were equally disreputable, so we got off comparatively lightly.

The pier master—well known to me, as he had formerly been a clerk in the British Honduras Government Service—told us that on the piers and wharves unskilled labourers were being paid five dollars gold daily, while skilled stevedores, with overtime, sometimes made as much as twenty-five dollars in twenty-four hours. I wonder what proportion of professional men—lawyers, parsons, doctors—either in England or the United States make such incomes as these?

We caught the 10.30 train for Merida, arriving in little over an hour, after an extremely unpleasant journey in a crowded carriage—hot as an oven, and permeated by the fine limestone dust of the peninsula, which induces in new-comers, till they get used to it, an unpleasant state of suffocation

Merida is one of the prettiest, cleanest, gayest little capitals it has been my good fortune to visit. In many ways it reminds one of Monte Carlo in the season. The warm climate, the scrupulous cleanliness of the streets and plazas, the flowers, music, and sunshine, the crowds of pretty, well-dressed girls, the numbers of prosperous-appearing idlers, the absence of poverty, squalor, and ugliness, and the perpetual air of *festa*, are all common to both.

The Plaza de Independencia is the main plaza or square, and the chief place of rendezvous of the town. Its north side is occupied by the State Executive Palace, its south by the Montejo Palace, its west by the Municipal Palace, while on its east side stands the fine old sixteenth century cathedral, where, though the devout are allowed to enter and pray in front of the altar, Mass is no longer celebrated, as all the padres, with the exception of one or two in Merida and Campeche (who, however, do not celebrate the Mass, but confine themselves to the performance of baptisms and weddings) have been expelled from Yucatan, amongst them the Archbishop, who is at present in exile in Cuba, and whose fine old palace adjoining the cathedral has now been converted into Government offices.

Carrancista soldiers, under General Alvarado, did a great deal of damage in the cathedral when they entered Merida, burning the magnificent, priceless old seventeenth century reredos and gilded carving of the altar, and practically destroying the ecclesiastical library, which contained four copies of the first edition of Cogolludo's *Historia de Yucathan*, a work indispensable to the student of Maya archæology. In the somewhat remote hope that these might have been preserved by some marauding soldier, we inserted an advertisement several times in the *Voz de la Revolución*, the principal paper and official organ of the Government in Yucatan, offering to purchase copies of Cogulludo, without result, however ; and, indeed, no Mexican soldier would have looked upon four ancient volumes as worthy loot, and, like Bishop Landa, when dealing with MSS. of the aborigines three centuries previously, would probably have cast them into the fire, as in his opinion likely to perpetuate a pernicious and worn-out religious system.

The façade of the Montejo Palace is a very fine one, decorated with many statues of Spanish ladies in the dress of the period, knights in armour, and scantily-clothed Indians. All the carving is said to have been done by native Indian sculptors, and this is probably the case, as we realise from the remains they have left behind their remarkable cleverness in stone work of all kinds. The decoration of the hated conqueror's palace with statues of the haughty Spaniard in full armour triumphing over their own half-clad chiefs, exhibited, moreover, on the façade of the principal house in the principal square, for all who passed to see, must have been a bitterly hateful task to the Indian artists, whose pride of birth and the length and purity of whose descent equalled the proudest Castillian of them all.

The plaza is slightly raised and asphalted ; like the streets, it is kept scrupulously clean, and is covered with beds of beautiful sweet-smelling flowering shrubs and trees, amidst which are walks supplied with free seats, while at night, from eight to ten, the whole place is brilliantly illuminated. An excellent band plays, and it is then that all Merida comes forth to enjoy itself. Some ride slowly round and round the outer zone in automobiles, looking at the crowd, listening to the band, and exchanging smiles, nods, bows, and finger twiddlings with their friends passing on foot, or in other autos. Others promenade round the inner zone, or sit on the seats, to see and be seen, while neat, polite little boys flit silently amongst the crowd, selling dulce and cigarettes, or carrying tiny boot-cleaning outfits ready to give one's shoes a shine for the modest sum of 50 cents, for no Meridano seems to get his boots cleaned in the morning, or at his own house, but waits till he goes abroad and engages a bootblack, of whom there are swarms throughout the city.

It is a curious fact that amongst a people so fond of inno-
cent pleasure private entertainments are conspicuous by
their absence. Dinners at their own houses are rare, and
dances of still less frequent occurrence. Even foreigners
bringing letters of introduction to native families are
rarely entertained at their private houses, but feasted—on
an elaborate scale, it is true—at clubs, hotels, or restaurants.
One reason for this, I believe, is that on more than one
occasion foreign travellers who have been entertained at the
private residences of the native aristocracy have, on writing
their experiences later, given most unflattering—and, it
must be admitted, unfair—descriptions of the home life
and morals of the Meridanos.

Everywhere the country is in a transitional state. The
old order is giving place to the new, and the Mestizo and
peon (the latter, till freed by Alvarado, a virtual slave)
are breaking down the barriers of caste which separated
them from the Spanish Yucatecan, and gradually becoming
free citizens of a free Republic. At one time the Indians
and Mestizas, or women of mixed Spanish and Indian blood,
were compelled to wear a distinguishing costume consisting
of the *huipil* (a long, loose, sleeveless cotton garment cut
square and rather low at the neck), and a *pik*, or cotton petti-
coat reaching to the ankles. These *huipils* were always
kept scrupulously clean, and often exquisitely embroidered
by the owners at the neck, armholes, and bottom of the
skirt with gaily coloured cotton in all sorts of fantastic
devices. Their magnificent black hair, ribbon adorned,
was worn braided, hanging down the back, sometimes
covered with a shawl, while the richer ones were often
loaded with jewellery—chains, rosaries, earrings, rings, and
brooches. This undemocratic regulation has now been
abolished, and Indians and Mestizas dress as they like. The
garments of their ancestors are, however, hard to cast off,
and many of the elder women, even in Merida, still cling to
them, with the result that one not infrequently sees an
old mother promenading about the plaza in bare head,

moccasined feet, and loose *huipil* and *pik*, arm in arm with her daughter in high-heeled shoes, elaborate coiffure, surmounted by a still more elaborate hat, and clothed in the latest importation in the way of gowns from the U.S.A.   It must, however, be admitted that the mother's costume is by far the more becoming, as well as comfortable, for the female Yucatecan of all classes almost invariably possesses a figure short and somewhat broad, with practically no waistline marked by nature, eminently unfitted for the clothes of modern civilisation.

Many Indian workmen may still be seen wearing a short striped apron, the distinguishing badge of their class, which formerly they were compelled to wear, and now continue, apparently from sheer inability to break a centuries-long custom, though the compulsion no longer exists.

At the best hotels, if one asks for the excellent corn cake of the country he is regarded with mild contempt as an unprogressive countryman, and, indeed, the toothsome tortilla has in the city been largely superseded by atrocious white bread.   Even *posole*, the native drink made from ground corn and drunk all over the Maya area for the last 2,000 years, is now offered for sale at the little kiosks and stalls round the plaza in the form of *posole helada*, or iced *posole* !

The whole country was practically bone dry, no alcohol except beer and light wine being on sale.   The former is so very mild that it would be impossible to drink sufficient of it to induce intoxication, while the price of the latter is so prohibitive that no one but a millionaire could afford to buy sufficient of it to produce the same result.   In consequence of this strict prohibition an unfortunate contretemps occurred to us.   Morley had six bottles of claret on board the *Lilian Y*, which he insisted upon landing, and which we brought safely through the Customs, quite ignorant that any duty had to be paid on them.   These wretched bottles of claret proved a white elephant to us, as we lugged them about all over the country, though no one thought of drinking any. On returning from Chichen to Merida, however, they were, as usual, bestowed in our grub box, which an over-zealous Customs official, who had had some misunderstanding with Muddy, insisted on searching. He said nothing at the time, but telegraphed the authorities in Merida, who arrested the unfortunate Muddy, who was in charge of the luggage, on his arrival, and hauled him off to the police station. We meanwhile had taken an auto for the hotel, as Muddy had always proved himself capable of clearing the baggage.

The next we heard of the matter was the arrival of a small policeman an hour or so later to tell us of Muddy's plight, and the retention of most of our luggage in the police station, whither we hurried at once. We found Muddy sitting peacefully on a bench in the office, quite undisturbed. Nothing, however, would induce the sergeant to let him depart till the arrival of the Chief of Police, who, we were told, was closeted in his office, and would appear before long. We sent out for some food for Muddy, and, not liking to desert him, Morley and I took it in turns to sit up with him till about 2 a.m., when, as it became obvious the chief was not on the premises at all, we retired to the hotel to bed, which was just as well, for he did not arrive till 11 a.m. next morning, when he very politely expressed his sorrow for the inconvenience we had been put to, and dismissed Muddy in triumphant possession of the claret.

One is loth, however, to criticise the Yucatecans, for their kindliness, cleanliness, hospitality, and cheerful optimism far outweigh their minor faults ; and whereas the latter are ephemeral, and rather the result of a rapidly developing civilisation than temperamental, the latter are permanent, and ingrained in the Yucatecan character. Nearly everyone in Merida can speak Maya in addition to Spanish, and an astonishingly large proportion of the people have at least a working knowledge of English ; so much so that it behoves one to be remarkably careful not

Ml

to make adverse criticisms aloud in that language of the native manners and customs. Morley overheard an Indian urchin shouting to one of his companions : " Conex, conex, jugar baseball, ten catcher, tech pitcher "—" Come along, come along to play baseball, I catcher, you pitcher "—Maya, Spanish, and good Americanese, all mixed in one sentence.

On the 27th we were received in the State Executive Palace by His Excellency Carlos Castro Morales, Governor of Yucatan. What struck us most forcibly at first sight of him was his immense and colossal size, for, though not very tall, he was tremendously broad and thick, yet extraordinarily active for a man of such vast bulk. He smoked brown *orozus*—Mexican cigarettes—from morning to night, the stub of one serving as a light for its successor. These were covered with paper impregnated with liquorice, and the tobacco they contained was so saturated in saltpetre that it burnt like a time-fuse, which it strongly resembled in flavour and smell. The Governor was at one time an operative on the Yucatecan railroad, and, being a man of considerable ability, was put in by the Socialists, as Governor. He proved a success from the first, and never has the country enjoyed such prosperity, and never were the labouring classes so free, and never have they received such wages as during his régime. He was very pleasant and agreeable to us, asking many questions as to the object of our visit, and showing no mean knowledge of the archæology and former history of the country. Indeed, he put me right in the spelling of the Maya word " Chachac " in the title of a little pamphlet of mine he had read, and which should have been written " Chachac," to denote the Maya explosive " Ch." We found that he spoke with equal facility Spanish and Maya. On my expressing regret at seeing all the churches closed and padres banished, and asking if he were a Catholic, he struck his great chest with his fist, like a drum, and shouted : " *No, Señor, yo no estoy Catolico, yo no estoy Protestante, yo soy Pensador libre* "—" No, sir, I am not a Catholic, I am not a Protestant, I am a Free Thinker "—

and as this matter of religion bid fair to lead to friction, we quickly changed the subject. He gave us each an open letter addressed to all Government officials and others throughout Yucatan, advising them to give us every aid and assistance in their power in the prosecution of our archæological work, and, furthermore, put the railroad automobiles at our disposal, to convey us to any ruins or places of interest which we might wish to visit ; and so with mutual expressions of goodwill we took leave of the most genial, human, and successful Socialist it has ever been my good fortune to meet. On numerous occasions we met Señor Don Juan Martinez, recently representative in the U.S.A. of the " Commission Reguladora de Henequen " of Yucatan, which practically controls the entire trade of the State. He had previously been Government Inspector of Ruins, and introduced us to his son who now occupied that office. Mr. Juan Martinez is an extremely intelligent man, with a thorough knowledge of English, very strong American sympathies, and an acquaintance with the ancient written Maya language probably unsurpassed in the Peninsula. He has translated MS. records in old Maya dating from just after the conquest, as well as portions of the books of Chilam Balaam, the ancient Indian historical records kept by each town at first in the glyphic system employed by the Mayas before the conquest, but later translated into Spanish by some educated Indian very soon after the conquest. It is greatly to be hoped that, having at least temporarily abandoned his labours as an ambassador of commerce, Mr. Martinez may be willing to turn his unique knowledge of ancient Maya to account, and publish some of the MSS., translations which he has made, of old Indian records and documents, which may otherwise be lost to the student of Maya archæology for ever. Mr. Martinez, junior, the present Government Inspector of Ruins, was extremely kind to us ; giving us letters of introduction to the local *Guardianes* of the ruins, who are all under his supervision : for the Government realising at

length the immense value and interest of these wonderful
memorials of the past, has placed one or more guardians or
caretakers in each of the principal ruins, who are paid by the
state, and whose business it is to keep the buildings clean
and free from bush, and to see that none of the statues,
inscriptions, stucco paintings, etc., are removed by visitors,
as they have been practically indiscriminately in the
past. It may be also that the Government were not
unwilling to demonstrate to outsiders that a Socialist
Administration can not only lead the State to a material
prosperity hitherto unknown, but alone of all the Govern-
ments which have ruled Yucatan since the time of the
conquest, is sufficiently enlightened to actually spend a
considerable amount of money in the preservation of her
artistic and archæological memorials. He also took us
round to the owners of ranches on which the ruins were
situated, or to their representatives in Merida, and from
them we obtained letters to their major-domos instructing
them to provide us with food, lodging, transport, or in fact
anything within their power which we might require.
Probably in no country in the world would hospitality have
been carried so far as the provision of free bed and board
for an indefinite period, for a number of practically unknown
strangers. But the land barons of Yucatan occupy in
many ways a unique position. Their vast estates, often
grants from the Spanish crown, dating back to the days of
the conquest, run to hundreds of thousands of acres, their
Indian and Mestizo peons are numbered by hundreds,
sometimes even by the thousand, while the country houses
where they spend the hot season are often so vast as to
resemble rather royal palaces than private dwellings. Their
revenues, which in former days were indeed meagre, being
derived from the few head of stock carried by their vast
stretches of stony arid land, have, since the introduction of
henequen, for the cultivation of which this land is peculiarly
well adapted, swollen in the most Aladdin-like manner, till
Merida is reported to contain more millionaires in proportion

to its population than any city in the world—not excluding Pittsburg.

We had several very interesting interviews with Don Francisco Juan Molina Solis, the historian of Yucatan, whose works, the *Historia de la Conquista de Yucatan* and *Yucatan durante la dominacion Española,* have a wide circulation amongst archæologists outside the Peninsula. Notwithstanding his great age he is now engaged in writing a history of Yucatan from the end of the Spanish rule to the present day. His knowledge of the conquest of the various tribes of Maya with whom the Spaniards came in contact, the cities and territories occupied by them, and of the early ecclesiastical history of Yucatan, is absolutely unsurpassed and unique. Indeed, he and Don Juan Martinez are almost the only survivals of a generation who regarded a knowledge of the wonderful history and literature of their own country as more important than a foremost place in the mad rush for wealth, which now alone seems to occupy the people of Yucatan.

At 6 a.m. on the morning of March 1st we left Merida by the Campeche railroad, with the object of visiting the ruins of Holactun, situated at a distance of about 100 kilometres from the capital, where we hoped to find, and possibly decipher, one of the three Initial Series dates known to exist in Yucatan ; after which we intended to go on to Campeche by rail, and there meet Held, who had already left by the *Lilian Y* from Progreso, with a view to calling in at, and examining, the coast towns between the two places. The trains from Merida to points throughout the peninsula all seem to start in the very early hours of the morning, an extremely awkward arrangement for travellers, as life at the hotels does not commence till between 7 and 8 a.m. with the service of tea, coffee, chocolate, and *pan dulce*, and to ask for anything of the sort before 6 a.m. would be looked upon by the extremely independent servants of the Socialist régime as nothing short of a British outrage. As we expected to be away for several days we had to take cots, blankets, a change of clothes, and photographic and drawing outfits, and by the aid of two of the clean, fast little public automobiles, the most efficient and the only really reasonably cheap service in Yucatan, just succeeded in getting our luggage registered (a Herculean task in itself) and catching the train. We managed to seize half a dozen good-sized cakes of *pan dulce*, which resembled very stodgy sponge cakes, at the station, upon which, without the aid of any liquid to wash it down, we made shift for breakfast ; but long, long before the train covered the 100 kilometres between Merida and Dzibalchè, the nearest station to the ruins, we were consumed by an overwhelming thirst, in no wise relieved by the heat and clouds of limestone dust in the carriage. On arriving at Dzibalchè, a parched-looking Indian town of possibly 4,000 inhabitants, with most of the adobe walled, leaf-thatched houses standing in large, dirty, untidy bush-grown lots, surrounded by unmortared stone walls, we hired the only cart at the station to take our baggage to the plaza, as being the most likely place in the town to hire horses, and trudged behind it ourselves in the blistering heat of the sun's rays reflected from the glaring white limestone soil.

On arriving at the plaza, what was our delight to find a little " Ford," known all over Yucatan as " Fotingos," the Aztec diminutive " *ingo* " having been first affixed to the " Ford " in affectionate appreciation of the wonders the little cars can do in this roadless land, and the resulting combination being later rendered " Fotingo " by the Indians. The owner, Señor Candelario, agreed to take us that day to the Rancho of San Luis, and from thence, if car made by mortal hands could accomplish it, on to Holactun, which had never been visited by motor. Parched with thirst, we enquired whether it were possible to get some light beer, but were informed that only through the President of the Municipality could this be accomplished, as in the state-wide prohibition Dzibalchè had suffered even worse than the capital, for the sale of both beer and light wines

was prohibited here. We made a bee-line for the house of
El Presidente, and found that he not only gave the permission, but dispensed the beer himself, and even so far
honoured us as to join in the consumption. We reached
the ranch house of San Luis safely soon after midday, over
a very rough road, covered in places with great blocks of
limestone six inches high, in others presenting perpendicular
limestone ridges a foot high to be surmounted. San Luis
is the property of Señor Sixto Garcia, at one time one of the
richest and most hospitable men in Yucatan, but now,
unfortunately, an exile in Cuba, where, we were informed, he
drove a taxi for a living in the city of Havana. It was
almost exclusively a cattle and horse ranch, and, though
running to thousands of acres of rough grazing, was one of
the smallest of his vast possessions. These great estates,
with immense tracts of land surrounding them, and their
hundreds of peons practically the property of the *ranchero*,
and actually transferred as assets with the ranch, have not
prospered under the new régime, except in the henequen
belt. The peons have been freed, and have either started
fincas, or small farms, of their own, or have gone off to other
employers, where they receive ten times their former wages.
A great deal of the land has gone out of cultivation, the
buildings are going to ruin, while the *rancheros*, formerly
little less than reigning princes, are now for the most part
eating the bitter bread of poverty in exile. San Luis
presented a melancholy picture of this type of ranch ; the
labourers' houses are all empty and falling to pieces. Where
formerly one hundred peons were regularly employed, the
place is now in charge of an old man who acts as caretaker of the owner's house, with one *mozo* to assist him,
while the pasture is rapidly growing up in tough, wiry bush.

On our arrival the old caretaker at once produced oranges,
and promised eggs and tortillas as soon as his wife could get
the fire going. A curious anomaly with regard to the orange
supply in Yucatan is that whereas at almost any village the
owner will give one a dozen oranges off his trees just as

freely as he would a glass of water, and with as little idea of asking for payment, yet the selfsame orange, carried perhaps a hundred yards to the railway station (and with no change except that its green outer coat has been neatly sliced off, leaving it in its white underclothes for more convenient manipulation, " More Yucateco," by slicing in two and sucking), sells for anything from five cents to ten cents gold to thirst-consumed passengers in this thirsty land. We had hoped to find a guide at San Luis, to the ruins of Holactun ; but, all the peons having departed, we were, of course, disappointed, so set out for Xcalumkin Savanna, a vast extent of low bush and grass, hidden somewhere within which we knew the ruins lay, in the hope that we might discover a guide there. The road was far worse than the one from Dzibalchè to San Luis ; indeed, in places it was evidently the dry and very stony bed of a torrent which passed through the close, scrubby bush of the country, where we were compelled to lower the hood, which was getting torn to pieces by the numberless thorns and spines which every bush possesses. Our skins were protected only at the cost of constant vigilance, and even then I nearly had my left eyelid torn off. Soon the last vestige of a road disappeared, and we found ourselves pushing through sour grass and scrub, bumping over hidden rocks, trees and holes, where never motor-car had gone before. Many times we halted, and were on the verge of turning back, though we doubted our ability to find the way again to San Luis, but Morley's enthusiasm where ruins were concerned drove us ever forward. We passed several ruins of small Maya temples of the usual type—quadrangular, with flat roof, Maya arched ceiling and ornamental cornice outside. All were in an advanced state of ruin, and none showed signs of sculpture of any sort, much less of an Initial Series inscription.

We encountered several Indians, both men and women, struggling along under their loaded *mecapals*, or packs, slung from the forehead, but they were half sullen, half shy,

TEMPLE OF THE INITIAL SERIES, HOLACTUN (XCALUMKIN).
The Initial Series is seen between the pair of columns.

[p. 185

HOLACTUN (XCALUMKIN).

SHOWING LOWER PART OF INITIAL SERIES, AND CARVED COLUMNS
WITH CARVED LINTEL ONCE PLACED OVER THEM.

[p. 185

refused to answer except in monosyllables, and all disclaimed any knowledge of the ruins for which we were searching. At length, however, our persistence was rewarded, as we came across a small cavalcade of Indian and Mestizo *cargadores* taking out corn on their wiry little ponies for sale in Dzibalchè, amongst whom were several who knew the ruins well, and volunteered to act as guides. As it turned out, we were no great distance from them, and soon had the " Fotingo " at the base of the plateau upon which they stood ; the first time in the world's history, as far as we know, that a motor-car has visited a Maya Initial Series *chez lui*. The temple, which stood on a small mound, formed one of a group of very similar temples in this part of the savanna, and, though by no means the largest or most imposing of them, was the only one to contain any kind of stone sculpture. It consisted of a single large room entered by a triple doorway, to the left of which was a much smaller room or sanctuary. The ceiling of both rooms is formed by a Maya arch. The walls are covered by a mosaic of small pyramidal stones, the smooth quadrangular bases of which project outwards, and fit nearly together, while the pyramidal ends are buried in the substance of the walls, which are very thick, and composed of a mass of mixed mortar and rubble. These stones, which line the interior, act in no sense as a support to the building, and in the figure it will be seen that many of them have fallen away without impairing its stability, a peculiarity of most Maya temples, where the walls are, as it were, monolithic, for which the squared stones covering the interior merely form a tessellated lining. The central and right-hand door jambs are neatly sculptured on their outer surfaces, each with a double row of six glyph blocks, making twenty-four glyphs in all. While parts of these are decipherable, including several numerical coefficients, period ending signs, and lunar counts, the meaning of the inscription as a whole cannot, with our present knowledge of the glyphs, be elucidated. The same may be said of the inscription on the stone lintels. The left-hand jamb has sculptured upon that surface of it which faces the doorway a human figure, probably a priest, in very elaborate costume, consisting of enormous feather-decorated headdress, large round ear-plugs with dependent plumes, gorget of jewelled mosaic work, maxtli, or apron, decorated with bows, tags, and fringes, and large sandals, very elaborate and ornate. In his right hand he holds a ceremonial wand, and in his left a plume-decorated shield.

By far the most interesting feature about the temple, however, is the Initial Series inscription, which in several respects is absolutely unique. As will be seen, it occupies a raised band on separate square stones, stretching from about half-way up the arch to the cornice which divides the arch from the wall, immediately opposite the doorway, where the light of the sun would fall most clearly upon it. The inscription contains eight glyphs, the topmost being the introducing glyph, which always precedes Initial Series inscriptions, and consists essentially of the katun sign, with three dots or scrolls as a superfix, and the same as a subfix. (In the photograph only the katun sign and three dots are visible.) This is the most important of all glyphs to recognise when doing archæological work in the Maya area, and every member of the expedition, from the humblest Indian up, should be as familiar with it as with the ubiquitous tortilla, if no Initial Series date is to be missed, as this sign alone is sufficient to prove without doubt that the inscription which follows is an Initial Series date. Immediately beneath it is a glyph consisting of two grotesque heads, the one on the right hand being undoubtedly the head variant for a cycle, or period of 400 years of 360 days; the one on the left is the head variant for the numeral denoting the number of cycles elapsed, and is unfortunately unknown to us, never having been encountered in any other Initial Series inscription. The cycle coefficient, however, must be either 9, 10, or 11, as these three cycles comprise all Maya history in which the Initial Series might be used here, and

INITIAL SERIES AT HOLACTUN (XCALUMKIN).

The Initial Series commencing with the Introducing Glyph (the lower part of which only is shown) is to be read from above down.

[p. 187]

HOLACTUN (XCALUMKIN) : FIGURE ON JAMB OF DOORWAY IN TEMPLE OF THE INITIAL SERIES.

[p. 186]

as the number is neither 9, nor 10, the head equivalents for which are well recognised, it must, by a process of elimination, be 11. The next glyph beneath the cycle glyph shows two grotesque faces in front of a third grotesque face, which represents typically the head variant of the katun, or 20-year period sign. The two faces are the head variants for the number of katuns elapsed. Unfortunately, these are encountered as numerical coefficients for the first time. As 2 is the least frequently encountered number in the inscriptions, the fact that they are two in number may lead us to accept them provisionally as indicating two katuns. The glyph beneath the katun has unfortunately been a good deal defaced owing to the scaling off from the edges of the two stones upon which it is inscribed of a considerable amount of the carving, owing to the tremendous super-incumbent pressure of the roof falling chiefly on this point. The lower jaw of the right-hand face marks it as that of a head variant of the tun, or year sign, while the lower part of the left-hand face most closely resembles that of the head variant for eight, making 8 tuns. Below the tun sign the head variant for the uinal, or month sign, preceded by the head variant for four, is very clear, and below this the head variant for the kin, or day sign, preceded by the numeral nine written thus ⋮| is clearer still. The whole inscription then reads thus: 11.2.8.4.9, being 11 cycles, 2 katuns, 8 tuns, 4 uinals, 8 kins, or 1,601,369 days after the date 4 Ahau 8 Cumhu, the day upon which Maya chronology commenced.

Beneath the cornice, as a continuation of the band containing the Initial Series, is a further band containing eight double glyph blocks, reaching from the floor of the temple. The uppermost of these obviously records the day 7 Muluc, the seven being written above the sign for the day Muluc, denoting the day upon which the Initial Series ended. The month, however, and the position of the day in the month upon which it ended, are unfortunately omitted, though they can easily be worked out and arrive at 17 Tzec—that is, the day 7 Muluc occupying the 18th position in the month Tzec was the day upon which ended the Initial Series 11.2.8.4.9. The eighth or lowest of these glyph blocks contains a glyph which denotes an oxlahuntun, or 13-tun period, ending in 2 Ahau. On the left-hand door-jamb, not shown in the photograph, the same sign is again seen, preceded by a torch-like glyph designating a period ending.

We may then take it that the contemporary date of the temple is the next oxlahuntun ending in 2 Ahau following the date 11.2.8.4.9.7 Muluc 17 Tzec, which the temple is erected to commemorate, or, in other words, it was erected in 11.2.13.0.0, to commemorate an event which occurred in 11.2.8.4.9, or 1,711 days previously. Now the Initial Series is 11.2.8.4.9, and corresponds to 1012 A.D., while 11.2.13.0.0 corresponds to 1017 A.D., consequently the temple was erected in 1017 A.D. to commemorate an event as to the nature of which we have no indication, though such may well be recorded in the numerous indecipherable glyphs on the jambs, which occurred in 1012 A.D. This Initial Series is in many ways remarkable. In the first place, its position in a band along the arch of the ceiling and down the side of the wall is unique, Initial Series being almost invariably inscribed upon monoliths or panels. Next, it forms one of the only three known Initial Series hitherto discovered in Yucatan ; and lastly, its contemporary date is no less than 16 katuns and 3 tuns, or approximately 318 solar years later than the next latest Initial Series, namely, that of Tuluum, which, it will be remembered, is 10.6.10.0.0. As we know, the cumbersome method of Initial Series dating in Yucatan had rapidly given way to the more convenient, if less accurate, method of period ending, calendar round, and katun procession dating ; and it seems almost incredible that in this one situation throughout the whole country the ancient method should have been reverted to after a desuetude of over three centuries. There can be little doubt but that the priests, though using the more handy methods of dating, still retained a knowledge of the " long count," and could give the position of any day in it, but that they should employ this knowledge, so far as we know, but once in three centuries, is truly remarkable.

The date 1017 A.D. occurred soon after the commencement of the Triple Alliance between the rulers of Uxmal, Chichen Itza, and Mayapan, ushering in the golden period of the Maya rule in Yucatan, which was to last for two centuries. It probably marked also a renaissance in art, architecture, and religion, and no doubt a wide extension of the population, now all at peace, and still pouring in thousands into the peninsula, especially in the neighbourhood of the three main towns of the alliance. Holactun is only about sixteen miles to the west of Uxmal, and was no doubt one of the settlements founded about this time, so that there is nothing historically improbable in the date recorded by the Initial Series—quite the contrary—in fact, its historical probability is a further argument in favour of the reading being a correct one.

We spent a couple of days at the ruins photographing, sketching, and exploring other small ruins in the vicinity ; and though we discovered quite a number of small temples, that of the Initial Series was the only one containing any sculpture whatever. The whole of the great Xcalumkin savanna must have been at one time densely populated, as ruined temples and buildings are to be found all over it, and what is now a sea of coarse grass and low bush, broken at long intervals by the small maize patch of some solitary Indian settler, was, at the time of the conquest, a vast cultivated plain, the bottom lands covered with fields of waving corn, and the higher points occupied by the palm and adobe houses of the people, which have completely disappeared centuries ago, and by the stone temples of their gods, now rapidly falling into ruins.

CHAPTER XII

Inconvenience of Sleeping in a Liquor Store even when Closed—Natives
Turn Night Into Day—Superiority of Yucatecan Women of the
Bourgeois Class to the Men Exemplified in our Hostess—Heavy
Municipal Taxation—No *Curas* in the Villages Now—An Officious
Jefe—Arrival in Campeche—The Hotel Guatemoc, Formerly the
Governor's Palace—Campeche, Formerly a Prosperous City, now
Suffering from Dry Rot—Great Wall Surrounding the City—Two Fine
Old Churches—Trouble in Clearing from and Entering Mexican
Ports—Port of Campeche Silting Up—We Leave Campeche—An
Unfortunate Accident—Arrival at Champoton—Rumour of German
Wireless—Archæological Interest of Champoton—Strangers in Town—
A Terrible Trek Across the Peninsula from East to West—The Campo
Santo—Champoton a Decaying Town—Difference between Yucatecan
and Campechano—We Leave Champoton—Seiba Playa—Return to
Merida—Difficulty in Obtaining Old Books in Merida, dealing with
Yucatan—Set Out for Xcanchacan—A Light-hearted Crowd of
Natives—A Vast Ranch—Absolute Power of the Owner over his
Servants—Indian Girls at Xcanchacan—Henequen Cultivation and
Preparation of the Fibre—Stele with Important Katun Date at the
Rancho—Arrival at the Ruined City of Mayapan—Primitive Means
of Drawing Water—Destruction of Mayapan and Slaughter of the
Cocomes—Some of the Reigning Family Probably Escaped.

WE returned to Dzibalchè from the ruins every night,
having been lent the former liquor store of the town to sleep
in. This was an immensely lofty room, with doors opening
on to two streets, and would not have been uncomfortable
but for the fact that when the doors were left open pigs,
dogs, and children entered at all hours of the day and night
to investigate, whereas if they were closed the haunting smell
of new rum became too much for us who had not acquired a
taste for it early in life. We dared not keep a light burning
at night, as we found that old topers from the neighbourhood were attracted by it, under the impression that prohibition had ceased, the drought was over, and the *cantina*
again dispensing their favourite liquor. They routed us
out at first at all hours of the night, and were never pleased

and not always civil at finding three sleeping *gringoes* instead
of the hoped-for drinks. The Maya of Yucatan, like the
people of India, have a curious disregard of the divisions
of the day and night. They can sleep almost anywhere and
at any time, while at no matter what hour of the night one
may sally forth into the village streets, quietly-gliding, cotton-
shrouded figures of men and women will be encountered
going about on mysterious errands, and, when camping in
the bush, they will sit half the night in interminable conversation and tale telling, the gentle clicks of their remarkable language, insistent and monotonous, soon acting as a
peaceful lullaby to the listener. At 3 a.m. or even earlier
the subdued scrunch of *nistamal* being ground by the lady
of the house on her stone hand-mill for the breakfast corn
cakes becomes audible, to the accompaniment of the same
gentle but ceaseless click of conversation, punctuated in
this case by restrained gusts and gurgles of feminine laughter,
of which one may guess that they themselves, their out-
landish manners and customs and appearance, are the main
cause.

Candelario—or Candy, as we generally called him—very
kindly gave us early coffee in the morning at his home
before leaving for the ruins, and dinner—or, rather, supper—
on returning. These dinners form one of the pleasantest
memories connected with the whole trip, and it must be
admitted that we both fell violently in love with Mrs. Candy
the first day we met her. Pretty, gentle, tastefully dressed,
well educated, intelligent, and natural, she hardly appeared
a fitting mate for her husband, who, though a kindly and
excellent little man, was, after all, only an ordinary peon,
who by thrift and hard work had managed to purchase a
Ford, with which he was then making a very good living.

We had noticed time and again that the Yucatecan
woman of the bourgeois class is almost invariably more
refined and better educated than her husband, and Mrs.
Candy was but a more convincing proof of this fact. She
acted as hostess with the utmost tact and freedom from

affectation, chatting to us about the European War, Mexican and local politics, the position of women in Yucatan, and even Maya folklore and archæology, on all of which subjects she was evidently well informed, and capable of expressing an intelligent opinion. She spoke Maya and Spanish fluently, and English to some extent, and possessed a delicate sense of humour, a rare and priceless gift in a woman of any nationality. While we talked, Candy sat silently listening, nor could he be induced to join in the conversation ; but it was delightful to see how devoted the two were to each other— more like young lovers, indeed, than the parents of two charming babies. Yet Mrs. Candy was born in Dzibalchè of parents of very much the same social status as her husband. She had been educated there, and had never been farther than Merida ; and where she and a thousand other young Yucatecan girls of the same class acquired their gentle manners, good taste, intelligence, and sympathy is difficult to surmise, unless they were heritages handed down from their great ancestors who ruled the land before the coming of the Spaniards. Everyone we encountered in Dzibalchè was most bitter in their denunciation of the exactions of the Mayor, who was a nominee of the Federal Government and not one of themselves. Everything was taxed to the utmost farthing, and even if one asked a few friends in to dine or dance, a fee for so doing had to be paid to the Municipality, or the omission was sure to be followed by a heavy fine. We started to explore the fine old church, which we found open that day, as the only *cura* in the State had come over from Campeche to celebrate a wedding ; a state of things which we could not help contrasting with that of Stephens' day, when every village had its own *cura*, who almost invariably acted as kindly, cultured host to the explorer and to whose good offices not a little of the comfort and pleasure of his trip through Yucatan was due. Hardly had we entered the church when a constable came along from the " *Jefe* " to say the church was the property of the Municipality, we were trespassing in it, and must come along at once and answer for our crime. We told him to go and inform the *Jefe*, with our compliments, that we carried letters from the Governor of the State requesting all officers of the Government to assist us by every means in their power in our archæological investigations, and that under the circumstances we could hardly report to His Excellency on our return that the Chief of the Dzibalchè Municipality had done his best to carry out these orders. The message evidently proved effective, as we were molested no more during our stay in the town. On the 3rd we took sorrowful leave of Candy, his wife, and a group of friends whom, though newly made, we really regretted leaving, and made a triumphal procession to the railroad station in the motor-car, where we found the *cura*, a stout, red-faced, full-fed looking individual surrounded by a group of female members of his flock, who seemed unwilling to part with him, and were pressing on him light refreshments for his tedious forty-five mile train journey.

We arrived at Campeche in excellent time for a late breakfast, and made our way at once to the Hotel Guatemoc, which has a great reputation for what Yucatecans term " sea food," including fish, lobsters, oysters, and crayfish. Here we were pleased to encounter Held, who had come round on the *Lilian Y* by sea, sailing all the way in order to economise gasolene, and putting in at every little fishing village and settlement *en route*. We had an excellent breakfast, consisting of turkey, soup, oysters, lobster salad ; and afterwards an hour's siesta in a really magnificent and palatial chamber, for the old hotel had been the Governor's palace in the brave days of the Spanish occupation, and still showed traces, in its decoration and the spaciousness of its rooms, of viceregal occupation. We had a bath in a real bathroom, where we simply stood in a drained enclosure and allowed floods of rainwater—not the miserable, strictured trickle usually afforded by the shower pipe in Yucatan—to deluge our thirsty skins, which had not enjoyed such a treat since leaving Merida. In the cool of the evening we strolled

NL

forth to see the town, which to the visitor straight from Merida forms a strange contrast to that busy, bustling, up-to-date little city. Campeche, with its narrow, dirty streets, iron-barred windows, and air of perpetual siesta, is obviously a relic of the past, a typical ancient Spanish town, where people and city are succumbing peacefully and painlessly together to the dry rot of old age. Yet the city in its day has seen more stirring times probably than any city in the peninsula, for it was the great objective point of buccaneers of the sixteenth and seventeenth centuries who haunted the shallow bay of Campeche, awaiting the passage of the richly freighted galleons and plate ships of Spain on their way from Vera Cruz to Cuba and to Europe. Many of these carried millions of dollars' worth of bullion, sufficient to enable a whole ship's company to retire from their hazardous profession and live in the odour of sanctity for the rest of their lives. Campeche was stormed and taken by English and French buccaneers on no less than three occasions within twenty-six years, till in 1692 the citizens, assisted by the Spanish Government, built a great wall round it. This took seventy years to complete and cost 250,000 dollars (a vast sum in those days, before the introduction of facile millions). It was 26ft. high by 12ft. thick, and was surrounded by a deep moat. It covered an irregular seven-sided polygon, with bastions at each angle and massive forts along the water-side. The greater part of it has now been pulled down, and the work of demolition is still proceeding, yet enough remains to show what a vast undertaking it must have been for a comparatively small population. We passed two magnificent old churches. One, whose façade is decorated after the Moorish style in exquisite coloured tiles, has had a modern stone house built within a few yards of it, completely obscuring the ancient decoration, while one of its towers has been converted into a lighthouse. In the other the one remaining *cura* in the State, who had accompanied us from Dzibalchè, still officiates from time to time. On returning to the " Guatemoc " we anticipated, after our excellent breakfast, an equally excellent dinner, but were somewhat disappointed to find that it consisted only of the cold remains of the morning's turkey, and when breakfast next morning dwindled to eggs and bread and butter (the last supplied by ourselves from a tin, as none was to be obtained in the town), we concluded it was about time to move on. On reaching the Custom House we discovered that the same wearisome and expensive business of clearing the *Lilian Y* had to be gone through again. She had just arrived from Progreso via Rio Jaina, fifteen miles away, and was bound for Champoton, some forty miles to the south ; all in the same country, and, excepting Progreso, in the same State ; yet a fresh clearance, bill of health, and all the endless papers connected with clearing from a port had to be taken out. All through our trip we had found this business of clearing the ship the greatest nuisance. Though we had travelled throughout the entire trip from one Mexican port to another, at each place fresh papers had to be got out, entailing endless delays. Yet our boat was a small one, carried no cargo, and had the highest recommendations from the principal authorities with whom we came in contact. She had the misfortune, however, to be English registered, and the Mexicans freely admit that they wish to retain their coastal traffic for their own boats, and had we been Mexican registered we should not have encountered these delays and heavy fees. The Administrador of the Customs recommended us to an agent whose business it was to get the clearance, bill of health, etc., assembled and in order from the various Government Departments where they were issued. After some trouble we ran him to earth, and found a very ancient gentleman, with long white beard, of stately demeanour and very deliberate action. After a time we got him going, and about midday arrived at the Customs Office with all our papers in order, and so at length got safely away. We could not get even the shallow-draft *Lilian Y* up to the wharf in Campeche, as the water is gradually silting up ; indeed, the port does but little business now, and unless dredging operations are undertaken will soon do none at all.

We arrived off Champoton in the afternoon, and Morley, Held, and myself went ashore. It is a town of 1,000 to 1,500 inhabitants, situated at the mouth of the Rio Champoton, along which a good deal of the products of the *hinterland* bush, chiefly chicle, rubber, and logwood, are brought out. We had heard before setting out on our trip to Yucatan that Champoton was a hot-bed of German spies, who ran there openly a wireless outfit. We discovered that the wireless rumour originated in two 60ft. posts, which carried the Mexican telegraph wires across the mouth of the river sufficiently high up to admit of sailing boats passing underneath, and which at a glance from the sea strongly resembled wireless *aerials*. The only foundation we could find for the Hun rumour was the presence of a manager at a ranch some way inland, who, it was reported, might be a German, as he was certainly not a native Yucatecan ! Champoton is a place of some historical and archæological interest, owing to the fact that it is the site of the sojourn of the Itzas between their first exodus from Chichen Itza, about 700 A.D., and their return to that city two centuries and a half later. There are considerable traces of ruins in the neighbourhood, but all in a very poor state of preservation, partly, no doubt, owing to the fact that they have been systematically wrecked to obtain building stone. Only two strangers lived in Champoton ; one a *cura*, whose occupation had departed on the closing of the churches by the Government, but who had turned his talents to account as a billiard-marker ; the other a black boy, a native of Belize, who had been working for the American Chicle Company at Bacalar, on the eastern side of the peninsula, at the time of the great hurricane. Like many more chicle bleeders, he had been shut in the bush by the obliteration of all roads and trails owing to the complete flattening out of the forest under the tremendous force of the hurricane. Most of these men had made their way out after weeks of incredible toil and hardship, but many never made their way out at all, leaving their bones to whiten in the bush. The case of this boy was, however, perhaps the most remarkable of all, for though a frail youth of poor physique and no great intelligence, and with no particular knowledge of bush craft, he made his way clean across the base of the peninsula from east to west over a practically trackless stretch of forest and swamp, with no inhabitants beyond, at great intervals, a few chicle and rubber bleeders. He must have covered in all nearly a couple of hundred miles before he happened to encounter a band of chicle bleeders not far from Champoton. He had managed to subsist on such leaves, fruit, roots, and insects as he could pick up along the route, and, of course, was never at a loss for water. When found he was reduced to very little more than skin and bones, and his mind was somewhat fogged as a result of the terrible privations. How long he had taken over the journey he was unable to say, as he had lost all count of time, but such a trip accomplished alone, and without food or equipment of any kind, postulates tremendous vitality and dogged perseverance, which one would hardly have expected to find in a youth apparently so poorly equipped, both mentally and physically. We shipped him on the *Lilian Y* and promised to take him back to his family in Belize, whom he had not seen for many months, and by whom he had presumably been given up as dead ; but at Progreso, finding wages high and prospects good, he left us silently, nor stood upon the order of his going.

The *campo santo*, or burial-ground, at Champoton is about the only thing worth visiting in the place. It is very neatly kept, and the dead, or at least those of them who were well-to-do in life, are provided with miniature houses, some of them almost large enough to have been used as habitations by the living, kept nicely painted and whitewashed. Champoton, like Campeche, is suffering from the dry rot of old age. On the outskirts of the town the arcaded ruins of the former Governor's palace and of ecclesiastical buildings are seen falling rapidly into ruins, while many of the larger and better-class houses are empty. For some reason the Campechano, though of practically the same race—mixed Indian and Spanish—as his brother the Yucateco, is quite lacking in the energy and commercial acumen of the latter, and is content to accept as his watchword the good old Spanish proverb, " *Mañana, no hoy* "— " To-morrow, not to-day "—which for the last three centuries has been the *bête noire* of Latin Americans.

We left Champoton that night and turned back towards Campeche, having reached the southern limit of our trip, and the last place in this direction at which we might expect to encounter relics of the ancient Maya civilisation. We anchored off Seiba Playa, about twenty-five miles north of Champoton, and spent the night on the *Lilian Y*. Next morning early we went ashore in the pram to visit the *pueblo*, which is an exceedingly primitive village of 800 Mayas and Yucatecans, with one solitary black man, who seemed to be retained as a sort of curiosity. The only industries are fishing and agriculture. The people are self-supporting, and rarely come in contact with anyone from the outside world, so that our advent was looked upon as quite an event.

We were told here of ancient ruins a few miles back in the bush, but, on learning that they were mere heaps of stones, made up our minds that it was hardly worth while visiting them.

Strolling along the beach, we picked up some perfectly gorgeous shells, many of them in excellent preservation, with their colours bright and undimmed, and some of them species which we had not observed before. This would be a conchologist's paradise, as for some reason the sandy bay, bounded by rocky promontories, seems to act as dumping-ground for every variety of shell-fish known in the Gulf of Mexico. We were followed along the beach by a little queue of children, who were greatly entertained at our picking up quantities of what to them were too common

even for playthings, and who evidently regarded us as
un poco loco, or a little crazy.

We reached Campeche about noon, and lunched again at
the " Guatemoc " on a rich selection of sea products.
While at table in the restaurant of the hotel we had forcibly
brought home to us what one notices at all eating-places in
Yucatan—the constant annoyance to which guests are
subjected from all sorts of casual strangers, who come up
and address one on the flimsiest pretext.   The natives are
so used to this as apparently not to object to it in the least.
On this occasion we were attacked in turn by four im-
portunate sellers of the *Voz de la Revolucion*, the Government daily paper ; three boot-blacks, who, although our
boots had been operated on in the plaza just before coming
in, were insistent on giving them another polish ; two
unequivocal beggars seeking *caridad* ; and one gentleman in charge of a subscription list for the relief of
a destitute old man—not a bad bag for one solitary
half-hour !

We took the afternoon train for Merida, where we arrived
the same evening quite pleased to find ourselves back again
in the " Gran Hotel."   We spent the whole of Wednesday,
the 6th, in Merida, chiefly in visiting book-shops and private
dealers in books in a vain quest after the *Historia de Yucathan*
by the Provincial Diego Cogolludo, containing information
concerning the manners, customs, and history of the Maya
absolutely indispensable to the student of Maya archæology.
We were unable to obtain a single copy of either volume
for love or money in Merida, but succeeded in obtaining,
through a bookseller from Mexico City, an edition of the first
volume published in Campeche in 1842, and of the second
published in Merida in 1845, bound in a single volume.
We heard only of one copy of the original edition, for
which the owner asked 1,500 dollars, but the work in any
form is exceedingly difficult to acquire, as only 100 copies
of the Campeche edition were published, and but 200 of the
Merida edition.   Books dealing with the antiquities of the

country are difficult to obtain in Merida, while the prices
asked are simply outrageous. Such works as John L.
Stephens' *Incidents of Travel in Central America, Chiapas,
and Yucatan,* and his later volume, *Incidents of Travel in
Yucatan,* sell for four or five times what they can be bought
for in Europe or the States at any book-dealers, while
Molina Solis' *Historia de la Conquista de Yucatan,* published
in 1896, but now out of print, sells at more than ten times
its original cost. In Yucatan, books, like every other
commodity where the stranger is concerned, are taxed
for all that the traffic will bear.

We caught the 5.30 a.m. train on the morning of the 7th
by an exceedingly narrow margin and were again reduced
to sticky, thirst-provoking sponge cakes, snatched up *en
route,* to break our fast. However, this did not matter so
much, as our destination was only about twenty miles from
Merida—the ruins of Mayapan, situated on the *rancho* of
Xcanchacan.

On arrival at the station we changed on to a mule-drawn
flat car running from the main line up a narrow gorge to
the ranch house, on which we squeezed ourselves, in amongst
a great crowd of laughing, chattering Indian girls and children,
wives and kiddies of labourers on the ranch, some of them
going up there to do light work themselves. A gayer and
more light-hearted crowd it would be impossible to imagine ;
everything was treated as a joke specially got up for their
benefit. The loss of my hat from a puff of wind gave rise
to roars of laughter, and even the derailing of the car, which
might have resulted in a nasty accident—and did result
in half an hour's tedious wait in the sun—only produced an
increase of hilarity. An endeavour on Held's part (who
always improved the shining hour on these lines) to carry on
a mild flirtation with his pretty neighbour through the
medium of about ten Maya words, and that language of the
eyes and lips which is the same all the world over, was a
source of pure joy to all beholders, including Morley and
myself.

The ranch house, one of the largest in Yucatan, is an immense one-storied stone mansion over 300ft. long, with a deep, tiled piazza in front, whose vault-like coolness, enhanced by a gentle breeze, proved a delightful change from the glaring heat of the sun outside. The rooms were large, lofty, well ventilated, stone-floored, and consequently very cool and comfortable, but it must be admitted that from a European point of view they were bare and sparsely furnished ; no pictures, carpets, knick-knacks, or ornaments— just the bare chairs, lounges, and hammocks. The estate belongs to the Peon family, one of the oldest and richest in Yucatan, who hold their titles from the Spanish Crown, and whose occupation goes back practically to the conquest. For size it could put many a European principality to shame, with its hundreds of thousands of acres. At one time the power of the owner was that of an absolute monarch, for he administered the high justice, the middle, and the low over his labourers—or, rather, slaves—whose ancestors had been made over to him by the Crown after the conquest of the Indians, and who were themselves just as much his property as the acres upon which they toiled.

We sat in the shade of the great corridor, as Stephens had done nearly eighty years previously, and watched, as he had done, the Indian girls going to the well, situated in the great stone yard on the opposite side of the *hacienda*, for water. All were extremely graceful, slow and deliberate in their movements, and with heavy *tinaja* balanced on the head, lightly supported by one upraised, beautifully-modelled bare arm, arrow-straight figure, and majestic walk, were worthy models for a sculptor.

The majority were of the usual Maya olive or light bronze colour, with thick black hair, dark-brown eyes, and beautiful complexions, but not a few showed a strain of Andalusian blood, and one or two were light-haired, blue-eyed, and fair complexioned—throwbacks, perhaps, to some Norwegian buccaneer ancestor who had harried the coast 200 years ago. Some passed us with eyes demurely cast upon the tiles, others with a smirk possibly of greeting, but more probably of amusement at our—to them—strange appearance, while a few unmistakably threw us what John Held classified as the " glad eye," in response, I think, to his expansive smile.

After a rest we took a tour of inspection round the *hacienda*. On every side, as far as the eye could reach, were vast fields of henequen, or Agave Americana, from which is derived the sisal fibre, practically the only export of the country, which makes it, for its size and population, one of the richest in the world. These aloes are planted in rows at regular intervals ; each one stands from 3ft. to 4ft. high, and consists of a central core, attached to which are great, thick, tough, dark-green leaves, 3ft. to 4ft. long, 5in. or 6in. broad, each tipped at the point with a huge black thorn. The outer leaves are cut from each plant at frequent intervals and carried to the mill, where they are beaten and scraped till all the pulp is removed, and only the beautifully white silky fibre remains. This is hung on wires in the sun to dry, and all round the *hacienda* were drying-grounds, with children at work changing the hanks of fibre from side to side on the wires till they were dried all over by the sun. Lastly they are compressed in hydraulic presses into great bundles bound with hoop iron, in which form they are exported to the U.S.A., where, converted into thin, loosely-woven rope, they bind the sheaves of corn cut by the reapers from Canada to Mexico.

The whole vast estate is covered with a network of light railroad, on which the labourers ride to work, and along which the stacks of cut leaves are brought in to the mill.

On returning to the *hacienda* we discovered an extremely interesting relic of the past—no less, indeed, than a stone stele about 6ft. high, brought by a former owner from the ruins of Mayapan, and carefully built into the wall of the corridor, where, preserved from the weather, it should last practically for ever. The top of the stone is rounded, and the upper third of its surface is divided into thirty-six more

MAYAPAN: XCANCHACAN STELA BUILT
INTO THE WALL OF THE HACIENDA,
SHOWING THE DATE KATUN 10 AHAU,
OR 1438 A.D.

[p. 203]

Chichen Itza.
Plan of the Ruins

1. Cenote of Sacrifice.
2. Ball Court.
3. Temple of Jaguars.
4. Castillo.
5. Market.
6. Chichanchob.
7. Cenote.
8. Caracol.
9. Akabsib.
10. Monjas.
11. Hacienda.

PLAN OF THE RUINS OF CHICHEN ITZA, YUCATAN.

[p. 201]

or less equal spaces by incised lines, which probably originally each contained a painted glyph. Below this is a zone
of incised geometrical ornamentation, followed by a band
consisting of ten quadrangular spaces, and below this again,
roughly and crudely cut in low relief, are seen two human
figures. The figure on the left as one looks at the stele is
much the smaller, and stands upon a low altar, or stool.
His headdress is composed of a highly conventionalised
bird, and he holds in both hands an indeterminate object,
which he is apparently offering to the figure on the right.
This is undoubtedly meant to represent Cuculcan, or the
Long-nosed God, one of the most popular deities throughout Yucatan. (Compare the face of the god as shown here
with the representation of him in the painted stucco at
Tuluum). The god holds in his right hand a ceremonial
club, or baton, while his left arm is held in front of him
semiflexed. He wears the usual feather-decorated headdress, and large round ear-plug, with pendant.

The most interesting and important part of the whole
sculpture, however, is the date glyph, which is quite clear
and unmistakable. It is situated between the upper part
of the club held in the right hand of the figure of the god
and the headdress of his worshipper, and records the date
10 Ahau ; that is to say that the stele was erected
to commemorate the end of Katun 10 Ahau. A
crack filled in with light-coloured cement passes
obliquely across the centre of the stele, and this crack
crosses the Ahau sign about its centre.

There is recorded in the books of Chilam Balam, in which
are given the procession of the katuns and the most important events occurring in each, one date with meticulous
accuracy, namely, the death of a certain native chief named
Napot Xiu, which is said to have occurred in a Katun 13
Ahau, while yet 6 tuns (periods of 360 days) were lacking
before the end of the katun, on the day 9 Imix, which was
the 18th day of the month Zip. The chronicler further
states that this event took place in the year of our Lord

1536. It is obvious, therefore, that the end of this Katun 13 Ahau occurred 6 tuns later, or somewhere in the year 1542 A.D. The Maya did not number their 13 katuns from 1 to 13, but in the following order : 10, 8, 6, 4, 2, 13, 11, 9, 7, 5, 3, 1, 12, 10, so that, granting the end of Katun 13 Ahau fell within the year 1542, it is obvious that the end of Katun 10 Ahau, counting backwards, fell 5 katuns, or 100 tuns, or 36,000 days earlier—that is, within the year 1438 A.D., which is the contemporary date of this stele. Of course, it must be remembered that a Katun 10 Ahau recurred every 13 x 20, or 260 tuns, that is, every 256 years, so that it fell also in the year 1182 A.D., but both on stylistic and historical grounds this date may be rejected.

After an excellent breakfast provided by the major-domo, Morley, Held, and myself, accompanied by a guide, set out on horseback for the ruins of Mayapan.

At first the road led through vast and apparently interminable fields of henequen, criss-crossed in all directions by light railroads, but at length we got beyond the henequen zone into a vast, flat, sterile plain, covered with short grass burnt yellow by the sun, interspersed with stones and patches of low prickly bush. It must be admitted that the name of the ranch, Xcanchacan, or Kanchacan, derived from the Maya, *kan*, yellow, and *chacan*, a plain or savanna, expresses well its appearance. We passed the remains of a great stone wall, now completely in ruins, which our guide told us surrounded a more or less square enclosure two miles in each direction, and followed it up in both directions for a short distance, but as there was nothing to be gained by making a complete circuit, and, moreover, the going was very bad, we soon continued on our way to the little ranch house close to the ruins, where we off-saddled and set out on foot for a great mound standing up commandingly from the plain, less than a quarter of a mile away. We encountered a few half-starved cattle, horses, and mules, whose living on this scorched pasture, which did not look as if it could carry one head of stock to twenty acres, must, indeed, have been a poor one, and at the little ranch house we observed water being drawn by a wheel turned by a patient horse from a deep well, which flowed into troughs for the benefit of the stock. This primitive contrivance is very rare in Yucatan now, as nearly all the water used is raised from the bowels of the earth by American windmills, fleets of which form the most prominent objects scattered over every town, and without which even the smallest *hacienda* is rarely found. Of all the ruined sites of Yucatan, Mayapan is perhaps the most disappointing to the archæologist and explorer visiting it for the first time with some historical knowledge of its former importance amongst the Maya.

From about 1000 A.D. to 1200 A.D. this city formed, with Chichen Itza and Uxmal, a Triple Alliance which ruled the whole peninsula during the golden period of the Maya occupation of Yucatan. About 1200 A.D., owing to a quarrel between the Halach Uinic, or ruler of Chichen Itza, and his ally of Mayapan, war broke out between the two cities, which ended only by the calling in of Toltec mercenaries from Chiapas to assist the armies of Mayapan, who were getting decidedly the worst of it. This ended in the complete overthrow of the Itzas and the domination of the Cocoms, the ruling family of Mayapan, over their former allies of Chichen Itza, and, indeed, over the whole Maya area. The Cocoms then became the overlords of all the petty kings and caciques, and compelled them to reside for a certain period every year in the city of Mayapan, around which they built a great stone wall, remains of which we passed on our way to the ruins, where each vassal lord had his own palace and temple, his own priests and retainers, and outside the walls of which he was allowed to house servants and stewards, who collected his revenue and supplied the wants of himself, his priests, and his more immediate retainers. This remarkable state of affairs lasted for no less than 250 years—till the year 1450 A.D., in fact, the vassal chiefs and their subjects being kept well under subjection by the Toltec mercenaries and their descendants, to whom the Cocoms appear to have handed over the city of Chichen Itza. At length, driven desperate by the overbearing arrogance of the Cocoms and by the exaction of their Toltec mercenaries, the subject lords of Yucatan revolted against the Cocoms, and under the leadership of the ruler of Uxmal made war upon them. This set the whole country in a blaze, and a fierce civil war raged amongst the Maya for a number of years, till sometime during Katun 8, or about 1448 A.D., the city of Mayapan was taken and utterly destroyed, the whole of the royal family being slain with the exception of one son, who was absent in Honduras. Though, according to the native chroniclers, the whole Cocom family was exterminated with this one exception, the probabilities are that several other members of the royal family escaped, and fled the peninsula, for there exists to-day amongst the Indians of British Honduras and of the province of Peten, in Guatemala, families of Cocoms so much superior to the other Indians in physique, appearance, and mentality, as to give one the impression that they belong to a different race. They are, moreover, in some cases associated in the minds of the other Indians with a vague idea of royalty or nobility possessed in the old days. The destruction of Mayapan must, indeed, have been complete, as the contemporary accounts relate, for at the present day hardly one stone is left standing upon another, and practically all that remains is the great stone-faced pyramids, or substructures, upon which the temples stood.

CHAPTER XIII

ON our return to Merida we determined to remain there for
a few days while laying in a stock of provisions for our stay
at Chichen Itza, the largest and most spectacular ruins of a
New Empire Maya city throughout Yucatan. On March
7th we left the capital by one of the usual uncomfortable
5.30 a.m. trains for the town of Dzitas, the nearest point on
the Yucatan railroad to Chichen Itza, from which it is
distant about twenty miles. On arriving in Dzitas we found
that two methods of reaching the ruins were available—by
" Volan Coche " or on horseback. The Volan, as it is
usually called, was, before the coming of the railroad,
practically the only means of transport throughout Yucatan,
and a more uncomfortable conveyance it would be difficult
to conceive. It consists of a high wooden cart entirely
devoid of springs, and drawn by two, three, or four mules.
The passenger lies, sits, or reposes as best he may at the
bottom of the cart, which, with the sides, is well padded

with mattresses and pillows. The driver, usually an Indian, squats in front and drives. The roads are simply broad tracks cut through the bush over the limestone surface. Great boulders and ridges of limestone are left, and over these the volan jolts and rocks, taking everything in its stride, the mules keeping up a good hand-gallop most of the way. To the new-comer it is perfect torture, as he is thrown from side to side and up and down in the volan like a shuttlecock, and it is quite useless to try and stop the driver once he has started the mules, as he takes no notice whatever of the most piteous cries, till he has reached his destination. Having had considerable experience with the volan, we determined to send on our luggage by one of them while we proceeded on horseback. But even here we were unfortunate, for the only four horses available were miserable little skinny, thirteen-hand ponies, so dejected and worn that we hesitated to mount them, especially as the saddles were on a par with the mounts, and the bridles and stirrup leathers of rope. Soon after starting, finding that I was riding with my knees nearly up to my chin, I endeavoured to lengthen the stirrup ropes, but discovered they were not adjustable, so changed horses with Morley, whose legs were better adapted by nature to the short stirrups. We were passed by a volan going at a great pace, occupied by an enormously stout woman and a child ; they were being volleyed about in all directions by the jolting of the vehicle, but did not appear to mind it in the least, though I could not help wondering what would have happened if the lady had landed on the child.

Our progress was slow and uncomfortable, and by the time we arrived at the ruins we were quite tired out, as constant urging had been necessary the whole way to get the unfortunate little ponies to move at all. Our first view of the ruins, however, amply compensated us for all our trouble, as, coming suddenly round a bend, we had presented before us, perhaps a quarter of a mile away through a broad straight cutting in the bush, the splendid structure known

CHICHEN ITZA: LINTEL IN WATER TROUGH AT HACIENDA.

The uppermost line of the inscription shows plainly the lower part of the 11 Kan and 14 Cumhu, as well as the winged Cauac tun sign.

[*p.* 209

THE MONJAS, OR HOUSE OF THE NUNS, CHICHEN ITZA,
WITH THE IGLESIAS AT THE RIGHT.

[*p.* 210

as the Castillo, perhaps the most spectacular monument now standing in the Maya area, and certainly one of the best preserved.

Passing the Castillo, we arrived shortly at the Hacienda or Casa Principal, the house of the owner of the ranch, which had been placed at our disposal during our stay. It is a fine, large, cool house, having extensive verandas, built about the middle of the eighteenth century with stone taken from the ruins. The first owner was a recluse who had amassed a large sum of money in gold coin. He lived at the *Hacienda*, attended only by a Belize Negro man and an old Spanish woman. Feeling that his end was near, and not wishing that his relatives should benefit by his death, he sent these two old retainers off one morning to Valladolid, the nearest town, with instructions to take the whole day off. On returning at night, they found the old man dead in bed, and the treasure gone, the presumption being that he had found just sufficient strength to get up and secrete the treasure, either in the house or somewhere near at hand in the ruins, but, the excitement proving too much, he had returned to his bed to die.

On being notified of the old man's death, the relatives at once instituted a search for the treasure, half pulling the house down and digging the floor up in the hope of finding a secret hiding-place, and even going so far as to excavate in some of the closer buildings amongst the ruins ; all to no purpose, however, as they found nothing. Ever since it has been a favourite sport amongst the Indians, and other visitors, to take an occasional dig, in the hope of coming across the treasure accidentally.

Around the house was an immense stone yard used at one time for cattle, but now empty except for our ponies. Inset in a stone water-trough which had been constructed for the cattle to drink out of is a large slab of stone from the ruins, set in upside down, upon which is inscribed a calendar round date with the wrong numerical coefficient in front of the month sign, a most unusual mistake for a Maya sculptor to make.

OL

I elected to sleep in the yard that night, as it was much cooler, but regretted my decision, as in the early hours of the morning I was awakened by a painful stinging and nipping all over my body, and discovered that I had been attacked by myriads of large brown ants known as the " marching army," who had crawled up the legs of the cot and were endeavouring to make a meal off me. I jumped out of bed, brushing as many off as possible, woke the others, and with all the servants of the *hacienda* we attacked the invaders with torches made of dry palm leaf. We must have burnt millions of them, but still more millions came on, and it was only after a couple of hours' strenuous work that we succeeded in driving them from the yard and returned again to bed. These ants are a terrible scourge in Yucatan, and will often drive the Indians from their homes, when they pass through, devouring everything *en route*. Birds and animals in cages are left as balls of feathers, or fur, and bones, and no doubt if a man or woman were unable to escape nothing would be left of them but bones. They possess, however, one advantage in that they eat up all scorpions, cockroaches, tarantulas, and other noxious insects which always infest thatched houses.

Next morning, directly after coffee we started a survey of the ruins, beginning with the Casa de Monjas, or Convent, which is quite close to the *hacienda*. This building received its name from the fact that it was supposed to have been a convent occupied by the Maya maidens, who, like the vestal virgins, served the gods and were sworn to chastity for life. There is, however, no proof forthcoming that it was specially used for this purpose. It consists of a solid block of masonry apparently without any chambers in its interior, upon one side of which is built a wing containing nine chambers with arched Maya roofs. The great solid structure adjoining the wing was apparently constructed only to support two ranges of buildings. The first is approached by a stairway passing up the solid central block 56ft. wide and 32ft. high, leading to a range of rooms extending all round the structure, with a platform, 14ft. wide in front of them. From this platform ascends a second stairway of fifteen steps leading to a second range of rooms, now in a very bad state of preservation. The total height of the building was 65ft. Closely adjoining the wing is a small structure known as the *Iglesia*, or church, 26ft. long, 14ft. broad, and 31ft. high. The outside of this is decorated with gigantic stone faces of the long-nosed god, one of which is very clearly seen in profile in the illustration. The nose curves up somewhat like an elephant's trunk, and forms the chief ground for the somewhat fanciful theory that the ancestors of the Maya, who built the ruins of Copan and Yucatan, came originally from India, whence they carried with them the tradition of the elephant reproduced in their sculpture. The most interesting point about the Monjas perhaps is that a great excavation 30ft. deep, which has been made in one side of it by a former proprietor, for the purpose of taking out building stone, shows that the great central core is entirely solid, and, furthermore, that it has on two occasions been added to, the original core having supported quite a small, unpretentious temple, the second an extension of this, while the last consisted of the addition of the great stairway, the upper range, and the lower range containing nine rooms.

The Monjas was probably constructed during the great period of the New Empire, i.e. between 1000 and 1200 A.D., and it clearly indicates how rapid must have been the growth of the city when within a couple of centuries a simple temple underwent such tremendous extension and elaborate sculptural decoration. Close to the Monjas is seen the building known as the Akatzib, or " Writing in the Dark." It faces east, and measures 149ft. by 48ft. The façade is quite plain, and in the centre of the building, which contains in all eighteen rooms, is a solid mass of masonry, to the platform, upon the top of which originally led a great stone stairway, now in ruins. From various indications it would appear that this building was unfinished, and that it was contemplated to build a second range of buildings upon the top of the great central solid core, an enterprise probably stopped by the Toltec conquest of the city. The name " Writing in the Dark " is derived from the presence of some hieroglyphic inscriptions in the southern room, none of which, unfortunately, give the date of the erection of the building; they are difficult to read, as the room is almost in darkness.

Proceeding northward from the Monjas, at a distance of 400ft. stands the building known as the Caracol, from the spiral stairway in its interior, the only structure of this kind found throughout the Maya area, with the single exception of one at Mayapan, now a mere heap of ruins. It is circular in form, and stands upon the upper of two terraces. The lower terrace measures 223ft. by 150ft. Its summit is approached by a broad flight of stone steps, on each side of which, forming a balustrade, is a gigantic stone serpent, their heads resting upon the ground. The upper terrace measures 80ft. by 55ft., and its summit is reached by another flight of sixteen stone steps. Upon the summit of this terrace stands the Caracol, a circular building 22ft. in diameter. One side and a great part of the roof have fallen in. The roof must originally have sloped inwards almost to an apex. At each of the cardinal points is a small door opening into a circular passage 5ft. in diameter, the inner wall of which is pierced by four more doors, placed at intermediate points and opening into a second circular passage 4ft. in diameter. The centre of the building is occupied by a solid core of masonry. The whole structure is in such a tottering state that it is very dangerous to explore it, as the least movement brings down loose stones, and very little would be required to bring the whole structure down on the head of the explorer.

One hundred and fifty yards north-west from the Caracol stands the building known as the Chichanchob, or Red House, one of the most compact and best-preserved buildings amongst the ruins. It stands on a terrace measuring

CHICHANCHOB, OR RED HOUSE, CHICHEN ITZA.

[p. 212

CHICHANCHOB, OR RED HOUSE, CHICHEN ITZA.

[p. 212

62ft. by 55ft., faced with cut stone, the rounded angles being formed by much larger stones. It is approached by a stairway 20ft. wide. The building itself measures 43ft. by 23ft., and possesses three doorways opening into a passage or corridor which runs the whole length of the building. Behind this are three small chambers, each with a door of its own opening into the front corridor. Extending along the whole of the upper part of the back wall of the corridor is a band of hieroglyphics, all in a very bad state of preservation, but not, so far as may be judged by those which can still be deciphered, dealing with time counts.

Not far from the Red House stands one of the most interesting buildings at the ruins, known as the High Priests' Grave. It consists of a stone-faced pyramid approached by a stairway, on each side of which were the extended bodies of gigantic stone serpents, forming a balustrade, their heads, with open jaws and extended tongues, resting upon the ground, their tails containing the Crotalus rattle held upright. The illustration showing an Indian standing beside one of the heads gives a good idea of their size. On the summit of the pyramid stands the ruins of a small stone temple supported on square stone columns. Upon one of these columns is an extremely interesting inscription reading 2 Ahau 18 Xul, and just beneath this Tun 11, 2 Ahau. This means that the contemporaneous date of the temple fell upon a day 2 Ahau, the 19th day of the month Xul in the calendar round, and that in the Initial Series count this fell upon a Tun 11 ending in 2 Ahau. Now the only Initial Series date which would fit in with these data is 11.19.11.0.0, 2 Ahau 18 Xul, which occurs in the year 1350 A.D. The date of the High Priest's Grave consequently is 1350 A.D. A short time ago excavations were made in the stone floor of the temple at the summit of the pyramid, as it sounded hollow beneath. On removing the large slabs, a circular opening was disclosed leading into a stone-lined chamber, which contained a human skeleton with a number of ornaments and some pieces of pottery. On removing the slabs from the floor of this chamber a second one was disclosed beneath it, in which were also found human bones, accompanied by some very beautifully carved ornaments (beads, earrings, gorgets, etc.) of polished green jade. Beneath the second chamber a third one was discovered, also containing human bones, together with three large pearls, contained in a small saucer, which had unfortunately lost all their lustre after nearly five centuries of burial in this damp vault. The bones were in such a poor state of preservation that they crumbled away on being touched, and it was found impossible to preserve them. A tradition existed that this mound was the burial-place of the High Priests of Chichen, and that from the lower chamber an underground passage passed to the Cenote of Sacrifice. No trace could be found of the passage, but it may exist, as working in the confined space and impure air of this lowest chamber—especially excavating, which throws up clouds of impalpable dust—is extremely difficult. I am strongly of opinion that the pyramid was the burial-place, not of the priests, but of the reigning Toltec family of Chichen at the time of its erection, and what leads me to this conclusion is that amongst the débris from the three chambers, which the excavator had left on the floor of the temple as worthless, I discovered the petrous portion of the temporal bone (the most indestructible part of the whole skull) of a child of about five years of age. Now if this had been the mausoleum of the high priests, no child would certainly have been buried there, but if it had been the royal mausoleum, probably all members of the royal family would have been interred within it.

Passing to the north of the Castillo we come to the Ball Court. This consists of two parallel walls each 274ft. long, 30ft. thick, and 120 ft. apart, faced throughout on their inner sides with neatly-cut square blocks of stone. To the north of the Ball Court, and facing the space between the two walls, is a small building standing on a terrace and approached by a flight of steps. It is 39ft. long, and contains but a single chamber. The front is supported by two

SERPENT COLUMNS BY THE SIDE OF THE RUINED STAIRWAY LEADING
UP THE PYRAMID OF THE HIGH PRIEST'S GRAVE, CHICHEN ITZA.

[*p.* 213

CHICHEN ITZA : HIGH PRIEST'S GRAVE, A ROYAL
MAUSOLEUM. DATED COLUMN SHOWING IN-
SCRIPTION COMMENCING 2 AHAU 18 XUL.

[*p.* 213

elaborately sculptured columns, while the back wall is covered from floor to arch with sculptured figures in low relief, now much defaced. At the opposite end of the court stands another building, facing the space between the walls. This is 81ft. long, and contains a single room. It was supported on a series of elaborately sculptured square columns, now in ruins. In the centre of each wall, 20ft. from the ground, and exactly facing each other, was a great stone ring 4ft. in diameter and 13ins. thick, the diameter of the hole being 19in. Round the borders of each are sculptured intertwined serpents. These courts were undoubtedly made for playing the Mexican game of *thlachtli*, which was unknown to the Maya till introduced about 1200 A.D. by the Toltec conquerors, for ball courts are found only at the two cities where Mexican influence was strongest, namely Chichen and Uxmal. The acoustic properties of the Ball Court are very remarkable, though whether they were intentional on the part of the builders it is impossible now to say. The lowest tones of a speaking voice in the North Temple can be heard quite plainly in the South Temple, though nearly an eighth of a mile separates them, and it is perfectly delightful, especially on a fine, calm, moonlight night, to sit in the South Temple and listen to the sweet voice of one of the native Maya girls singing a native song, as it almost appears as if she were standing at one's elbow to sing.

Herrera the historian, in describing Mexican games, gives the following vivid account of the ball game, or, as he calls it, tennis :

" The King took much delight in seeing sport at Ball, which the Spaniards have since prohibited because of the mischief which often happened at it ; and was by them called *Tlachtli*, being like our Tennis. The Ball was made of the gum of a Tree that grows in hot countries, which, having holes made in it, distils great white drops, that soon harden, and being worked and moulded together,

turn as black as pitch. The balls made thereof, though
hard and heavy to the hand, did bound and fly as well as
our Footballs, there being no need to blow them ; nor
did they use chaces, but vy'd to drive the adverse Party
that is to hit the wall, the others were to make good, or
strike it over. They struck it with any part of their
body, as it happened, or they could most conveniently ;
and sometimes he lost that touched it with any other
Part but his Hip, which was looked upon among them
as the greatest dexterity ; and to this effect, that the
ball might rebound the better, they fastened a piece of
stiff leather to their hips. They might strike it every
time it rebounded, which it would do several times one
after another, in so much that it looked as if it had been
alive. They played in parties, so many on a side, for a
load of mantles or what the gamesters could afford, at
so many scores. They also played for gold and leather
work, and sometimes played themselves away as has been
said before. The place where they played was a ground
room, long, narrow and high, but wider above them,
below and higher on the sides than at the ends, and they
kept it very well plastered, and smooth, both the walls
and the floor on the side walls they fixed certain stones,
like those of a mill with a hole quite through the middle,
just as big as the ball, and he that could strike it through
there won the game, and in token of its being an extraordinary success, which rarely happened, he had a right
to the cloaks of all the lookers on, by the ancient custom
and law amongst gamesters, and it was very pleasant to
see, that as soon as ever the ball was in the hole the
standers by took to their heels, running away with all
their might to save their cloaks, laughing and rejoicing,
others scouring after them to secure their cloaks for the
winner, who was obliged to offer some sacrifice to the
idol of the Tennis Court, and the stone through whose
hole the ball had passed. Every Tennis Court was a
temple having two idols, the one of gaming and the other

SERPENT COLUMN ON SUMMIT OF HIGH PRIEST'S GRAVE.

[p. 213

MAYA INDIAN IN RUINED SANCTUARY OF HIGH PRIEST'S GRAVE.

[p. 213

of the ball. On a lucky day, at midnight they performed ceremonies and enchantments on the lower walls and on the midst of the floor, singing certain songs or ballads ; after which a Priest of the Great Temple went with some of their religious men to bless it, he uttered some words, threw the ball about the tennis court four times, and then it was consecrated, and might be played in, but not before. The owner of the Tennis Court, who was always a Lord, never played without making some offering and performing certain ceremonies to the idol of gaming, which shows how superstitious they were, since they had such regard to their idols even in their diversions. Montezuma carry'd the Spaniards to this sport and was well pleased to see them play at it, as also at cards and dice."

This description by Herrera of the game of tennis as played at the court of Montezuma can leave no room for doubt that the game was introduced by the Toltec conquerors from Mexico, as the courts, the rings, and the temples of sacrifice, with a few minor variations, are exactly as he described them. In clearing out the Ball Court enormous quantities of fragments of large clay incense burners, with the figure of a god in high relief done in appliqué on their outer surface, were found. These were buried amongst the dust, vegetal mould, and débris of falling walls, and had evidently been placed there since the abandonment of the Ball Court, probably in early Spanish times, by a few poor remnants of the Maya, who, as we have seen at Chacmool, still carried on the worship of their ancient gods in forests, ruins, and secret places notwithstanding the cruel persecution of the Spaniards, and especially of the priests.

At the southern end of the east wall of the Ball Court stands the temple known as the Casa del Tigres, or Temple of the Jaguars. The lower story consists of a single room with vaulted roof, supported in front by two elaborately sculptured columns. The back wall is covered by very

elaborate sculpture in low relief, showing a procession of
Toltec warriors painted in red, green, and yellow, every
detail of their plumed spears, shields, and other arms, their
elaborate headdresses, their ornamental sandals, and even
their crests or coats of arms which are placed by the side
of each, is brought out with the utmost fidelity, and in the
absence of any other evidence this painted, sculptured wall
would prove conclusively that Chichen was at one time
under Mexican dominion. Unfortunately, a great number
of the stones from this magnificent painted sculpture have
fallen, and we hoped to be able to find them all amongst
the piles of débris which litter the floor of the chamber.
This hope, however, we were compelled to abandon on
finding several of them built into the wall of the church at
Pistè, an Indian village a couple of miles distant from
Chichen. The upper story of this temple is decorated by
a most elaborate cornice, showing a procession of jaguars
following each other all round the temple. The position of
the animals—head forward and front paw upraised as they
creep along—is most realistic. The front of this upper
story is supported by two immense serpent columns, one
of which is shown, with an Indian standing beside it. These
serpents represent Quetzalcoatl, the hero god of the Maya,
whose name signifies the " Feathered Serpent," and on both
the head and the square column which represents the body
of the serpent conventionalised feathers can clearly be seen.
The single room of this upper story is covered with stucco,
upon which are painted in green, yellow, red, blue, and
brown, in a highly realistic manner, scenes from the domestic
and religious life of the inhabitants, warriors with shield
and spear, dancing men, women about their domestic
occupations, dug-out canoes on lake or sea, musicians,
priests offering sacrifices, houses, figures of gods, and
religious ceremonies.

One hundred and twenty yards to the south of the temple
of the Tigers stands the Castillo. The pyramid upon which
it is erected measures at the base 197ft. by 202ft., and stands

THE BALL COURT, CHICHEN ITZA.

[*p.* 214

CHICHEN ITZA, CASA DEL TIGRE,
OR TEMPLE OF THE JAGUARS. [*p.* 217

75ft. high. It is approached by four stairways, the one on the north is 44ft. wide, and those on the other sides 37ft. wide. The northern stairway was evidently the main approach to the temple, as on each side of it are two great serpent balustrades whose heads rest upon the ground. Both stairway and balustrades are now in ruins. The stairway on the west side has been restored, and one can reach the temple on top by means of it, though as the steps are very narrow and high the ascent is not easy, and numerous accidents have happened, especially to half-intoxicated Indians who have rashly undertaken the ascent without assistance. The platform at the summit of the mound measures 64ft. by 61ft., and the temple which stands upon it 49ft. by 43ft. The temple possesses four doors facing the four cardinal points, each with a lintel of carved sapote wood, now a good deal weathered after their 500 years' exposure to the weather, and jambs of stone upon which are sculptured in low relief the figures of warriors with plumed headdresses, ear-plugs, and nose-ornaments. The northern doorway is by far the most important, as from it no doubt started the processions of priests accompanying the victims to the Cenote of Sacrifice. It is 20ft. wide, and divided into three by two elaborately sculptured columns 8ft. 8in. high. It leads into a corridor 40ft. long and 17ft. high, in the rear wall of which is a door giving access to what is undoubtedly the most remarkable room throughout the whole ruins. It measures 19ft. 8in. by 12ft. 9in., and is 17ft. high. Within it are two elaborately carved square stone columns 9ft. 4in. high and 22in. in diameter, and they support great sapote beams also very elaborately carved. Unfortunately, a great part of the surface of these beams has crumbled away from dry rot, and the best preserved piece of carving has been attacked by some vandal with an axe, perhaps a couple of feet of it removed, but a much greater area, of course, completely destroyed. One can only hope that there is in the future a special hell reserved for the type of person who will do this wanton and irreparable damage, and, above all, for those who are unable to leave a ruin or a monument without recording, as conspicuously and in as prominent a place as possible, their name and the date of their visit. From the top of this temple a magnificent view is obtained of all the surrounding country. Far as the eye can reach in every direction nothing is visible but an endless sea of virgin bush, flat as a table, and silent as the grave. To the east of the Castillo is found the curious structure known as the Market-place, or " The Group of a Thousand Columns." It consists of groups of three, four, or five columns standing on long, elevated terraces. Each column is composed of round, flat stone discs, and as their number is approximately a thousand they have been called " The Group of a Thousand Columns." Most of them have fallen, and round all of them quantities of débris have collected, in some cases covering them to a height of 5ft. or 6ft. The group encloses on three sides a quadrangular space of considerable size. It is broken at intervals by temples and pyramids, and within the enclosed space are also a few small temples. There can be but little doubt that these columns formed an arcade surrounding a central market-place, and that at one time they supported a roof, possibly of cement, but more probably of palm leaf, carried on sapodilla beams. The group of columns, with their subsidiary temples, the Castillo, the Ball Court, the Temple of the Tigers, and numerous other smaller temples and pyramids, all stand upon one vast low terrace, which was at one time covered with stucco. The whole group, viewed from the summit, must in the days when the city flourished have presented a perfectly magnificent spectacle.

CHICHEN ITZA.
Castillo from the West

[*p.* 219

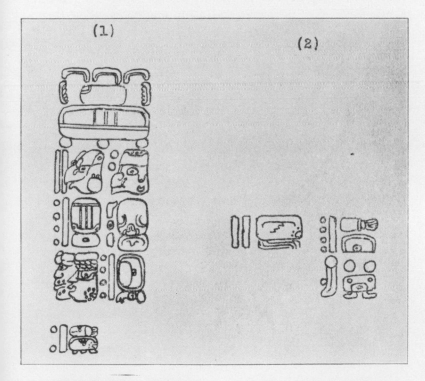

CHICHEN ITZA.   INSCRIPTION ON INITIAL SERIES LINTEL.
(1) UNDER SURFACE OF LINTEL.   (2) FRONT OF LINTEL.

[*p.* 226

CHAPTER XIV

The Cenote of Sacrifice—A Weird Pool—The Most Sacred Spot in Yucatan —Sacrifice to the Rain God of Young Girls—Wonderful Treasure Recovered from the Cenote, with Skeletons of Girls—Objects Found— Wide Distribution Geographically of Art Treasures—Sacrificial " Killing " of Objects before Throwing in the Cenote—First Historical Account of the Ruins—Montejo's Ill-fated Occupation of Chichen Itza—The Spaniards Escape by a Ruse—The Temple of the Initial Series—The Chacmool Temple—The Temple of the Atlantean Figures —The Temple of Two Lintels and its Date—The Temple of the Owl and its Date—Dated Buildings Found Covering the Three Periods of the City.

To the north of the Castillo lies the Cenote of Sacrifice, one of the most interesting sights at the ruins. It is a great circular well nearly 300ft. in diameter, with perpendicular sides descending 70ft. to the surface of the water, which is 70ft. deep. The bottom is covered by a layer of thick brown mud 30ft. deep. It is a gloomy, repellant and mournful place, surrounded by thick bush, where a weird silence always exists, unbroken by the cry of an animal or the song of a bird. The surface of the water is of a dark greenish colour, without a ripple even in the highest wind. A stone dropped in produces a dull booming reverberation around the whole great cavity. It is from this *cenote* that the city took its name Chichen Itza, i.e. Chi, mouth, Chen, well, Itza, of the Itzas, the branch of the Maya who first occupied the site. From the Toltec conquest at the end of the twelfth century it was regarded as the most sacred spot in Yucatan, and hither came devotees from all over the Maya provinces to sacrifice to the god of rain. At ordinary times the sacrifices consisted of the most valuable and beautiful products of the land—jade, turquoise, and gold jewels, stone and wood carvings, weapons of flint and obsidian, beautifully decorated pottery, gold vessels and gold inlaid ornaments, and pieces of incense made from the gum of the white acacia of all sizes and shapes. During times of stress and especially during droughts, which must have been particularly dreaded by the inhabitants of this arid land, the most beautiful of their maidens were sacrificed to the god by being thrown into the *cenote* from the temple on its margin, the remains of which still exist. These sacrifices, till a few years ago, were regarded as merely traditionary ; then systematic dredging of the mud at the bottom of the *cenote* was undertaken, with the most astonishing results. The top layers of mud when brought up by the dredges yielded absolutely nothing, and operations were about to be abandoned, as it was supposed that tradition was, as usual, lying, when a few light-weight Maya artifacts appeared mixed with the mud. The deeper the dredges went the more things were brought to light, amongst them some of the most wonderful products of Maya art, including gold vases, cups, and bowls of all sizes, weapons, implements and ornaments of gold, jade, and obsidian, many thousands of pieces of incense, some contained in the vessels into which they had been poured while liquid, others spherical lumps, exquisitely carved round shields, and throwing sticks of hardwood, covered with a thin layer of gold following the contour of the carving, carved jade plaques, and, perhaps most interesting of all, great numbers of the skeletons of young girls, in a wonderful state of preservation, and coloured a dark brownish yellow by the mud in which they had been buried for so many centuries. Thus, then, the tradition handed down by Landa, Bishop of Yucatan, soon after the conquest, in his writings on the Indians and their customs, proved true in every particular. The reason why no objects were found in the upper layers of mud was probably that these had accumulated during the 400 years which had elapsed since the conquest of Yucatan, when, of course, no sacrifices were made in the *cenote*. From the Castillo—undoubtedly the principal temple during the Toltec occupation—to the *cenote* stretches a straight, broad, elevated road, along which the girl victims marched to the sacrifice. They were accompanied by many priests in procession, and by bands of players on musical instruments, while the people in their thousands lined the sides of this *via dolorosa* and the edge of the *cenote* itself. The victims, who were probably partially drugged, seem to have gone to their fate, not only without fear, but with actual joy, as they believed that they would within a few moments enter their heaven, a joyous, fertile land ruled over by the beneficent rain god, where sickness, sorrow, and death were unknown. If, as occasionally happened, one of the victims survived till midday at the bottom of the *cenote*, either by swimming or clinging to the side, she was rescued, being regarded as a messenger sent back with a communication from the god as to the kind of sacrifices necessary to procure the much-desired rain. One of our principal amusements while at Chichen was picking up pieces of jade from the margins of the *cenote*.

When the dredges came up full of mud from the bottom this was dumped on the ground and felt over by hand, by Indians, under very close supervision. Notwithstanding these precautions, however, a considerable number of gold ornaments, bells, beads, etc., and some beautifully carved jade objects, were stolen. Most unfortunately, nearly all the objects offered as sacrifices to the rain god were " killed " before being thrown into the *cenote* ; that is, the jades were smashed, often into tiny pieces, the flints and obsidians were broken, the gold objects were hammered together into compact masses, and the lumps of incense were partially consumed, frequently with a jade plaque or a few beads on top of them, which were necessarily calcined and blackened.

Thus it happened that thousands of small pieces of jade and turquoise were left amidst the mud on the margins of the *cenote*, and after every heavy fall of rain these are washed out and may be picked up. I found several beads of beautifully polished translucent green jade, one piece with half a Maya glyph of the day Ahau inscribed upon it, and hundreds of fragments of blackened and calcined jade which had been burnt in the incense before being thrown in. Some of the objects sacrificed are evidently heirlooms, which had been handed down in the great Maya families for centuries. This applies particularly to the jade plaques, some of which can, on stylistic grounds, be dated back to the Old Empire, and were at least 600 and perhaps 1,000 years old when they were thrown in.

Turquoise from as far north as the Pueblo region is found side by side with gold ornaments from as far south as Nicaragua. The *cenote* must, therefore, have been regarded with extraordinary veneration both by the Maya and their conquerors, while either the rain god cult extended from the Pueblo region to Nicaragua, or, what is more probable, the Maya carried on commerce with the people of both these regions, and sacrificed the more precious of the objects obtained from them in the *cenote*.

The first historical mention of the ruins of Chichen Itza was when, in 1528, Francisco Montejo penetrated them with his soldiers from the east coast, starting from opposite the Island of Cozumel, shortly after he had been appointed Adelantado, or Governor of Yucatan. Montejo decided to settle at Chichen Itza, as he considered that the strength of the great buildings as fortresses would enable him to defend them against any attack launched by the Indians. Here he made the fatal mistake of dividing his forces, sending one section off under Davila to Chetumal, where the existence of gold had been reported. Though the ruins were probably at this time abandoned, for since the middle of the previous century the Maya had degenerated greatly in every way owing to the constant internecine wars between the small rulers of the peninsula, yet nevertheless there must have been a dense population around Chichen Itza, for we are told that, in making the distribution allowed by the Royal Charter, not less than 2,000 fell to any of the *conquistadores*. The Indians, enraged by the brutal treatment of the Spaniards and the constant drain on their stocks of provisions, at no time much more than sufficient to support themselves, determined to get rid of their oppressors at any cost. With this end in view they first of all cut off the supply of provisions completely, and when the Spaniards sent out foraging parties, these were set upon and exterminated.

Immense numbers of Indians now began to collect round the Spanish fortification, and the Spaniards, seeing that they must either fight or die of starvation, sallied forth and fought the most sanguinary battle ever recorded in Yucatan between the Indians and their conquerors. The Spaniards were victorious, but at a terrible cost, for 150 of their number were killed, and hardly one of the survivors was without a wound.

Surrounded by Indians, unable to obtain food, the situation was obviously untenable, so they had resort to a ruse to make good their escape. One dark night, after the Indians had been well tired out by constant sallies during the day, and were off their guard, the Spaniards tied a dog to the clapper of a bell, and placed some food beside him just out of his reach. The dog, endeavouring to follow them, and later to get at the food, kept the bell constantly going, while the Indians, imagining the Spaniards were sounding an alarm, waited daybreak before attacking them again.

In the meantime the Spaniards had marched quietly out and made their way towards Silan, where the cacique was friendly towards them, and eventually assisted them in making their way to the coast. From that date to the middle of the eighteenth century no further mention is made of Chichen Itza, but the probabilities are that the Indians were left pretty much to themselves, as the accumulation of fragments of incense burners in the Ball Court, sure sign of a return to idolatry and an absence of priestly influence, would tend to show.

PL

We found innumerable smaller temples and other structures at Chichen Itza, many of which possessed some point of special interest, though compared with the larger buildings they were in themselves insignificant.

Of these the most important was the Temple of the Initial Series. Situated a considerable distance to the south of the *hacienda*, this small ruined temple stands on a low pyramid, and forming one of its entrances are two Atlantean figures supporting a stone lintel, upon the front of which is sculptured in low relief the Initial Series 10.2.9.1.9. 9 Muluc 7 Zac, falling within the year 619 A.D. On the under surface of the lintel is sculptured a Tun 10 ending on a day 2 Ahau, which brings the contemporaneous date of this lintel to 10.2.10.0.0. 2 Ahau 13 Chen, falling within the year 620 A.D. This, however, it must be understood, is the contemporaneous date of the lintel only; the temple itself belongs to a much later period, for as the Atlantean figures—a purely Mexican innovation—show, it was not built till after the Toltec invasion about 1200 A.D. It follows, therefore, that the lintel must have been taken from an old Maya temple and reused in its present situation by the conquerors, without altering its original date. Had it not been supported on Atlantean columns, this lintel would undoubtedly have been regarded as dating the temple of which it forms part.

The Initial Series is extremely interesting, partly because it is the earliest one of the only three known in Yucatan, and partly because it fixes, without a shadow of a doubt, the earliest Maya occupation of the city.

Situated a short distance to the north-east of the Castillo is what is known as the Chacmool Temple. A few years ago, when the substructure upon which this temple stood was excavated, there was brought to light a gigantic human figure in a reclining position, the arms pressed to the sides, legs drawn up, and head looking backward over the shoulder, precisely similar in every respect to the one found at Chacmool, already described. Since then numbers of these figures

CHACMOOL STATUE, FROM ONE OF SMALLER TEMPLES, CHICHEN ITZA.

[p. 226

UXMAL : HOUSE OF THE ADIVINO.

[p. 248

have been discovered at the ruins, and there can be no doubt but that they were introduced by the Toltecs, and probably worshipped by them as gods.

The temple of the Atlantean Figures is situated just north of the Market-Place. It is a square building standing on a high stone-faced pyramid, both now in a very ruined condition. In the small back room as sanctuary of the temple are a number of Atlantean figures such as are found in great quantities all over the city. Here the use to which they were originally put is well shown, for four of them support a large rectangular slab of stone, evidently used as an altar, upon one side of the sanctuary, while on the opposite side a similar altar has fallen, leaving the Atlantean figures and top scattered on the floor. This temple is known locally as the Temple of the 'Mesas or tables, from the resemblance of these altars to low stone tables.

The Temple of the Two Lintels is interesting in that it contains one of the only four dates found at Chichen Itza. The inscription shown in the illustration reads 9 Eznab, a day, eleven, the month Yax, occurring in a Tun 13 ; which may be interpreted as the calendar round date 9 Eznab, 11 Yax, occurring in a Tun 13, and corresponding to the Initial Series date 13.7.12.16.18.9 Eznab 11 Yax, falling within the year 1107 A.D., which may be regarded as the contemporaneous date of this little temple. The tun sign given in this inscription is a winged Cauac, the meaning of which we discovered from data collected on this trip, a discovery which has helped immensely in the decipherment of the glyphs throughout the whole peninsula.

From a small structure situated quite close to the Temple of the Initial Series, and known as the Temple of the Owl because the head of that bird is sculptured upon it in several places, was taken a capstone, upon which was painted 1 Ahau ending a Tun 13, this would correspond with the Initial Series date 12.2.13.0.0. 1 Ahau, 18 Ceh, falling within the year 1411 A.D.

We had now found dated monuments corresponding to the three periods of occupancy of the city. The Initial Series date on the Temple of the Initial Series—620 A.D.—goes back to the first Maya settlement after the hegira from the Old Empire. The Temple of Two Lintels, 1107 A.D., corresponds to the Great Period, between 1000 and 1200 A.D., when the League of Mayapan existed.

The High Priest's Grave, 1350 A.D., and the Temple of the Owl, 1411 A.D., correspond to the latest or Toltec period of the city.

A small temple situated close to the Temple of the Owl is of interest, as from the inner walls of two of the rooms project gigantic phalli, the only indication throughout the whole city that phallic worship was ever practised by the Maya.

To archæologists used to exploring ancient Maya cities two facts stand out as remarkable at Chichen Itza—the absence of small burial-mounds and of potsherds. Usually Maya sites are covered with potsherds, and such small articles as clay beads and spindle whorls, arrow-heads, and pieces of obsidian knives, flint hammerstones and scrapers, and similar comparatively valueless indestructible objects.

At Chichen Itza, however, nothing of this kind is found, and even potsherds are extremely rare. One reason possibly is that a very durable kind of cement used in the ruins was composed largely of broken-up potsherds, most of which may have been collected and used for this purpose. This would not, however, account for the complete absence of all small artifacts so common at most other Maya sites.

The city was occupied for nearly 1,000 years, and at one time its population was probably in the neighbourhood of 250,000, so that at a very moderate computation at least one million persons must have been buried in and around it, from the date of its foundation on to the Spanish conquest, including kings, priests, and nobles, and yet, with the exception of the High Priest's Grave and one other sepulchral temple, no burials have been found up to now.

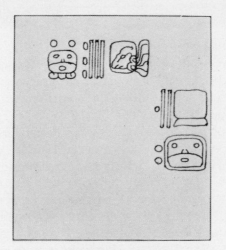

CHICHEN ITZA.
Text from High Priest's grave. Above 2 Ahau 18 Xul;
below Tun 11, 2 Ahau.

[p. 213

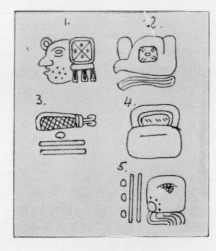

CHICHEN ITZA.
Temple of the two lintels.

1. 9 Eznab.   2. "A Day."
3. Eleven.   4. Month Yax.
        5. Occurring in Tun 13
or 11.7.12.16.18., 9 Eznab 11 Yax or 1107 A.D

[p. 227

The small mounds in the neighbourhood of the city are not, as one might expect, sepulchral, but almost invariably formed substructures for small temples. What, then, did the inhabitants do with their dead?

All round the city are found quarries, mostly shallow excavations in the limestone, from which had been taken the vast quantities of stone required for the construction of the buildings. In many of these quarries great blocks of stone still remain, some of them partially squared, just as they had been left by the builders.

It is difficult to form a true conception of the extent of the city. We found ruins three miles to the north of the *cenote* and a couple of miles to the south of old Chichen, while paved roadways branch out to ruins to the east of the city. All except the few central buildings are buried in dense bush, and till this is cleared and burnt it is impossible to say for how many miles the ruins extend in each direction.

We had thoroughly enjoyed our stay at the ruins, our only regret being that we could not remain longer, but this was out of the question, and it will require years of systematic work in clearing and excavation to bring all its hidden secrets to light.

We found *garapatas*, or ticks, the most troublesome pest at Chichen, where they abound in every part of the bush, and vary in size from a large split pea to a small pin's head. On returning from work in the ruins at dusk we always had a rub down with gasoline and afterwards a good bath with soap and water, thus ensuring a peaceful night. Indeed, if we got badly covered with ticks during the morning's work we often had to resort to a midday rub down and bath as well. One horrible pest seems to be peculiar to this locality, as I have never seen it in any other part of Central America. This is a beetle about $1\frac{1}{4}$in. in length, with a long proboscis, which it digs into one's skin. It usually attacks early in the morning, and fortunately gives warning of its approach with a loud booming noise, but as it is extraordinarily quick one is not always able to avoid its attack, even when duly warned. The puncture inflicted does not itch or give any trouble for the first twenty-four hours, but after that for two or three days it swells to a painful lump, which itches intolerably, and may not completely disappear for several weeks, and may even suppurate.

STONE ALTAR SUPPORTED ON ATLANTEAN COLUMNS, CHICHEN ITZA.

[p. 227

STELE REPRESENTING TWO NATIVES CLAD IN LOIN
CLOTHS, CARRYING THE CARCASS OF A DEER SLUNG
ON A POLE.

[p. 227

CHAPTER XV

ON Saturday, March 17th, we left Chichen early in the
morning on horseback, sending our luggage on with Muddy
by volan for Dzitas.   It came on to pour with rain when
we had gone about eight miles, and for the last half of the
journey never let up, so that we arrived like drowned rats.
We were given the Cabildo, or combined Court House,
Police Station, and Lock-Up, to sleep in ; a fine, large, airy
clean, whitewashed room, with an earth floor, where we
were very glad to get into dry clothes and hang up our
hammocks. Tea and food were our first thought after
changing—both difficult to obtain, as all the shops close
every day at noon by order of the Municipality.   The tea
we managed to obtain by giving a Turk two dollars gold to
open his store and sell us ¼lb., but as we heard he was fined
ten dollars for doing so it cannot have been a very profitable

transaction. Tortillas, sponge cakes, eggs, and *longanis*, or native sausage, Muddy managed to procure by a house-to-house tour, so we did not do so badly. A bugle and drum reposed in the corner of the Cabildo, and, knowing by bitter experience the horrible custom in all Yucatecan villages, where a few soldiers are stationed, of sounding révéille at cock crow every morning, and prolonging the agony for a quarter of an hour, we carefully wet the drum-heads and poured water into the bugle. To no purpose, however, as next morning before five we were awakened by the well-known racket right outside the door of the Cabildo. It was a trifle spluttering at first, and the bugler was using horrible language in Maya, while the drum was decidedly flat, but the volume of noise was unimpaired, and I think we got an extra long performance.

Next morning the stores were open, and we bought some provisions from a tiny shop next the Cabildo, outside which were collected several litigants waiting till we had finished early tea for the Court to open. At breakfast-time the Judge, who kept the little store where we bought our provisions, very courteously adjourned Court till we had finished, when we discovered it was time for us to get on to the railway-station.

The more one sees of Yucatan, the more it reminds one of Ireland ; the same soft, fragrant, indescribable atmosphere found nowhere else in the world, the same straggling villages with their whitewashed thatched cabins, with the same pig, the mainstay of the family, running in and out at will, and the same kitchen midden under the window ; the same happy-go-lucky, kind-hearted, hospitable, super-stitious, irresponsible people, equally ready for a row or a spree, hating the one the Mexican, the other the Sassenach with a bitter, hereditary racial hatred.

From Dzitas we took train to Ticul, another large village, whose inhabitants are nearly all Indians and Mestizos. The national flag was flying half mast high on our arrival, and on enquiring the reason we were informed that it was in

mourning for the anniversary of General Alvorado's entrance to Yucatan four years previously,when the Yucatecans
were, after a bitter lesson, subjected to the Carranza Government.   Surely nowhere else but in the Emerald Isle could
the conqueror be thus insulted publicly without after-
thoughts of reprisals !   But Mexico now justly regards
Yucatan as the goose which lays the golden eggs, whose
laying abilities are not to be lightly interfered with.

We slept that night at Ticul, where, as there is nothing
approaching an hotel, we were glad to be able to hire hammocks in the house of a merchant from whom we had hired
a " Fotingo " to take us to the ranch of Tabi next day.
Our host was an enormously stout man, and at the usual
Yacatecan supper of chicken, beans, eggs, tomatoes, chili,
and tortillas entertained as with the half-dozen sentences
in English of which he was the master.   He was like all
Yucatecans, extremely anxious to learn the language, but
as an opportunity of conversing with a citizen of the U.S.A.
only occurred about once a year, while I was probably the
first Englishman he had encountered, his progress was
naturally slow.   The whole family sat around at the lesson,
and gave us some useful hints in Maya pronunciation in
return.

They were all very stout, and soon after we had retired
to our hammocks all commenced to snore in different keys;
though doubtless, being used to each other's little idio-
syncrasies, none of them apparently kept the others awake.
For me, however, the noise rendered sleep impossible, and
though I had no compunction in waking our host, I hesitated
to enter the señorita's room for that purpose, lest my motives
be misunderstood, so retired with a small cot and rug to the
patio, or yard, to keep the house dog company, though even
his reception was far from friendly.

We made a very early start next morning with the
" Fotingo," in which the driver engaged to take us as near
as the auto could go to the mouth of the great cave of Loltun.
From this point we would walk to the cave, while he
QL

went on to the ranch at Tabi, where we were to join him later.

Arrived at the point, Morley, Held, myself, and Muddy started with a guide for the cave, which we were assured was but three short kilometres away. After walking over a rocky road for nearly an hour in the broiling sun we thought we must be approaching our destination, and, on asking the guide, were told : " *Pues, señor, no es mas que una legua* "—" Well, sir, it's not over a league ! "

In another forty minutes, however, we reached the mouth of the cave, a comparatively small and not very impressive-looking hole in the ground. Entering, we found ourselves in a sloping passage, scrambling down which, we arrived at a ledge from which a ladder, constructed of two tree-trunks, having steppers tied on with strands of liana, led to the floor of the cave. It proved to be a vast, rock-strewn chamber, with many stalactites hanging from the lofty roof, the floor covered by a layer of soft brown earth. From the chamber, at various levels, innumerable passages led away in all directions, some low, narrow tunnels only large enough to squeeze through on all fours, others vast galleries, lofty and spacious as the nave of a cathedral.

We followed one of the largest, and shortly came to another great rock-strewn chamber, with an opening to the outer world through its roof, perhaps 40ft. overhead, partly obscured by an exquisite tracery of creeping vines covered with flowers and leaves. The name of the cave—" Loltun," or " Flower Stone "—may have been derived from these, or possibly from the fancied resemblance of some of the stalactitic formations to flowers.

We passed numerous petroglyphs, both on the walls of the cave and on the rock outcropping from the floor. They were, however, very roughly executed—mostly geometrical devices, as circles, lines, and squares, with a few crude human figures. At frequent intervals basins for the accumulation of the constantly dripping water have been cut in the rock formation, and these having in the course of centuries become encrusted with lime salts, now present the appearance of great smooth monolithic fonts, ever full of ice-cold water to refresh the weary traveller.

The earth covering the floor of the cave, near the overhead openings, is full of relics of the ancients—pottery, beads, potsherds, fragments of idols, charcoal, pieces of bone, bone needles and borers, malacates or spindle whorles, broken grindstones, and a great variety of indestructible débris. It is evident that these rooms, being light and dry, were at one time occupied by the former inhabitants; indeed, it is probable that those unfortunate Indians who fled from their Spanish conquerors took refuge in this vast catacomb, from which a whole army corps could never have dislodged them.

Away from the skylights the cave is pitch dark, and the atmosphere chill, musty, and oppressive. The extent of the whole subterraneous system must be enormous, as on one occasion a party well equipped with torches, and leaving a thread track behind to guide their return, travelled for two days on one of the main galleries without finding an end to it.

In a chamber under an opening into the cave about a mile from the one by which we first descended is the only date discovered up to the present, carved very plainly on the rock. This consists of a 3 Ahau, signifying that it was executed at the end of Katun 3 Ahau, which might correspond to either of the two dates 12.1.0.0.0. 3 Ahau, 18 Kayab (that is, 1379 A.D.), or to 11.8.0.0.0. 3 Ahau, 18 Chen (that is, 1123 A.D.).

It is practically impossible to say which date should be accepted as contemporaneous, as no doubt the cave was well known to the natives centuries before the earlier and after the later.

We did not explore any of the innumerable galleries very far, as, knowing well their vast extent, we were afraid of getting lost. Moreover, though the skylights are numerous, they are for the most part mere holes in the roof, with no means of access from below, those by which it is possible to leave or enter the cave being few, and situated miles apart. Indeed, wandering in these interminable pitch-dark passages and galleries one would be far more likely to fall into a pot-hole or crevasse than to stumble on to an exit leading to the open air.

There is a tradition handed down amongst the modern Indians that during one of the innumerable internecine wars amongst the Maya which followed the breaking-up of the central authority in Mayapan, the inhabitants of a certain village were driven to take refuge in this cave by a band of their enemies, who pursued them even into this last refuge, and that of neither pursued nor pursuers was any trace ever again seen, not a single survivor returning to tell the fate of the rest. Some believe that all fell over a precipice in one of the unexplored galleries ; others that all lost their way and died of starvation ; and others, again, that all were poisoned by irrespirable gasses. Whatever their fate, the possibility of encountering at any turn several hundred rag-clad skeletons, shrouded in the impalpable dust of centuries, does not detract from the eerie feeling one experiences in traversing these dark and silent galleries.

On emerging from the cave, we made our way to the *hacienda* of Tabi, a magnificent stone palace with a broad corridor 300ft. long, from which opened huge, cool, spacious rooms. It was flanked by a fine church, while at the back were vast stone corrals full of cattle, horses, and mules. The village occupied by the labourers was close to the house, but here—as elsewhere in Yucatan—the houses were falling into ruins, and the peons had deserted the *rancho* for better-paid work, or to start small *fincas*, or farms, of their own. The sugar mills and distillery, amongst the finest in Yucatan, were closed—in fact, work on the *hacienda* was confined almost exclusively to stock-raising.

We were entertained by the major-domo with the usual lavish hospitality of the country, and dined with him and several of his staff, who having a Chinese cook, and a free run on the resources of the *rancho's* gardens, stockyards, and hen-houses, did themselves uncommonly well. We contributed as our quota to the feast a few small luxuries in tins and bottles, which even in Merida were exceedingly difficult to procure.

Amongst the other luxuries of the *rancho* was an enormous stone tank, with several feet of water in it, fed by guttering from the roof, in which one could not only enjoy a bath, but a fair imitation of a swim, and where, if a warm bath were desired, it was only necessary to wait until late afternoon, when the sun had heated the water to about blood heat.

Even at this paradise amongst *ranchos*, however, we were not to enjoy a peaceful night, for soon after we had retired to our hammocks pandemonium broke loose amongst the horses in the corral, and an equine battle royal raged, which must have lasted a couple of hours. The squealing, neighing, and shrieking of the animals, punctuated by the drum-like thud of hoofs on ribs, the bellowing of the cattle in the neighbouring corrals, the shouting and swearing of the stockmen trying to quiet the disturbance, combined to produce a terrific din, while a great bunch of milling animals dimly visible by the light of flaring torches, made a scene difficult to describe, and impossible to sleep through. At last things quieted down gradually, but next morning the effects of the battle were plainly visible in the form of two dead stallions lying side by side in one of the corrals, the earth floor of which, torn up by their hoofs, resembled a ploughed field, their carcases were already being fought over by a pack of great mangy, half-savage dogs, and flocks of sopilotes, or black vultures, tearing the skin and flesh to get at the entrails.

Near the gate of the great *patio*, or yard, which surrounds the *hacienda*, is a very remarkable stele representing two Indians clad only in loin cloths, carrying, slung on a pole, the carcase of a deer, above which, on a rounded arch of stone, is sculptured a row of hieroglyphics, now so weather-worn as to be completely indecipherable. This stele is quite unique in the nature of the event recorded, the free and unconventional treatment of the subject, and the fact that the figures are not merely executed in relief upon the face of the great flat stone, but perforations have been made in it following the main outlines. The whole, in fact, shows strong Spanish artistic influence, and it would almost seem as if it had been executed after the conquest by Indians, who, coming in contact with the Spaniards, had absorbed some of their notions of art. The hieroglyphics at the top probably described the nature of the event depicted below. Some Goth, as may be seen, has recently given the whole a coat of limewash in two colours.

This stele, with several other inscribed stones about the *hacienda*, was taken from ruins in the vicinity, which have been completely torn down to build the house, church, labourers' homes, and corrals, so that nothing remains now but mounds of débris.

Early next morning we started in the " Fotingo " for the ruins of Kabah, over a road which had never before been negotiated by a motor-car, and which everyone at the *rancho* warned us was impassable. Our impedimenta were even more extensive than usual, as in addition to cots, bedding, food, cooking utensils, photographic apparatus, suit-cases, etc., which constituted our normal outfit, we had to carry a good supply of water in demijohns, as none was to be procured at Kabah. By dint of walking most of the way, removing the largest rocks from the road, and pushing the car up the worst rocky ridges, we managed to cover the five miles or so to the *rancho* of Santa Ana in about two hours. Here we stopped for a rest, and the major-domo had a large bag of oranges picked for us from a very prolific little orange-grove in the *rancho*. Like most of the other *haciendas* we had seen in Yucatan, this showed signs of having once been a fine, prosperous estate, now gradually undergoing a process of slow degeneration.

From Santa Ana to Kabah the going was better, and we passed innumerable ruins, plainly visible on each side of the road through the thin bush which surrounded them. These were mounds, stone-faced pyramids, and fallen temples, but all in a very dilapidated condition, nor did we anywhere come across a large aggregation of ruined buildings denoting a former city site.

The ruins of Kabah are buried in a dense growth of low, thick bush, with a few narrow, indistinct paths, used by the Indians, passing through it here and there. The most conspicuous object is a great pyramid situated in the centre of the ruins, 60 yds. in diameter at the base, and 80ft. high. It had originally been faced with cut stone, and the summit reached by stone stairways like the Castillo at Chichen Itza and the House of the Dwarf at Uxmal. These had now, however, completely fallen away, leaving only a vast mound of ruins covered with bush, and showing traces of ruined buildings only at the summit. From the top a magnificent view was obtained over the whole surrounding country, bounded, except to the west, by ranges of low hills, and showing the grey bleached walls or ruins visible in all directions through the parched green of the low scrub.

Wherever one goes in Yucatan ruins are found in extraordinary abundance ; indeed, one cannot help realising that the whole country in the days of its magnificence must have been literally so covered with cities, both large and small, that their suburbs almost joined each other, leaving hardly a square mile which did not contain a stone palace or temple, round which clustered the thatched huts of the workers. The whole country, as one of the *conquistadores* puts it, resembled a garden.

A quarter of a mile to the east of this pyramid is a great stone-faced terrace approached by a flight of steps 20ft. high. Upon this terrace are the ruins of many buildings, one of which measured 107ft. by 106ft. at the base, and rose to three stories, each smaller than the one beneath it. The summit was approached by a broad stone stairway supported on the half of a Maya arch, springing from the ground, and leaning against the wall of the building. We used one of the small stone-faced rooms of the lower story as a store-room and the arched space beneath the stairway as a kitchen, for being open at both ends, there was always a good draught passing through to carry off the pungent wood smoke.

On the opposite side of the platform stood a long building approached by a broad, steep flight of stone steps, and possessing a most elaborately decorated façade, the sculpture reaching from the platform to the roof of the building. This resembled very closely the façades of the *Iglesia* and part of the Monjas at Chichen Itza, and consisted of reproductions of the face of the long-nosed god in rows, one above the other. The nose resembles an elephant's trunk, the teeth are square and jagged, and the pupils of the eyes are formed of round stone tenoned in, most of which have now fallen from the hollow eye-sockets.

Two somewhat remarkable stone heads found among the ruins are seen resting in the lower cornice of this façade.

The interior of the building contained a front and back row of apartments, the front measuring 27ft. by 10ft. 6in. ; the back 27ft. by 10ft. The inner room is on a higher level than the outer, and is approached by two stone steps. In front of this building is a square structure discovered by Stephens, upon some of the stones of which he describes hieroglyphics. This was almost completely covered by earth, and we had to dig the stones out very carefully one at a time.

The only intelligible glyphs we found were an Imix ⊕ repeated several times, and an Ahau ⊕ ; both, however, without numerical coefficients. It would appear that the inscription had gone all round the structure, and that the stones containing it had got out of their proper places.

As it would have required much more time than we had at

KABAH : THE DOOR ON THE RIGHT IS THE ENTRANCE TO OUR
SITTING-ROOM.

[*p.* 240

KABAH : FAÇADE ORNAMENTED WITH FACES OF THE LONG NOSED GOD.

Two of these are shown, the left eye of the face on the left side
still retaining in situ the stone which served as the pupil.   Beneath
these are seen two stone heads dug from the ruins.

[*p.* 240

our disposal to excavate this building thoroughly, find all the stones, put them in their proper sequence, and decipher the inscription, we buried them again for future reference on our next visit to the ruins.

Just to the south-west of the central pyramid stands a great solitary arch with a span of 14ft. It is placed upon a slight elevation, and, as it is quite unconnected with any other building, was no doubt intended as a triumphal arch to commemorate some victory. It is constructed on the cantilever principle, and the upper part has fallen, but it is nevertheless a very imposing structure, and the span is unusually large for an arch of this type.

To the south-west of the central pyramid is a great stone-faced terrace 300yds. long by 30yds. wide, buried in the dense bush, upon which stand the ruins of two buildings. The first, 217ft. long, with seven openings in front, and what had at one time been a very elaborately sculptured façade, is now almost completely in ruins.

The second building was 142ft. long, and consisted of two stories, the upper set back from the lower and approached by a great arched stone stairway.

At the time of Stephen's visit in 1841 the lintels of these doors, cut from sapodilla wood, were all *in situ*, and in fairly good preservation ; now throughout the whole ruin we did not find a single wooden lintel ; all had been torn down, in some case bringing with them the buildings to which they belonged, and adding very materially to the rapidity with which this once great city has fallen into ruins.

Stephens himself is not to be absolved of blame in the matter, as from the second of the buildings on this terrace he removed a beautiful carved sapodilla lintel in three pieces, the vast gap which has been left in the process still bearing mute and pathetic witness to this act of vandalism, now seventy-seven years old. The lintel, which was removed to New York, was unfortunately destoyed by fire, with a great part of the large collection made by Stephens, soon after its arrival in the U.S.A.

Close to the great terrace Stevens found a comparatively small stone building with sculptured figures on the doorjambs, facing each other, representing small kneeling figures in front of large, elaborately clad warriors, beneath each of which was a row of hieroglyphics in excellent preservation.

We looked forward to finding at least a period ending date amongst these, by which we might accurately date the city, and our disappointment was great at finding the building a mere heap of great stones, with the jambs probably buried beneath hundreds of tons of rubbish, and utterly beyond our power to disinter with the time and labour at our disposal.

Kabah was probably a purely Maya city, as no Chacmools, serpent columns, Atlantean figures, or other indications of Toltec culture are to be found anywhere within it, whereas the Maya long-nosed god is very conspicuous on the façades of the temples. Stylistically it is extremely like the Monjas at Chichen Itza, and was probably erected within a few years of that building—that is, during the Maya renaissance between 1000 and 1200 A.D.

We slept in the open during our stay at Kabah, without even a mosquito net, and though on one occasion I was annoyed by a vampire bat hovering around my head, none of us were attacked by these pests while asleep.

These are, from the explorers' point of view, thoroughly delightful ruins to visit, as there are neither mosquitoes by night nor ticks by day to annoy one. The great drawback is the lack of water, for the nearest supply is three miles away, and has to be brought in on the back of an Indian, who received four dollars gold per day, and refused to make more than a single trip daily, carrying quite a small waterjar. We had to dispense with personal ablutions entirely, and towards the end of our stay it got to be a question of washing the plates or going without tea; but the plates seemed to do very nicely with a scour from a palm leaf, supplemented by a polish from a piece of newspaper, whereas tea, after our exertions in the sun, was absolutely indispensable. We were greatly puzzled as to how the ancient inhabitants, who must have been numbered by tens of thousands, obtained their water-supply, till we observed in the stone-paved courts, in front of some of the temples, openings nearly blocked up, leading to large, cement-lined, subterraneous water cisterns beneath the courtyards, the drainage from which must have filled them very rapidly.

CHAPTER XVI

Visit to Uxmal, the City of the Tutul Xiu—The Casa del Gobernador—
We Take Up our Abode on the Uppermost Terrace—A Romantic
Spot—Mausoleum of the former Kings of Uxmal—Graffiti on one of
the Walls—Removal of the Sapodilla Lintels from the Casa del
Gobernador—The House of the Dwarf—Uxmal Visited by Padre
Cogolludo—The Ruins Still Venerated by Modern Indians—Casa de
las Monjas—Description of the Building—Inscription in One of the
Rooms—Painted and Dated Capstone—Other Capstones on which
We Could Not Read the Dates—Stele with Time Count Engraved
upon It—The Ball Court—Inscribed Rings—Probably Record the
Shifting of the Month Coefficient by One Day—Accounts of the
Unhealthiness of the Ruins Not Justified—Held's Unpleasant Job
of Copying the Capstones—Visit from Indian Pilgrims—Two Pretty
Girls—An Aboriginal American Royal Family—End of our Work in
Yucatan—What We had Accomplished During the Trip.

ON Friday, the 22nd, we returned to Tabi, where we spent
the night, proceeding next day by an excellent road to the
ruins of Uxmal.   This, owing to its proximity to Merida,
and the facility of reaching it, is probably the best known
and most frequently visited ruined city in Yucatan.   In the
number of its buildings, the beauty of its architecture and
sculpture, and the area which it covers, it is second only to
Chichen Itza.   It was the capital city of the Tutul Xiu, a
branch of the Maya, and from 1000 to 1200 A.D. formed,
with Chichen Itza and Mayapan, the third member of the
Triple Alliance.   After the conquest of Mayapan its inhabitants, for some unknown reason, deserted it *en masse*, and
retired to the insignificant provincial city of Mani, never
again returning to the magnificent palaces, temples, and
public buildings which must have cost them such a tremendous outlay in time and labour.

On arriving at the ruins we took up our quarters in the

KABAH : FACADE OF ONE OF THE MAIN TEMPLE.

[p. 240

UXMAL : WEST RANGE OF MONJAS.

[p. 249

UXMAL : MONJAS LOOKING TOWARDS CASA DEL ADIVINO, WHICH
IS SEEN IN THE BACKGROUND.

[p. 250

building known as the Casa del Gobernador, or House of the Governor, one of the finest aboriginal buildings on the American continent. The structure itself is 322ft. long by 39ft. broad. It contains twenty-four rooms in all, which are divided by a wall running the whole length of the building into a front and back range. The front façade is divided into an upper and lower zone by a projecting cornice, the lower being quite plain, the upper most elaborately decorated by complicated sculptural devices, amongst which are seen the head of the long-nosed god, seated human figures, probably rulers or high priests of the city, geometrical devices, together with a band of glyphs representing constellations over the main doorway. There are eleven doorways in this façade opening into the front range of rooms, the back rooms being reached by doors opening from the front range or from the sides, as the back wall is quite plain and undecorated, and possesses no doorways. The rooms are ceiled by the corbel arch, and the roof is flat.

This building stands upon the topmost of three great stone terraces, the lowest 575ft. long and 3ft. high, the second 545ft. long and 20ft. high, and the uppermost, upon which the building stands, 365ft. long by 19ft. high. The first terrace is approached from the ground level by an inclined plane, while the third terrace is approached from the second by a broad stone stairway, on the side opposite the inclined plane.

We spread our cots on the uppermost terrace, and took up our residence here during our three-day sojourn at the ruins. It afforded a cool and airy lodging, free from bush and its attendant ticks and red bug, while the open doors of the palace rooms presented a desirable retreat in case of rain, and a magnificent view over the whole of the ruined city was always before our eyes from this lofty perch.

We often sat up long into the night discussing our day's work and discoveries, entranced by the spectacle spread out before us, bathed in a flood of tropical moonlight, the grey ruins standing out ghostlike from the darker background of shadowy, mysterious bush, and the dead silence of the night broken only by the murmur of our own hushed voices, the mournful note of the nightjar, or the distant scream of a jaguar seeking his supper in the surrounding forest.

A short time before coming to Yucatan I had purchased two magnificent stucco heads, painted red, white, and black in the devices used by the aborigines to decorate their faces, upon which were modelled the ear, nose, lip, and forehead ornaments used by them. These were taken from a vault below the floor of one of the back chambers of the Casa del Gobernador, and probably represented the king of the city and his queen, who had been buried there, as they were undoubtedly intended as portraits of a man and a woman. We saw the closed-in opening of this vault, and it seems probable that each of the other rooms contains beneath it a sepulchral chamber, in which are interred the remains of a king or high priest, with his jewels and orna-ments, accompanied by his life-sized statue, showing his official dress moulded in stucco, and painted in the original colours, for the two heads which I purchased were said to have been broken from statues of this descripton. This opened up wonderful possibilities in the excavation of the floors of the chambers, though the fate of the original explorer was not encouraging, as we heard that he had been fined 5,000 Mexican dollars for his pains, and the guardians of the ruins, who are always in evidence, keep an uncommonly close watch on all strangers visiting them.

Seated over the actual burial-places of the former kings and priests of the city, we could, on these hushed moonlit nights, almost visualise life as it was lived there some eight or nine centuries ago, for the palace dated back to the days of the Triple Alliance. We saw again the stately houses of the nobles restored to their pristine magnificence by the dim light of the moon, gorgeously attired men and beautiful women moving about in the stone courtyards.

The great Temple of the Adivino, perched just opposite to us on its lofty pyramid, a procession of white-robed priests leading a sacrificial victim up the steep terraced sides, while packed thousands of the common people pressed around the base, waiting for the headless body to be rolled down the stairway to them ; these same commons toiling and sweating under the scorching sun, all day and every day, on the erection of the vast palaces and temples, and to supply the wants of the caciques and priests who ruled them with the iron rod of superstition ; the courtyard of the monastery, which lay just beneath us, full of grave monks and minor priests, occupied with their daily devotions and sacrifices, the painting of their religious and astronomical manuscripts, and probably the treatment of the sick ; and lastly the Halach Uinic, or king himself, almost a god to his people, palanquin borne, surrounded by a richly dressed throng of minor chiefs and soldiers ascending by the great stairway to his palace, now occupied by three members of an alien race. These visions invariably faded as the moonbeams which induced them gave place to the chilly wind of early dawn, reminding us that it was long past time for sleep if we were to do any work that day.

In one of the front rooms, deeply scratched on the plaster of the front wall, we found Maya graffiti, one of which is shown in the illustration. The ear-plugs, elaborate feather headdress, and sandals, are all typically Maya, and it was probably the work of some Indian during the sixteenth or seventeenth centuries, as we know from the Padre Cogolludo that for at least a century after the conquest they were in the habit of returning secretly to Uxmal to burn incense to and worship their ancient gods. If only the artist who drew these graffiti had taken the trouble to write beneath them the current katun and calendar round date, as well as the date in our era, with all of which he must have been quite familiar, what a vast amount of controversy he would have saved amongst Maya archæologists.

The lintels of these doors were originally of sapodilla

wood, but have unfortunately all been removed within the last century, after withstanding for nearly 1,000 years the climate of Yucatan, so destructive to all woody material. Their removal has caused many of the doorways to partly fall in, and has hastened the decay of the ruins by centuries. Here again Stephens was the chief offender, as he shamelessly admits having removed the only carved sapodilla lintel from Uxmal for transport to the U.S.A., where it met with the same fate as the Kabah wood carving, and was destroyed by fire.

The Casa del Adivino, or House of the Diviner, sometimes known as the House of the Dwarf, stands upon a great stone-faced pyramid 88ft. high, and measuring 235ft. by 155ft. at the base. The house or temple itself is long and narrow, 72ft. in length by only 12ft. in breadth, and is divided into three small rooms, which do not communicate with each other. The outside is badly ruined, but still retains a façade elaborately ornamented by complicated stone sculptures, chiefly geometrical in character.

The temple is surrounded by a platform 5ft. wide, approached on the east side, from the ground, by a great stone stairway 70ft. wide, containing ninety narrow, high steps. On the west side, the one shown in the illustration, 60ft. up the side of the mound, a door opens upon a stone step leading to a small two-roomed temple, quite undecorated. This is approached by a flight of stone stairs from the ground level, which are now completely in ruins. They were supported upon a great corbel arch resting against the side of the sub-structure, and, when whole, must have presented a very imposing appearance.

Padre Cogolludo visited Uxmal one hundred years after its conquest, and ascended the House of the Dwarf by the great stairway on its eastern side, where he says that " on attempting to descend, his sight failed him and he was in some danger." He states that in the rooms of the temple still remained the idols of the Indians, and that he found offerings of cacao and copal incense which had been made

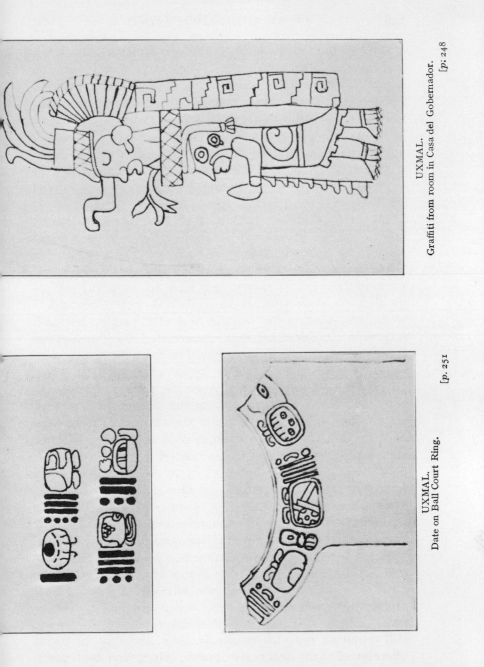

UXMAL.
Graffiti from room in Casa del Gobernador.

[p. 248

UXMAL.
Date on Ball Court Ring.

[p. 251

to them quite recently. The ruins of Uxmal appear to have been resorted to by the Indians, for the purpose of sacrificing to their ancient deities, up to a recent date, and even now the " *Noh nah ti Uxmal*," or ancient houses of Uxmal, are invoked in one of the prayers of the Cha Chac ceremony, as carried out by the modern Indians when sacrificing to the *chacs*, or gods of fertility, in order to ensure a fruitful maize harvest.

The Casa de las Monjas, or Nuns' House, was probably originally a monastic institution. It consists of a great quadrangular range of buildings surrounding a stone-paved courtyard, measuring 258ft. by 214ft., which is entered by a very fine corbel arch 16ft. 8in. wide. The inner façades of the building towards the courtyard are elaborately decorated above the cornices by stone sculpture, the face of the long-nosed god being, as usual, a very prominent decorative motif. Each of the four buildings surrounding the court-yard contains a front and back range of rooms, all roofed by the Maya arch. These apartments, which open on to the courtyard, are almost exactly alike in size and shape, and number eighty-eight in all. Upon the plaster in one of them we found written this inscription, in Spanish.

> Mi espiritu contemplando
> De esas ruinas la hermosura
> Las admiro con ternura
> Y las dejo suspirando
>
> —*Manuel Gomez.*

Literally translated, this runs :

" My soul contemplating the beauty of these ruins, I admire them, and leave them with a sigh."

A delightful sentiment, and not badly expressed, O Manuel, but it is the visitor who does the sighing when he contemplates the virgin white wall of the chamber defaced by a daub of large black painted letters, no matter how appropriate the sentiment they record.

In the north-east room of the quadrangle we discovered a
RL

capstone with the date 5 Imix, 19 Kankin, occurring in Tun 18, Katun 13, painted upon it,which corresponds with the Initial Series date 11.12.17.11.1., or to 1219 A.D. in our era. This capstone occupied the central position in the corbel arch which formed the ceiling of the room. In some instances we found that the image of the god to whom the temple was dedicated had been painted upon the capstone, together with the date of its erection. In most cases these paintings, which were executed in red, blue, green, black, and white, had become almost obliterated by damp, and were quite illegible, but where this had not occurred they fixed the date of the erection of the building containing them with absolute accuracy. We found several more painted capstones in the ruins of the Monjas ; on all of these, however, the dates were too much defaced to admit of our reading them.

It will be observed that this temple was erected at the very end of the Great Period of the New Empire, just about the time, in fact, when the Triple Alliance between Chichen Itza, Mayapan, and Uxmal was broken up, and before Mexican influence had had time to be generally felt. On the north side of the quadrangle we unearthed from a heap of rubbish the face of a stele, with four glyphs, each possessing numerical coefficients and evidently recording a date, engraved upon it. This is shown in the illustration, but the glyphs were unfortunately too much weathered by their long exposure to be deciphered.

Between the Monjas and the Casa del Gobernador the ruins of the Uxmal Ball Court are found. These are much smaller and less elaborate than the one at Chichen Itza, measuring only 128ft. by 70ft. The remains of two great stone rings 4ft. in diameter, fixed in the walls by tenons exactly opposite to each other, are still *in situ*. The outer portions of these rings have been broken away, apparently wantonly, and, though we searched very carefully in the great pile of rubbish beneath each of them, we were able to recover only a few of the missing fragments.

Sculptured on the north surface of each ring is a period ending date, and these we were fortunately able to make out, as enough of the inscription remains to make its meaning perfectly clear. It reads 10 Imix (the 10 being the head variant for that number) 17 Pop, in Tun 17, ending in a day 12 Ahau, which corresponds to the Initial Series date 11.15.16.12.14., or 1277 A.D. On one ring the date is written 10 Imix, 17 Pop, and on the other 10 Imix, 16 Pop. We know from the Maya records that at some period between the Old Empire and the books of Chilam Balaam the month coefficient was shifted back one day; thus Imix, which occupied the seventeenth place in the month during the Old Empire, in the books of Chilam Balaam occupies the 16th; and it is not improbable that this very important inscription records the date of this change. The date 1277 A.D. was approximately seventy years after the break-up of the Triple Alliance, and the Mexican mercenaries had already been for that period in Yucatan—long enough, evidently, to introduce the purely Aztec game of ball to the inhabitants of Uxmal, though one does not, as at Chichen Itza, find other evidence of their presence, in the form of Chacmools, serpent columns, and Atlantean figures, and the probabilities are that, except so far as the game of ball was concerned, the people of Uxmal came but little under their influence.

Our discoveries in Uxmal had more than realised our most sanguine expectations, in a city where no date had ever previously been discovered, and to the ruins of which an immense antiquity, amounting sometimes to thousands of years, had been ascribed, we were able to fix the date of at least two of the most important buildings—the Monjas and the Ball Court—in their correct position in Maya chronology and in the Christian era.

We had received many warnings as to the unhealthiness of the ruins, the prevalence there of malignant types of malaria and dysentery, and the plague of mosquitoes; but, as a matter of fact, our stay there was one of our pleasantest experiences in Yucatan. The weather was dry and warm, and mosquitoes were conspicuous by their absence, while never once did we have to retire under a roof for either cooking, eating, or sleeping. The cuidador, or Government guardian of the ruins, followed us about everywhere we went at first, but, realising at length that we were really what we gave ourselves out to be—merely crazy *gringoes*, wasting precious hours in sketching, photographing, and copying inscriptions—he soon left us entirely to our own devices.

Held, who was always complaining that when a job involving anything like real work turned up he was invariably the goat, actually had this woeful plaint justified at Uxmal ; for we had to erect an exceedingly tottery and insecure scaffolding beneath each of the painted capstones, upon which he had to lie flat on his back gazing upwards at the roof, while he made an exact reproduction of the painting and glyphs, with every probability of being precipitated to the stone floor, 15ft. beneath, if he indulged in even the most circumspect movement to relieve the constraint of his position.

During the second day of our stay at the ruins, a party of Indians of all ages and both sexes came from the large Maya village of Muna, on a pilgrimage to a shrine near the ruins, where the *santo* possesses a considerable local reputation for healing the sick and granting the petitions of his devotees. They were greatly interested in our camping outfit especially the culinary part of it, and stood round in an admiring circle watching Muddy prepare our lunch, exchanging light badinage with us meanwhile in Maya, about one word in five of which we understood.

They were nearly all of the usual Maya type—long black hair, dark eyes, and olive complexions—but two of the girls, each aged about sixteen, presented such a remarkable contrast the one to the other as to fix our attention almost exclusively on them. The one was pure Maya, with large brown, expressive eyes, long black lustrous hair,

straight, well-formed nose, rather prominent red lips, and
exquisite light olive complexion ; while the other, with blue
eyes and ropes of yellow hair hanging down her back, might
well have passed for a Norwegian and, indeed, was
probably a throw-back to some Norse, buccaneer ancestor,
who tired of his roving life, had settled amongst the
Indians a couple of centuries or so previously.

These two young ladies were by no means shy, and their
comments on us in Maya—which perhaps it was as well we
could not understand—were a source of pure joy to the other
members of their party. Muddy was the only one of our
party who had a really comprehensive knowledge of collo-
quial Maya, and I noticed that even he could not refrain from
snickering at some of their essays, though he refused to
translate, saying they were merely Maya jokes which did not
bear translation into English. They so far honoured us as
to try some of our canned peaches and apricots—which
they liked—and sardines and cheese—which they didn't—
and spent a good part of the afternoon with us, their
dazzling smiles, pretty faces, engaging manners, and broken
Spanish amply rewarding us for their earlier criticisms.
Both were barefooted, and skipped about like deer amongst
the sharp broken stones of the ruins, and, though they had
never worn shoes, their feet were not only beautifully
formed, but small and high-arched, which is most unusual in
those who have gone barefooted from infancy.

Uxmal was our last ruined city, and we left it with real
regret, for on returning to Merida our two months' trip
would be over. I should have to return to Belize in the
Lilian Y, while Morley and Held continued on to the ruins
of Palenque, in the State of Chiapas.

As before stated, the Tutul Xiu were the ruling family in
Uxmal from the date of its foundation till it was deserted for
the new capital at Mani. About two generations ago the
last few surviving members of this once great family—the
only aboriginal American royal family now in existence—
removed from Mani to Oxcutzcab, where two descendants

in the direct line still live, and were visited by Morley, who procured from them the following genealogical tree :

GENEALOGICAL TREE OF THE XIU FROM 1790

Anares Xiu—Antonia Us
b. abb. 1790
    Buenaventura Xiu—Francisca Baezu
    b. abb. 1815
    Bernabe Xiu—Maria Quijada   Anselmo Xiu
    1839—1911   d. a child of 2.

1   2   3
Jacinto Xiu—Calalina   Ildefonso Xiu—Alvina Gerardo—Natividad
   1860   Chulim   1861—1911   Perez Xiu   Chulim
      Bernabe Xiu   Nemensio Xiu—Edwarda Mis   Marcellino—Isidra
      d. a child   Xiu   Cocom
                Dionsio Xiu   Marcellino Xiu
                a child of 3   a child of 2
                in 1918   in 1898
                             Roberto Xiu
                             d. in 1911 at
                             25 unmarried
             Devero Xiu—Romana Uman   Bonafacio Xiu
                             boy of 12 in
                             1918

From Bernabe Xiu (1839–1911) the chronicle of Oxcutzcab, which is now in the Peabody Museum, was obtained. It is a record of the Xiu family as far back as 1600 A.D., when Gaspar Antonio Xiu was interpreter under the Spanish Crown. He was a son of Ah Kin Xiu, and grandson of Francisco Montejo Xiu, who offered his allegiance to Montejo, the Spanish Conqueror of Yucatan, at Merida in 1541. This Francisco Montejo Xiu was a direct descendant of the Tutul Xiu who, coming into the peninsula from the West, first founded the city of Uxmal, and with his people populated the western part of the Yucatan.

We reached Merida on the 25th, and Progreso on the following day ; at which port I boarded the *Lilian Y*, while Morley and Held set out a few days later for Chiapas and Tabasco.

From an archæological point of view our expedition had been extremely successful. We had discovered one large new ruined city at Chacmool, and two minor sites at Cancuen and Playa Carmen. We had elucidated the method of dating in use in Yucatan, and discovered the meaning of the winged

Cauac sign, the key of the problem ; while we had deciphered at least thirteen new dates, extending over a period of 800 years, from 619 to 1438, and practically covering the whole occupancy of the peninsula by the Maya tribes from the earliest immigration to within 100 years of the Spanish conquest. The annexed table drawn up by Morley gives the city and building in which each date was found, the date as actually recorded, and its position in the Initial Series and in Christian chronology.

NEW CHRONOLOGICAL MATERIAL FROM YUCATAN, MEXICO

	Site	Building	Record	Maya Era	Christian Era
1.	Cave of Loltun		3 Ahau	12.1.0.0.0 3 Ahau 18 Kayab or 11.8.0.0.0 3 Ahau 18 Chen	1379 A.D. 1123 A.D.
2.	Uxmal	Ball Court	10 Ix 17 Pop in Tun 17 ending on the day 13 Ahau	11.15.16.12.14 10 Ix 17 Pop	1277 A.D.
3.	Uxmal	Mon. Quad. West Range. North Room.	5 Imix 19 Kankin in Tun 18 of Katun 13.	11.12.17.11.1 9 Imix 19 Kankin	1219 A.D.
4.	Holactun	Temple of the I.S.	Tun 13, 2 Ahau 10.9.8.4.9 7. Muluc 11.2.8.4.9. 7. Muluc	10.9.13.0.0 2 Ahau 8 Uo or 11.2.13.0.0 2 Ahau 8 Yax 10.9.8.4.9 7 Muluc 17 Kankin or 11.2.8.4.9 7 Muluc 17 Tzec	761 A.D. 1017 A.D. 756 A.D. 1012 A.D.
5.	Mayapan	Stele 9	Katun 10 Ahau	12.4.0.0.0 10 Ahau 18 Uo	1438 A.D.
6.	Mayapan	Stele 8	13 Ahau, Tun 13	11.3.13.0.0 13 Ahau 1 Mac or 11.16.13.0.0 13 Ahau 3 Zip	1037 A.D. 1293 A.D.
7.	Chichen Itza	Temple of Two Lintels.	9 Eznab 11 Yax in Tun 13.	13.7.12.16.18 9 Eznab 11 Yax	1107 A.D.
8.	Chichen Itza	Temple of the I.S.	Tun 10 ending on day 2 Ahau 10.1.9.1.9. 9 Muluc 7 Zac	10.2.10.0.0 2 Ahau 13 Chen 10.2.9.1.9 9 Muluc 7 Zac	620 A.D. 619 A.D.
10.	Chichen Itza	High Priests Grave	2 Ahau 18 Xul, Tun 11 2 Ahau	11.19.11.0.0 2 Ahau 18 Xul	1350 A.D.
11.	Chichen Itza	Painted Lintel from Temple of the Owl.	1 Ahau, Tun 13	12.2.13.0.0 1 Ahau 18 Ceh	1411 A.D.
11.	Tuluum	Stele	9.6.10.0.0. 8 Ahau 13 Pax, end of a lahuntun 7 Ahau	9.6.10.0.0 8 Ahau 13 Pax 10.6.10.0.0 7 Ahau 18 Yaxkin	304 A.D. 699 A.D.

INDEX

A

Acumal, village near Tuluum, 41
Aguilar, Geronimo, connection of, with Cortez, 139–41
Ah Moo Chel, priest of Mayapan, 99
Ah Puch, Maya god of death, 128–9
Alcohol, effect on Indian temperament of, 49
Alfredo, Honduranian engineer of the party, 20 ; unpleasant experience of, 130–1.
Alvarado, holds an *auto da fé* at Isla de las Mujeres, 143
Alvarado, General, damage done in Merida by soldiers of, 173
Ambergris Cay, people of, 21
Anamix Chel, Lord of the Cheles, 165
Ants, a scourge in Yucatan, 210
Ascension, ruins of, 27
Ascension Bay, tiger tracks following racoon, 73–4 ; a sporting paradise—fish, game, and birds of—valuable logs driven into, 74–5

B

Bacalar, Spaniards in, 15 ; colonised by Maya, 92, 95–6
Belize, foundation and history of, 13 *et seq.*, starting place of expeditions—mixed population of, 13–4 ; logwood in, 14 ; Spanish trade, 14–5
Benque Viego, Indian village, 54

Blacadores Cay, *Lilian Y*, grounds at, 21
Boca Iglesias, difficulties of landing at ancient church, 156–60
Boca Paila, described, 62
Bravo General, reconquest of town of Santa Cruz by, 30–1
British Honduras, small settlers in, 16–7
Buccaneers, in Belize, 14–5

C

Cacicazgos, divisions of Yucatan, 99–100
Calendar, of the Maya, 112 *et seq.*
Campeché, history and description of, 192–4 ; natives of, compared with Yucatanese, 198
Canché Balaam, ruined shrine, 24–5
Cancuen, island, 142 ; described—buildings—a native iconoclast, ruin in, 148 *et seq.*
Candelario, Mrs., 191–2
Candelario, Señor, 182, 191–2
Canules, Toltec tribe, 99
Caribs, in Belize, 14
Carnegie Institute, 13, 20, 89
Carranza, damage done in Merida by soldiers, of 173
Castillo, the temple of Tuluum, described, 108–10 ; Initial series date on stele at, 120 *et seq.* ; correspondence of, with temple at Chacmool, 131–2
Catoche, Cape, 156

Diaz, Padre Juan, with conquistadores in Cozumel, 66 ; his diary, 105

Dogs in Yucatecan villages, 64

Dresden, Codex, Maya paintings and hieroglyphs in, 129–30

Dzibalchè, Indian town, described : Ford cars in, prohibition in, 182 ; strange sleeping-place in, 190 ; incident in church at, 192–3

E

Ek Ahau, Maya war diety, 130

El Meco, Espiritu Santo Bay, Maya temple at, described, 153–5 ; described, 23

Esquivel, Amado, v. " Muddy "

F

Flores, record of first Katun at, 93

Ford motor-car, much used in Yucatan, 182

G

Garcia, Señor Sixto, 183

George, 20, 21, 110

Gomez, Manuel, verses on ruin of Uxmal, by, 249

Grijalva, Juan de, discovers Cozumel, 67–8 ; voyage of, to coast of Yucatan, 105 ; chaplain of, on Tuluum, 134 ; at " Isla de las Mujeres " in 1517, 143

Guatemala, Maya established in, 91 ; earthquake in city of, 91–2

Guerrero, Gonzalo, apostasy of, 140

H

Held, John, 19, 20, 200 ; abilities of, as a caricaturist, 64 ; his unspeakable gramophone, 103 ;

visits the Castillo, 108 et seq., reproduces paintings and glyphs in Uxmal, 252

Henequen, or sisal fibre : exported from Silan, 163–4 ; importance of trade in—how the aloe plants are treated, 202

Herrera, on progress of Spaniards in Yucatan, 165 ; on Mexican games, 215–7

Holbox, Indian settlement, 160–1

Honduras, Maya established in first century in Western, 91

Howe, Dr., visits Tuluum, 106–7 ; leaves remarkable monolith at Castillo, 111–2

Hubert, 18 ; a spoiler of food, 78 ; his cookery, 102–3 ; disrated as cook, 111

Hunnac Ceel, King of Mayapan, 97–8

I

Icaiche Indians, their chief, subsidised by Mexican Government, 44

Independencia, wreck of the, 61

Insect pests, of Yucatan, 70–1

International Harvester Co., business done by, in Silan, 163

" Isla de las Mujeres," origin of name—reception by inhabitants of—Maya ruins in, 142 et seq.

Itzamna, 87, 95 ; apotheosis of, 97 ; priest-chief of Maya, 121 ; god of Yucatan, 127

Itzas, the, their place in Maya New Empire, 95 et. seq., alliance of, with Uxmal and Mayapan, 96–7

K

Kabak, ruins of—glyphs and pyramids of, 238–43

Kanchacan, visit to, 204–5